LIBERTY

The Evolution of an Idea

LIBERTY

The Evolution of an Idea

EDITED BY
KURT ALMQVIST, ALASTAIR BENN
AND MATTIAS HESSÉRUS

BOKFÖRLAGET STOLPE

CONTENTS

INTRODUCTION

Engelsberg Ironworks, where the Engelsberg Seminar is held each year, is situated outside the village of Ängelsberg in Västmanland, Sweden. Ängelsberg was earlier called Englikobenning after the *wohnsitz* (residence) of Englika – a German iron master in the fourteenth century. His grandson Engelbrekt Engelbrektson was supposedly born in a house just west of the present manor house of Engelsberg. He fought for Swedish freedom against the Danes in the 1430s. He is largely remembered by a song about liberty, probably dating from 1439. The song exists in hundreds of different musical arrangements and has been sung in Sweden over the centuries. It can be seen as a leitmotif for the Engelsberg Seminar of 2022.

Bishop Thomas's Song of Freedom

Freedom is the greatest thing
for all the world, both man and king.
The righteous free shall be.
The righteous free shall be.
If to yourself you will be true,
hold freedom dear as is its due.
All glory to the free.
All glory to the free.

Birds and beasts their lair defend
To keep it safe as they intend.
Now know what help to give.
Now know what help to give.
The Lord God gave you heart and soul,
Be not a slave; lift freedom's role
As long as you shall live.
As long as you shall live.

The first Engelsberg Seminar took place in 1999 with the topic 'The Swedish Success Story?' Much has happened since then; grander and more important issues than the possible successes of Sweden have been dealt with over the years.

But behind all these themes the common denominator has always been the question of the past, present and future of the West and Western civilisation and its values.

The Engelsberg Seminar of 2022 addressed the subject of liberty, so urgent and important for our culture and civilisation, and linked to the fundamental cultural core of the West. The culture of the individual, with its rights and obligations, and the culture of freedom and freedom of speech – with all its ramifications for our liberal societies – are challenged today by authoritarian contestants from across the world.

Stockholm, January 2023

Kurt Almqvist
President, Axel and Margaret Ax:son Johnson Foundation for Public Benefit

ORIGINS OF WESTERN LIBERTY

Christ and the Samaritan Woman,
Girolamo da Treviso, 16th century.

RECLAIMING CHRISTIAN FREEDOM
FOR THE MODERN AGE

Richard Chartres

The story of freedom in modern Western culture is often associated with the decisive break with the past effected by the French Revolution. A new vision of 'liberty, equality and fraternity' was substituted for the oppression identified with the Christian tradition. The Revolution sought to replace religion with politics as the real source of man's liberation. It was a shift which reflected a belief that evil is a consequence of society and not of original sin.

In this reading of the roots of the modern concept of freedom, the conventional view is that nothing very much happened between the death of Marcus Aurelius and the birth of Voltaire. There is some truth in this story of discontinuity, but many of the ideas which inform modern notions of freedom – ideas that are seen as 'self-evident' – are undeniably a secularised version of the Judaeo-Christian inheritance. The New Testament sets a high value on freedom and there is abundant evidence that the biblical narrative continues to inspire struggles for liberation.

Jesus Christ himself exhibited a remarkable degree of freedom from conventions. He was a religious teacher but neither an academic scribe nor an ascetic. He had no settled home, paid little special attention to his blood family, ate with all and sundry and was unusually open to children, women of dubious reputation, and even Samaritans. For Christians, as John Zizioulas writes, 'Christ is the whole reality of human being but he does not force himself upon us but appears among us as someone we can reject or accept as we like.'

Notoriously, some versions of Christianity have been highly controlling and coercive. Even if, from time to time, the distance between the Christlike ideal and ecclesiastical practice has prompted agitation for reform, nothing ought to obscure the repeated failure to do justice to the one who does not force himself upon us but appears as 'someone we can reject or accept as we like'.

There is a dramatic picture in Dostoevsky's *The Brothers Karamazov* of a confrontation between Jesus Christ and the ecclesiastical hierarchy which sought to rule in his name. The scene is set in Seville in the aftermath of a great *auto-da-fé* in which 100 heretics had been put to the torch. The Cardinal Inquisitor General recognises Christ in the crowd and imprisons him before he can protest. They have a rather one-sided conversation in which Christ is silent while the cardinal complains about his irresponsibility, and even lack of compassion, for the millions of spiritually second-rate people. 'I tell you that man has no more tormenting care than to find someone to whom he can hand over as quickly as possible that gift of freedom with which the miserable creature is born...even when all the gods have disappeared from the earth they will still fall down before idols.' Anyone in leadership is well advised to revisit this prison scene on a regular basis.

The Christian movement inaugurated by Jesus Christ, and first known as The Way, was a challenge to ancient notions of theocratic absolutism. Under the Pharaohs, the Inca, the Emperor of China, or under Caesar, the order of society was conceived to be part of the divine order. In St Matthew's Gospel, Jesus is shown a coin bearing the likeness of the Emperor Tiberius and the inscription, 'son of the divine Augustus'. In his response, 'render unto Caesar the things that are Caesar's and unto God the things that are God's', Jesus opens up a space for the secular life of the citizen, together with the need for a constant negotiation between the claims of a particular state or social custom and the service of the eternal God.

The early Christian community which sprang out of Christ's self-sacrifice was a new kind of social organism. It was not just a federation of groups for the study of the teachings of Jesus Christ – there were many such groups in the Roman Empire, living without any threat of persecution. Christians chose to call their community an *ecclesia*, the word used of the sovereign body of a Greek city state, summoned by authority and composed of adult, male, freeborn citizens. By contrast, the Christian *ecclesia* from the beginning included slaves, women and children. The community so constituted was believed to be the dwelling place of the Holy Spirit. Membership of the new community involved a freedom from existing social and political norms, which proved disruptive. It became clear that religious freedom for the Christian *ecclesia* was not just a private matter but one which required civic autonomy.

At the end of his famous 'I have a dream' speech, delivered from the steps of the Lincoln Memorial in 1963, Martin Luther King quotes from the words of St Paul, 'There is no longer Jew or Greek, there is no longer slave or free, there is no longer male or female: for all of you are one in Christ Jesus.'

This was a universalising of the vision of human dignity and freedom which permeates the Hebrew Scriptures. According to the book of Genesis (I:26–27), God created human beings in his own image and likeness. This is the source of the now secularised conviction that all human beings have an innate dignity and enjoy various rights. Man in Genesis enjoys a certain freedom, even in relation to God. God makes the animals, but Adam gives them names, which God accepts (Genesis II:19). Significantly in the Quran, it is God who teaches man the names of the animals.

In our day, the appeal to human dignity is frequently made as if it was a self-evident truth, even when other parts of the biblical revelation have been abandoned. Nietzsche took a more rigorously consistent position, arguing that 'Man in himself, the absolute man, possesses neither dignity nor rights nor duties.' It is culture and art that create beauty, and lives which come to possess dignity. Nietzsche's view of human worth and dignity is inegalitarian, and achieved rather than innate. In consequence, he thought that the ethics of compassion associated with the biblical view of humanity would disappear with the death of God.

God acts in history as liberator of the oppressed. There is constant reference to the experience of bondage (for example, Exodus XX:2) which leads on to prescriptions about Israelite behaviour towards foreigners (Exodus XXII:21, Deut.X:19, Exodus XXIII:9). Biblical liberty is not only to be enjoyed by a privileged caste but shared.

In the New Testament, the death of Jesus is the new Exodus (Luke IX:31); the passage to freedom. Freedom was liberation from captivity to a life enslaved to self-centred cravings and the desire to possess, which causes the individual to turn in upon himself (Gal V:1, Romans VIII: 21). It was freedom for life as persons enabled to embrace a right relationship with God-the-beyond-all, and with neighbours. Freedom *from* captivity was the precondition of freedom *for* a profound relationship with the other, in which we find our true humanity.

As a new kind of social order, and as strangers and aliens (1Peter II:11), the Christian church experienced persecution at the hands of the state. At first, Christians were taught merely to endure, but they were led eventually to articulate the case for religious freedom. The second century Latin theologian Tertullian coined the phrase 'religious freedom' [*libertas religionis*] in his Apology (AD 197). Then, in his public letter to the Proconsul of Carthage, *ad Scapulam* (AD 212), he wrote, 'it is a fundamental human right [*humani juris*]…that every man should worship according to his own convictions: one man's religion neither harms nor helps another man. It is assuredly no part of religion to compel religion – to which free will and not force should lead us.' This passage was not forgotten. It was written out in Thomas Jefferson's own hand in an annotation to the relevant section on religious freedom in his 1782 *Notes on the State of Virginia.*

Crucial to the development of civic freedom in the West was the collapse, in the fifth century, of the institutions of imperial government. The church had an opportunity to assert its freedom, and this set up a tension between the two authorities of church and state which strongly influenced the mediaeval debate on freedom and rights. At times, however, while denying the supremacy of Caesar, popes came close to claiming supreme power themselves.

Theocratic claims reached their high watermark in Boniface VIII's Bull *Unam Sanctam* (1302): 'It is altogether necessary for every human creature to be subject to the Roman Pontiff.' There was a strong response, not only by secular rulers, but by the supporters of a conciliar structure which could even discipline a pope.

From the twelfth century, representative assemblies met with increasing frequency, first in the church and then in the various monarchies of the West. The Fourth Lateran Council, convened by Innocent III in 1213, brought together great prelates, ambassadors of kings, envoys from Italian cities and elected representatives of cathedral chapters and collegiate churches. It put the representative principle into action with a prestige and on a scale which reverberated throughout Latin Christendom.

Medieval society was saturated with a concern for rights. The common gloss on Gratian's *Decretum* laid down that 'no one is to be deprived of his right except for very grave cause'. The problem is to determine when the doctrine of natural rights inhering in all individuals emerged from the medieval concern with the rights of particular persons and groups.

In the fourteenth century, William of Ockham appealed to the scriptural teaching on evangelical liberty, Paul's 'freedom with which Christ has made us free' (Galatians V:1), and applied it to freedom from tyrannical government, especially in the church. Not even the pope could subvert 'the temporal rights and liberties conceded to the faithful by God and nature'.

Thomas More appealed to Christian conscience as the basis for his refusal to swear the oath required by Henry VIII when he claimed Supreme Headship of the Church in England. More's example brings us to the fragmentation of the Old Western Latin Church in the sixteenth century. Revisiting the sixteenth-century Reformation era with an eye informed by all that has happened in the intervening centuries suggests an ecumenical agenda for repentance. As we reflect on the aftermath of the French Revolution, and especially on the twentieth-century rise of the messianic secular states in Germany and Russia, it is clear that one of the unintended consequences of the Wars of Religion was a disenchantment with the foundational place of the Judaeo-Christian tradition in the culture of the West.

The Reformation era resulted in an over-definition of mystery in the interests of polemics. The 'mainstream' churches were over-bureaucratised as they attempted to enforce uniformity within their territories. At the same time, they became more or less enthusiastic accomplices in the violent struggle of states and dynasties to establish themselves against rival powers.

It is also true that the scandalous denigration of the Jewish religion and people continued and even, in some places, became more acute. Wars of Religion persuaded many thoughtful people that competing Christian absolutisms provided a very questionable foundation for establishing public truth. Something more 'objective' was required, and the result was an impoverished form of 'enlightenment', which relegated the heart to the lumber-room of a cult of pure reason. Meaning was sacrificed to a rational pursuit of disembodied, mathematically established truth.

It is also fair to say, however, that in the turmoil of the Reformation era, there were new Bible-based assertions of liberty. Calvin in his *Institutes* (1536) echoes Luther's call for Christian liberty – liberty of the individual conscience from Catholic Canon Law and clerical control; liberty of political officials from ecclesiastical power and privilege; liberty of the local clergy from central papal rule.

The notion that there should be a separation of the offices and operations of church and state flourished in the various experiments in the new communities in America, especially associated with the names of Roger Williams, the founder of Providence Rhode Island, and William Penn.

In a letter to Lord Arlington, written from the Tower of London, Penn said, 'Force may make hypocrites but it can make no converts.' He quotes Tertullian and Lactantius and, like John Locke's *A Letter Concerning Toleration*, sums up a century of Christian argument about religious freedom.

St Peter said, 'Live as those who are free but do not use your freedom as a cloak for wrong doing; live as servants of God.' (First Epistle of St Peter II:16.) There are countless examples of what happens when there is an excessive focus on freedom from constraint, but less emphasis on freedom for life as persons who can bring other persons to fullness of life. Even the revolutionary poet John Milton, in the chaos of mid-seventeenth century social conflict and religious fanaticism, was moved to declare that 'Liberty hath a sharp and double edge, fit only to be handled by just and virtuous men.'

The phenomenon of ideologically or religiously inspired terrorism has forced us in our own time to think about the limits to freedom. But in 1945, contemplating the wreckage of Western civilisation, the evils of coercive regimes and ideologies were appallingly clear. In the post-war period there were, in consequence, efforts to enshrine in the law of nations protection for the freedom of the individual from external oppression.

Although the twentieth century saw the defeat (though who can say for how long) of race-centred fascism and class-centred communism, now there are different challenges, and in this fresh context we are called upon to restate the vision of human freedom. The world seems to have been re-imagined as little more than a global marketplace, committed to a project of growth without limit, with no end in view beyond the process itself. The consequences of this way of living have become clear in the many threats to the health of our planet and the human eco-system. But how can imaginations and desires shaped by advertising and economic imperatives be free to find delight and fulfilment in non-material relationships?

It has taken the passing of several generations to bring to light the soulless implications of the dominance of a form of radical positivism that recognises the empirical number-based sciences as the only valid form of knowledge. There are constant invocations of human dignity and the rights of the individual, but the reality is that each of us is increasingly subject to a seemingly irreversible extension of process and impersonal systematisation that leaves the deracinated individual with no place to stand from which resistance might be possible.

The glorious inheritance of democracy depends on the existence of a *demos*, a people with shared memories and a sure grasp of fundamental principles. As the various associations which incubate this shared culture are dissolved, *demos* becomes *ochlos*, a crowd of contextless people visited by gusts of indignation fanned by social media. It is a situation in which algorithmic influencers have a vast potential for manipulation in contemporary democracies and dictatorships alike. We are always fighting the last war and prosecuting extinct heresies while the stealthy advance of what Jacques Ellul calls '*la technique*' proceeds virtually unremarked.

Some see this as a hopeful development. Silicon Valley's Kevin Kelly sees technology growing into something self-aware and independent of its human creators, which he calls the 'technium'. In his book, *What Technology Wants*, he explains: 'It may have once been as simple as an old computer program, merely parroting what we told it, but now it is more like a very complex organism that often follows its own urges.'

As our systems become so large and our technologies so complex, it seems harder to steer them in our chosen direction, or to make them respond to human needs in our schools and hospitals. The cry 'take back control' is often simplistically directed at some particular institution or person, but it reflects our unease at the gathering strength of an inhuman force that seems to be, in some inexplicable way, independent of us, yet is, at the same time, acting within us. As Jacques Ellul asks, 'What does freedom mean in an age of "continually improved means to carelessly examined ends"?'

The western tradition of freedom permeated by a Judaeo-Christian belief in the dignity of all human beings once had the authority to champion liberation from sub-human instincts and arbitrary social forces. Now this authority is more often associated with repression or a mere expression of personal or class preference, while behind the curtain, the technium continues to advance.

Once the curtain is drawn aside, however, and the technium is revealed, a fresh re-statement of the human ideal of freedom is possible, drawing on the resources of centuries of reflection on Judaeo-Christian practice and the other wisdom traditions represented in this year's Engelsberg Seminar.

Thracian slave and gladiator Spartacus.
Engraving, 19th century.

SPARTACUS AND THE ENDLESS MARCH OF LIBERTY

Richard Miles

In 73 BC, 6,000 rebels were crucified on the orders of the victorious Roman general Marcus Licinius Crassus at regular intervals along the Appian Way, between the Campanian city of Capua and Rome. Crucifixion, if handled correctly, can be a long and agonising death lasting several days, and the rotting corpses would have stayed strung up for much longer than that. Even by Roman standards, this was a big statement to make.

This especially brutal treatment was partly the result of the humiliating defeats that the rebels had inflicted on at least five Roman armies, three of them led by consuls, over the previous two and a half years, and the huge amount of damage they had caused across southern and central Italy. At their height, their numbers had risen to 120,000 men and, at one point, it had looked like they might march on Rome itself. Some areas where they had passed through did not recover, either economically or demographically, for a century. Yet, far more significant was who they were. The rebels were slaves who had been marshalled by their charismatic leader, the gladiator Spartacus, into an extremely effective fighting force that terrorised Italy between 73 and 71 BC in what is known as the Third Servile War.

Spartacus, a Thracian, was said to have once fought as an auxiliary soldier for the Romans before being enslaved and sent to the gladiator school at Capua. There, in 73 BC, Spartacus had managed to escape with 70 comrades and sought sanctuary on the upper slopes of Mount Vesuvius. The Roman forces sent to recapture them were rebuffed when the rebels used ropes made of vines to scale down the sheer side of the mountain and launch a successful surprise attack on the Roman camp. Subsequently, another expedition was defeated, leading to the capture of Roman military equipment and a sizeable increase in the rebel numbers as other slaves learnt of their success and absconded, often murdering their owners before they fled. During the following winter, the slave army trained and armed their burgeoning number of recruits while raiding across southern Italy for supplies and booty. The spring of 72 would see Spartacus's greatest military success when, after an initial reverse, his forces defeated two Roman legions which had been dispatched against them.

The Roman senate, in a state of alarm, now sent Crassus with eight legions to put down the insurrection. The campaign started disastrously for Crassus when his deputy, Mummius, ignored his instructions to avoid engaging with the rebels, with the result that his army, made up of two legions, was defeated with extensive loss of life. However, Crassus doggedly forced Spartacus and his army southwards. By the last month of 71 BC, Spartacus and his army were trapped at Rhegium in the toe of Italy. After a failed attempt to evacuate his forces to Sicily, Spartacus broke the Roman blockade but suffered an emphatic defeat when Crassus's pursuing legions caught up with his army. A few days later, Spartacus's remaining forces made a final stand in Lucania, where most, including their leader, were killed, with the remaining 6,000 survivors meeting their gruesome fate along the Appian Way.

Spartacus is one of the most famous figures of the ancient world, the great freedom fighter, although his current celebrity has far more to do with Hollywood and Netflix than familiarity with the Roman and Greek writers who recorded his feats. In fact, the Spartacus that we know is very much a post-enlightenment heroic creation and was the subject of a plethora of plays, novels and works of art. In 1760, the French writer Bernard-Joseph Saurin's tragedy *Spartacus* drew parallels between the oppressive conditions of ancient Rome and those of his own times. Spartacus's celebrity as a freedom fighter dedicated to the overthrow of tyranny and the repressive social order grew further during and after the French Revolution.

Always understandably popular with revolutionaries, Toussaint L'Ouverture (1743–1803), leader of the Haitian revolution against French rule, was likened to Spartacus. In 1874, the Italian writer Raffaello Giovagnoli wrote his historical novel *Spartacus,* which drew parallels between Spartacus and Garibaldi. The early twentieth century saw Spartacus being adopted as a darling of the burgeoning socialist movement. Karl Marx had argued that Spartacus was among the greatest, if not the greatest, heroes of the ancient world and held him up as an example to be followed. The German socialist revolutionaries Rosa

Luxemburg and Karl Liebknecht named the Spartacus League after him. However, Spartacus has also had champions on the other side of the political spectrum, with Ronald Reagan casting him to be a great champion of freedom fighting against the oppression of the state.

Hollywood has had a long-held fascination with Spartacus. The 1960s saw Stanley Kubrick's muscle-bound Kirk Douglas in fighting pose with sword and shield, but Kubrick's Spartacus is an oddly puny affair, with much of the violence, anger and menace that are such a staple of the ancient accounts of the insurrection jettisoned for a saccharine love story and a life-affirming parable on camaraderie ('I am Spartacus!'). Kubrick's Spartacus is a rebel without a cause.

Far more interesting and complex are Roman attitudes to Spartacus. Here there is little trite allegory but vilification, unease and pregnant silence. Spartacus holds a very similar position in Roman historiography to that other great general who took the fight to Rome's Italian backyard, the Carthaginian general Hannibal, who had spent nearly a decade marauding across the peninsula some 130 or so years earlier, before also being penned in the south and defeated. Like Hannibal, Spartacus is admired for his courage, trickiness and skills as a general, while also being equally despised for his barbarity, impiety and cruelty. The two great foes of the Roman Republic often appear as something of a double act of favourite bogeymen in later Roman literature. The poet Horace, writing two generations later in a time of civil war, bemoaned how Rome was now completing what violent Spartacus had ultimately failed to do – its own destruction. Horace also somewhat whimsically wondered whether any of the fine Italian wines of the early 1970s had avoided being looted by 'Spartacus and his marauding bands'.

Roman attitudes towards Spartacus were a manifestation of a wider societal unease about slavery, although these were not founded on moral objection or a desire to end it as a practice. There are no champions of total emancipation in the Roman world. Considering how much slavery haunted the Roman psyche, it is fitting that the first Roman ghost story featured an apparition of a slave. According to the Roman writer Pliny, a Greek philosopher rented a house in northern Italy at a very cheap price because the landlord, a Roman senator, had been unable to let it due to a ghostly apparition, whose chains clanked around the house all night. The philosopher solved the mystery by following the ghost to a courtyard and marking the spot where it disappeared. The next morning the ground was dug up and a skeleton covered in chains was discovered. After the remains were removed and properly buried, the ghost never appeared again.

Spartacus's servility, his status as a non-human when matched with his defeat of a series of Roman armies, made him an extremely unsettling proposition for generations of Roman historians, particularly as an unwelcome reminder of Roman Italy's huge societal and economic reliance on millions of slaves (they made up around one third of the population). But, equally importantly, he represented the ambiguities and inconsistencies in Roman attitudes towards freedom and personhood.

For Romans, the most terrifying aspect of Spartacus's revolt was that his vast force was largely made up of faceless, expendable and extremely badly treated slaves, who toiled on massive agricultural estates in the Italian countryside, many chained together and living in barracks. Essentially treated like livestock, punishments for disciplinary infractions were often fearsome, with brutal floggings, branding and mutilations common. The Roman agricultural economy was addicted to slave labour. The wars of conquest of the third, second and first centuries BC against Carthage, the Hellenistic East and the Gauls, had brought a vast influx of slaves, with 75,000 captives from the first Punic War alone. The peasant farmers, who had once tilled the lands of Italy and been the backbone of Rome's armies, often returned home from many years of military service to find their families in debt and their small holdings bought up cheaply by the senatorial class, who had been the main beneficiaries of the wars of conquest. These new senatorial landowners created huge tracts of land across central and southern Italy called *latifundia,* where vast numbers of the new prisoners of war were put to work as slaves. Slave plantations were not the locations for the luxurious country villas that we often imagine them to be, but grim barracks and simple housing for the bailiffs and trusties that ran them. The surplus produce would be sold on to feed the newly landless poor of Rome, the former peasant farmers.

Romans' unease over slaves was not just a matter of their economic reliance on them, but also emanated from the intellectually ambiguous position that they themselves had adopted in relation to slavery. Ancient Rome was the most efficient enfranchising system that the ancient world has ever seen – barbarians could eventually become Roman, and slaves (legally non-humans) could transition to being free (legally human). Romans did free slaves in relatively large numbers, often for good service, in their masters' wills. Other slaves saved up money and bought their freedom. Manumission served as an important engine of Roman social and economic mobility, with some freed men becoming the backbone of Rome's business class and hugely rich themselves. Ex-slaves became slave owners. This point is well illustrated by the tombstone of a slave dealer and auctioneer, Publius Syrus from Mount Tifata in Campania, who had himself been a slave before being freed by his master and becoming his business partner. However, freedom was the lucky fate of just a privileged, talented and visible few. It was a Darwinian system, whereby those with skills and proximity to their masters – accountants, teachers, doctors, nurses – had a chance to earn their freedom, unlike the majority of invisible agricultural slaves marooned on distant plantations which the masters were very unlikely to visit.

However, even the privileged household slaves could come under suspicion. As the Roman stoic philosopher Seneca memorably said: 'So many slaves, so many enemies.' He goes on to describe how poor house slaves stood motionless and starving as their master greedily wolfed down expensive delicacies in front of them – any sound, cough or sneeze was met with a savage beating. Indeed, masters were most likely to be murdered by house slaves rather than their agricultural peers precisely because they had the opportunity to lay their hands on them. Such incidents were met with brutal collective punishment. When Pedanius Secundus, Prefect of Rome, was murdered by a slave, all 400 servile members of his household were marched out of the city and strangled.

Seneca was one of the few Roman authors to remind his friends of their slaves' humanity. Yet it is worth remembering that he was no Roman William Wilberforce. He was merely advancing a philosophical position and was a slave owner himself. Christianity made little to no difference to Roman attitudes toward slavery. When Augustine of Hippo, in the early fifth century AD, rescued the cargo of a slave ship that had docked at his port in North Africa, it was only because they had previously been free Christians.

Yet Seneca's reminder of slaves' humanity hints at the unease that lay behind Roman attitudes towards their slaves. They might be treated as livestock, but the fact that they all had the possibility of becoming free, however remote, suggested a capacity for humanity. Roman views here have all the weaknesses of a philosophical justification backfilling a legal judgement. It has been argued that the monstrous in the ancient world is always associated with something that has been touched by humanity. With Spartacus's revolt, the monstrosity of the slave in the Roman world was writ large.

With the coming of the autocratic rule of the emperors, the Roman senatorial elite were also served with uncomfortable reminders that the distinction between themselves and their slaves might be less than they thought. It would take an ex-slave, the Stoic philosopher Epictetus, to teach the Roman senatorial elite to preserve a tiny bit of freedom in a world where the emperor had the power of life and death over everybody. In Epictetus's eyes, the difference between slavery and freedom was minimal.

But what of Spartacus himself? What did he want? What were his aims? The answer is almost certainly not the one for which today's freedom fighters yearn. There is no evidence that Spartacus saw his mission as one of fighting against the cruel institution of slavery, nor the oppressive imperialism of Rome. The sources are agreed that he was simply fighting for his own and his family's freedom. Vengeance was also a strong motivation for the slave army, many of whom had experienced the extreme cruelty of the plantation system. Material gain also played a major role. Contemporary commentators were genuinely shocked by the wholesale massacres, rapes and other atrocities that the slave armies inflicted on the villas, towns and cities that had the misfortune to be in their path.

In his first novel, *The Gladiators*, Arthur Koestler, the famously repentant communist, viewed Spartacus as an allegory for the socialist leaders of his own age. Here, Spartacus's vision is a radical new utopian settlement called Sun City, where there are no slaves, ranks, gold or silver. For Koestler, Spartacus's fatal flaw (unlike his then-hero, Stalin) was that he was too weak with his men, unable to stop the rape and slaughter that was the fate of every settlement that the slave army captured. He had not ruthlessly eradicated internal dissent and thus failed the crucial revolutionary test, dooming the revolt to inevitable failure.

In his review of *The Gladiators*, George Orwell made the crucial observation that Koestler failed to nail Spartacus down, leaving him floating aimlessly in limbo somewhere between the 1930s socialist leader and the ancient man. Orwell was right. Koestler's Spartacus is a nowhere man, unable to articulate his motivations either as a historical or allegorical character. Orwell was particularly exercised by what he viewed as

Koestler's failure to bridge the cavernous moral divide to an ancient world, unlike Flaubert, who had been able to imagine himself in 'the stony cruelty of antiquity'. In contrast, Koestler's Spartacus is revealed as a would-be twentieth-century proletarian dictator in a tunic. Yet, it seems to me that here Orwell, for once, misses the point. Koestler's Spartacus is, in fact, the perfect portrait of a figure who floats between history and allegory, an empty void, like the upper slopes of Vesuvius, where he and his supporters first took refuge, now obliterated by eruptions. The real power of Spartacus is that he remains as impossible to pin down as the many conflicting forms of liberty for which he has been claimed as champion.

The School of Athens, Raphael, 1509–1511.

THE RELEVANCE OF ATHENIAN FREEDOM TODAY

Mark J. Schiefsky

F or about two centuries, between, roughly, 508 and 322 BC, the political system of ancient Athens was a democracy, a form of government in which all adult male citizens had a share in political decision making. The chief benefit of this system, as its supporters argued, was liberty. But what did liberty mean to the ancient Athenians, and can we learn anything from their history that is helpful for addressing the challenges of liberty today?

Distinctive features of Athenian democracy

Is it even appropriate to call ancient Athens a democracy as the term is understood today? There are obviously very significant differences, despite the fact that the modern word 'democracy' is a translation of ancient Greek *demokratia*. That term originally meant something like 'people power'. The first problem with assuming that it meant the same thing then as now, however, is that Athenian democracy granted a far larger share of power to the people than do modern representative democracies.

Male citizens in ancient Athens could debate and decide on political and legislative proposals in regular meetings of the citizen assembly. They had full power to decide legal cases as members of juries; such cases often involved political actors and issues, and there were no judges to shape or overrule citizen judgments. And they could hold political offices, most of which were distributed by lottery rather than by election. The average male Athenian would have participated in many of these activities on a regular basis.

We may contrast this with modern Western democracies, in which legislative decisions are delegated to representatives chosen by election, and great effort is made to separate the legal and political realms. In contemporary America, at least, political participation is generally restricted to occasional jury service and voting in elections, a pale shadow of the ancient experience.

In these ways, ancient Athens was far more democratic than modern societies that bear that designation. But, of course, it was also far less democratic in restricting political participation to men, who amounted to perhaps 50,000 out of a total population of 300,000 in ancient Attica. The exclusion of women, slaves and resident non-citizens from the Athenian political community meant that ancient democracy was, in fact, very far from rule by the majority of the population. Indeed, the number of slaves surely exceeded, on its own, the number of political decision makers. The issue becomes even more acute if one considers how many could actually participate in meetings of the citizen assembly; perhaps 5,000 or 6,000 adult males at one time.

Despite this limited participation, what set ancient democracy apart from other systems in antiquity was its extension of political power to all economic levels of the male citizen body. There was no property qualification for participation in politics in ancient Athens, and the city went to great efforts to ensure that those lower on the economic ladder would be able to participate, for example by providing pay for jury service. In this restricted sense, democracy was government by all, or at least all adult male citizens, even in antiquity. That was emphatically not the case for the other systems of government in the ancient Greek world, namely monarchy (rule by one) and oligarchy (rule by the propertied few). Thus, democracy came to be seen as self-government, a system in which the citizens governed themselves together, rather than a government in which one part of the polity exerted control over another. Moreover, there is a common ideological core that runs through both ancient and modern democracy. Ancient Athenian democrats appealed to values such as liberty, equality and the rule of law to justify and advocate for their system. Rule of law also meant equality under the law: both rich and poor had equal claims to legal protections. That was the ideal, of course, perhaps more often honoured in the breach than the observance. But the power of such ideas is undeniable; it was, after all, by appealing to ideals of liberty and equality that modern reformers succeeded in extending democratic participation to previously excluded classes in the last two centuries.

The Athenian concept of liberty

Thus, despite the very significant differences between ancient and modern democracies, we can view both as systems of government that attempt to put into practice basic commitments to principles such as liberty, equality and the idea of self-government by the people as a whole. Aristotle offers a succinct formulation of the importance of liberty (which we can treat as a synonym to 'freedom', both being possible translations of the Greek term *eleutheria*) to democracy in an important passage of his *Politics.* Although Aristotle was no supporter of democracy, he has a great deal to say about the arguments that were offered in support of it. The relevant passage reads as follows: 'A basic principle of the democratic constitution is liberty. People constantly make this statement, implying that only in this constitution do men share in liberty; for every democracy, they say, has liberty as its aim.' (*Politics* vi 2; 1317a40-b2.) (By 'constitution' or *politeia,* Aristotle means the political system as a whole, not a written constitution.) What was this liberty that could only be achieved in a democracy, according to these thinkers? In other words, what did it mean to be free in ancient Athens?

First, it meant that you were not a slave. In a society such as Athens, where slaves worked alongside free individuals on a daily basis, the possession of free status was obviously a crucial component of personal identity. Freedom in this sense applied not just to adult male citizens, but also to women and resident non-citizens.

Second, to be free in ancient Athens meant that you were not ruled by a tyrant, whether foreign or domestic. The spectacular success of Athens' resistance to Persian domination in the early fifth century BC fundamentally shaped the Athenians' sense of freedom. Moreover, this resistance to foreign tyranny went hand-in-hand with the basic origin story of Athenian democracy: the story of how the Athenians of the late sixth century BC did away with rule by the tyrant Pisistratus and his dynasty. Athenian texts of the fifth and fourth centuries BC are rich in descriptions of tyranny, understood as a kind of rule that is arbitrary, unaccountable, and supported by force rather than law. The possibility of such tyranny loomed large in the Athenian democratic imagination for the entire lifespan of democracy.

These two aspects of Athenian liberty – freedom from slavery and freedom from tyranny – are examples of 'negative' liberty, as defined by the twentieth-century political philosopher Isaiah Berlin. That is, they are situations of 'freedom from' certain kinds of external control, rather than situations of 'freedom to' engage in certain activities or to hold certain privileges. Berlin thought that the ancient world (ie the Greco-Roman world) primarily offered examples of positive, rather than negative, liberty; for him, negative liberty is chiefly a modern concept, associated with the problem of defining the limits of the authority of the state versus the individual. In conceiving of the issue in this way, Berlin follows earlier modern thinkers, such as John Stuart Mill and Benjamin Constant. The latter's influential 1819 essay, 'The Liberty of the Ancients Compared with that of the Moderns', argues that the 'ancients' (again, meaning the ancient Greeks and Romans) typically enjoyed a high degree of political liberty, but had to accept extreme limitations on personal liberty in exchange. In Constant's view, they were, in fact, slaves to the state in private affairs, because of the state's alleged role in controlling private life.

It is clear that these two negative liberties (freedom from slavery and freedom from tyranny) do not fully capture the concept of liberty that was important to Athenian democrats. The victory over the Persian empire was the common achievement of all the Greek city states, not just Athens; similarly, tyranny had largely disappeared from the Greek world by the fifth century BC, and the vast majority of states were either democracies or oligarchies. So, if liberty could only be secured in a democracy, as our Aristotle passage suggests, being free from tyranny and slavery wasn't enough to be truly free in ancient Athens.

Thirdly, being free in ancient Athens meant the ability to participate in politics. This is a kind of positive liberty in Berlin's sense, a freedom to do things and to have certain privileges. And it was obviously fundamental to democracy, insofar as the sharing of political participation across the economic spectrum of male citizens was the distinctive mark of ancient democracy. In the *Politics*, just after the passage quoted above, Aristotle neatly summarises this aspect of democratic liberty as 'ruling and being ruled in turn'. This is a kind of shorthand for all the forms of political participation that Athenians could engage in: voting in the assembly, jury service and the holding of offices.

Fourthly and finally, Athenian liberty involved personal freedom, the ability to 'live as you like'. Aristotle mentions this in the *Politics* passage as the second distinctive feature of democratic liberty, along with 'ruling and being ruled in turn'. It is clear from the attacks on democracy in sources such as Plato's *Republic* that individuals in democratic societies were thought to possess a high degree of personal freedom. Plato hated such freedom and thought it would lead to disorderly and superficial lives. Obviously, the democrats, and the majority of the Athenian male citizen body, disagreed. We can understand the ability to live as one likes as an expression of personal autonomy – again, a kind of negative liberty in Berlin's sense. The democratic system allows everyone to pursue whatever kind of life they want, without interference from others or the community as a whole.

Now, there is evidently a possibility of conflict between political liberty and individual liberty, so conceived. If political liberty involves submitting to rule by others (ruling and being ruled in turn), it requires some compromise in one's freedom to live exactly as one likes. As Aristotle puts it, from the principle of 'living as you like' comes the ideal of 'not being ruled': 'not by anyone at all if possible, or at least only in alternation'. (*Politics* vi 2, 1317b14–16.) While it would be better not to be ruled at all, at least democracy allows one to rule sometimes. The democratic bargain envisioned here is that one puts up with being ruled by others, since this comes along with the ability to rule in your turn; and this is enough to secure the freedom to live an otherwise autonomous life.

That is one way to reconcile the demands of individual and political liberty. In fact, these thinkers accepted the basic idea of tension between the two that Constant identified in his essay, though they gave more weight to individual liberty than Constant acknowledged. But the ancient sources on democracy also point in another direction, one which emphasises the interdependence of individual freedom and political participation, instead of the potential conflict between them. So, the state and its institutions provide individuals with the opportunity to live as they like and so to flourish; conversely, their participation gives legitimacy to the state, shapes its institutions, and allows it to flourish in turn. This is the basic point of view that underlies the Periclean funeral oration in Thucydides, with its emphasis on the harmony between public and private life, on the respect for individual talents, and on equality of opportunity regardless of social position or economic status (Thucydides 2.37). In contrast to the modern discourse of liberty, which typically views personal liberty as threatened by state power, and attempts to circumscribe the limits of the latter by means of a doctrine of rights, the ancient Athenian perspective tended to view the political community as a positive force for promoting liberty.

Although he was no democrat, Aristotle shares the idea that the state is not an impediment to human flourishing but, rather, an essential precondition of it. For him, the state is natural, not something imposed by force or coercion on a pre-existing 'state of nature'. Human beings, he says, are political animals, implying that humans can only attain their full potential to lead the good life when they associate with others in the city-state. The ability of individuals to flourish, to lead the good life, thus depends on their participation in a political community. Of course, Aristotle had a radically circumscribed conception of human nature that allowed for the existence of natural slaves and restricted the capacity for flourishing to a relatively small elite. But if we leave his particular prejudices aside, the conception of the state as an essential framework for securing liberty and human flourishing is one that some ancient democrats, such as Pericles, would have agreed with.

Relevance to contemporary challenges

The ancient Athenian discourse on democracy and liberty gives us the resources to think about the relation between the individual and the political community in ways that are free of the worries about state control that animate modern liberal theorists such as Berlin, Mill and Constant. This brings us back to another key difference between ancient and modern democracy: the lack of an explicit conception of rights in the former. Evidently, the Athenians found it possible to defend liberty, equality and the rule of law for two centuries without appealing to the notion of citizen rights. Athens was not, then, a liberal democracy in the modern sense. But this raises an important question: is the idea of rights the only or the best way to achieve the democratic goals of equality and liberty? The notion of the state as enabling human flourishing encourages citizens to think not only of what is owed to them – their rights – but also of their obligations and duties to others. Whatever we may think about the strengths or weaknesses of the ancient approach, it offers a fresh perspective that may help us to get past the divide between libertarians (for whom individual liberty is paramount) and communitarians (for whom the state takes priority).

For this reason, it is useful to reflect on the relevance of the Athenian concept of liberty today. Four aspects are particularly germane. First, while slavery as legal ownership of human beings may be a thing of the past, there are other forms of human bondage and forced deprivation of personal liberty that should command our attention today. Therefore, the ancient sense of freedom as the absence of slavery remains all too relevant. Second, at a time when the possibility of authoritarian rule looms both internationally and within states, we could do worse than reflect on the ancient Athenians' successful opposition to tyranny over some ten human generations. Third, that effort involved a sustained commitment to political participation on the part of the citizenry, and sustained efforts to promote participation on the part of those in government. This is a salutary lesson at a time of crisis in democratic participation that threatens to strip democracy of its legitimacy in the eyes of citizens. Clearly the Athenians understood that without a chance for citizens to participate in ways that they thought could make a difference, the project of self-government could not succeed. And, finally, the idea that individual liberty and political participation are mutually reinforcing, rather than at odds with one another, may help to overcome perennial disputes between liberal and communitarian approaches to politics.

The ancient Athenian promotion of liberty, without an explicit concept of rights, challenges us to broaden our perspective and consider not only the rights we have as democratic citizens, but also the duties we have to one another and to our political communities.

THE QUEST FOR LIBERTY

Miracle of the Cross at the Ponte di Rialto or
The Healing of the Madman.
Painting by Vittorio Carpaccio, 1494.

LIBERTY AND THE 'MYTH' OF VENICE

Alexander Lee

In 1364, the poet Francesco Petrarca (1304–74) hailed Venice as the 'one true home of liberty' – and with good reason. Throughout the Renaissance, this was precisely how Venetians liked to think about their city. By Petrarca's time, they had already begun to develop a rich mythology of their history and origins which made *libertas* – in the sense of political independence, rather than personal freedom – the very hallmark of Venice's identity. Like all myths, this was anything but stable. An organic outpouring of civic self-fashioning, it developed in fits and starts, as circumstances seemed to require, and its details could vary in the retelling, sometimes wildly so. Over the centuries which followed, it found expression in civic rituals and pageants, in official and 'popular' histories, in music, in poetry, even in the visual arts – and for that reason, employed a vocabulary which sometimes obscured as much as it revealed. Yet that Venice's liberty was special, even unique, no-one was ever left in any doubt.

Unlike every other Italian republic – the story went – Venice had been born in freedom. Reputedly founded by refugees on 25 March 421, it had resisted every foreign invader; and, despite much evidence to the contrary, its panegyrists maintained that it had never recognised a superior. As Paolo Sarpi (1552–1623) claimed in the early seventeenth century, Venice had only ever been ruled by her own laws. Whenever the doge appeared on public occasions, he was followed by the umbrella and sword which had reputedly been gifted by Pope Alexander III as a mark of the city's equal status at a meeting with the Holy Roman Emperor in 1177. And that wasn't all. As Venetians were fond of pointing out, they had never succumbed to a domestic tyrant, either. They had always governed themselves in peace and harmony. The mercantile elites who had dominated government since the late thirteenth century were kept in check by a complex system of balloting; factionalism was all but unknown; and though most people were excluded from the political process, the

Venetians liked to boast that there had never been any hint of popular unrest. As a roundel on the west façade of the Palazzo Ducale proclaimed, Venice had 'put the furies of the sea beneath its feet' – and had grown rich and powerful in the process.

No-one denied that this liberty was owed, in part, to the sea. As the diarist Marino Sanudo (1466–1536) pointed out, the rippling waves of the lagoon had protected the city more surely than any walls and had forced its people to work together in harmony, to boot. But for Venetians, such liberty was better understood in mystical terms, as a gift from heaven. It was no accident that the Republic often described itself in official documents as 'this holy city'. That Venice had been founded on the feast of the Annunciation was a sign that it lived under the Virgin Mary's protection; while the 'translation' of St Mark's remains from Alexandria in 827 or 828 – supposedly in fulfilment of a prophesy – was routinely trumpeted as proof that it had been marked for divine favour. As the historian Marcantonio Sabellico (1436–1506) proudly noted towards the end of the fifteenth century, the presence of the saint's relics was a guarantee of the Republic's endurance.

The fragility of liberty

Yet, in reality, Venice's liberty was remarkably fragile. However perfect its system of government might have seemed, however safe the lagoon may have felt, the Republic was unable either to eliminate the ambitions of unscrupulous men or avoid the envious eyes of its neighbours. Only a few years before Petrarca's letter, Doge Marino Faliero (1274–1355) had been executed after a botched plot to set himself up as a hereditary monarch; and less than a decade later, Venice came within a whisker of being conquered by its maritime rival, Genoa. And that was just the beginning. The more time wore on, and the more prosperous Venice grew, the more acute the threats to Venice's liberty became.

By the outbreak of the Italian Wars in 1494, Venice's neighbours, alarmed by its territorial expansion on *terraferma,* were openly talking about cutting it down to size. According to Niccolò Machiavelli (1469–1527), Italy would never know peace until Venice was destroyed. In 1508, the League of Cambrai was formed expressly to deprive it of its liberty; and in 1509, enemy cannon could be heard from St Mark's Square. Venice was in no position to defend itself. As Sallust said of Rome, wealth had made it complacent. Divisions began to emerge within the patriarchate; electoral responsibilities were frequently evaded; and the purchase of offices became common. Though evidence of popular sentiments is scant, there is some indication that the common people were growing restive; and as refugees poured in from the countryside, fears of civil unrest became so intense that soldiers were ordered to confiscate the weapons of anyone found wandering the streets near the Palazzo Ducale. A feeling of dread fell upon the Republic. It is no coincidence that in Sebastiano del Piombo's *Death of Adonis* (c.1512) – painted just a few years after the Venetian army was crushed at the battle of Agnadello – a dark cloud hangs over the city; while in Giorgione's *Tempest* (c.1509–10), the brooding storm evokes a sense of nameless foreboding.

A republic of virtue?

Venice was hence faced with a troubling question: how was it to reconcile its self-image with the true instability of its position? How, in times of crisis, was it to preserve its liberty?

Clearly, the Venetians couldn't stop their rivals from attacking them. Regardless of what their actual intentions may have been, no propaganda in the world was going to allay the suspicions and resentments aroused by its burgeoning empire. The answer, therefore, had to lie with the Venetians themselves. If they could somehow remain united – the logic went – bound together by a shared identity and common purpose, they would, at the very least, stand a fighting chance of fending off foreign domination. But how did you unite a people against the enemy? How could you stop them splintering into factions or succumbing to a domestic tyrant, like so many other Italian states in the past?

Throughout the peninsula, humanists preoccupied with this problem looked to the Latin and Greek classics for a solution. As was natural, their preferences varied according to taste. But many derived from works like Cicero's *De officiis* the view that liberty, along with domestic peace, rested above all on two foundations. The first of these was equity. No community, Cicero had argued, could govern itself in freedom unless everyone lived on the same legal footing. It was, therefore, vital to ensure that no-one received preferential treatment in the courts, and that wrongdoers were punished, irrespective of wealth or social status. This was obvious when you thought about it. Just imagine if there was no guarantee of even-handedness. There would be nothing to stop litigants from bribing judges and bartering influence – or to save the government itself from being corrupted. This also pointed towards the second foundation. Just as a people must be protected from harmful, partial influence, so the community must be governed only in the interests of the common good. By adhering to this principle, it would ensure that its weapons were used only against public enemies, and that all shared in its benefits.

If Venice was to remain free, it was hence clear that it would need to strengthen both. But how? From the mid-thirteenth century, humanists across northern Italy had come to believe that the key was virtue. Drawing on Cicero once again, they argued that since vice naturally inclined men to value the self above the social whole, neither equity nor the common good could exist without its opposite.

What specific virtues should be cultivated depended on who you asked. Some believed that there were seven of them: the four cardinal virtues (prudence, justice, temperance, and fortitude/magnanimity) and the three theological (faith, hope, and charity). Others preferred a smaller number, or a slightly different selection. But the challenge nevertheless remained the same. If liberty was to be preserved, you had to find a way of making citizens and rulers 'good'.

A great many letters, speeches, and treatises were devoted to precisely this issue, but it was in the ceremonial entry to the Palazzo Ducale – known as the Porta della Carta – that it found its most arresting solution. Carved by Giovanni and Bartolomeo Bon between 1438 and 1443, this acted as a visual *summa* of Venetian liberty. Above the portal, visitors saw an almost life-sized statue of the current doge, Francesco Foscari, kneeling before the Lion of St Mark. Meanwhile, on either side of the portal, four female figures represented the virtues of Temperance, Charity, Prudence, and Fortitude upon which the doge's just rule depended. The implication was hard to miss. Not only did this legitimise Foscari's government, but it also provided viewers with a laudable example to emulate. And that was not all. As the eye follows the tracery heavenwards, the rewards of virtue – and liberty – are made plain. Above a window, St Mark himself looks out benignly from his roundel, assuring liberty's survival, while at the very top, a personification of Justice sits on her throne, flanked by two lions. A more powerful endorsement of virtue could hardly be imagined.

Harmony, order and immortality

This all looked and sounded very impressive. But for the Venetians, it was only half the story. While no-one denied that the virtues were a laudable ideal, they were just that – an ideal, and to the pragmatic Venetians, that was always a little suspect. As Machiavelli famously pointed out, man is by nature a craven beast, in reality as inclined to the bad as to the good. No matter how compelling your rhetoric, rituals or art, you shouldn't bank on *making* people magnanimous, prudent, just or whatever, especially in times of crisis. As Paolo Paruta (1540-98) observed, empiricism, rather than idealism, was the only proper approach when government couldn't be sure of anything.

By the end of the fifteenth century, as the threat to Venice's freedom grew, Venetians recognised that something more was needed. Instead of extolling the virtues individuals *should* cultivate, panegyrists increasingly concentrated on valorising the Republic as it actually was. More particularly, they sought to craft an image of Venice, not as a place where equity and the common good might be strengthened, but as a polity which already embodied them both. This was, admittedly, not entirely new. Some aspects of this same idea can be found in rudimentary form in Venetian writings before this date. But from this point onwards, the presence – and durability – of liberty's foundations was demonstrated with reference to three clearly delineated ideas.

The first was order. As Gasparo Contarini (1483–1542) noted, this was by far the most essential quality of any free city. Drawing on Aristotle, he argued that the 'agreement and effective ordering of citizens' was 'the true basis and form of a republic', and that, in this, Venice excelled over all other cities. This did not mean mindless 'conformity to some abstract pattern of universal order', as William Bouwsma has put it. Rather, Contarini had in mind the kind of practical, everyday order which was assured by sensible government, and which made socio-economic life possible. Some idea of what this looked like is given by Jacopo de' Barbari's *View of Venice* (1500).

This enormous woodcut, printed in six blocks, each almost a metre wide, was designed to bring honour to Venice – and is so detailed that some scholars have speculated that it may have been based on a ground survey. But it was as much an idealised depiction of the city as a literal representation. The confusing warren of alleyways, beloved of brigands and thieves, was simplified; church towers were exaggerated; and some public buildings, such as the Palazzo Ducale, were made to seem taller or more imposing than they really were, especially in relation to private residences. This made Venice seem not only more comprehensible, but also more rational and orderly – a republic united by rules and laws; a city worthy of Neptune and Mercury's favour.

A second component was harmony. Closely connected with order, this entailed far more than the mere absence of conflict. It was also about ensuring everyone had a role, and that no-one shone more brightly than the rest. This found expression in the many, elaborately choreographed ritual processions which formed such an important part of the Venetian calendar. But it is perhaps most vividly illustrated by Gentile Bellini's *Procession in St Mark's Square* (1496). There is a deliberate *sprezzatura* to this painting. It is made to look as if we have just stumbled upon something quite natural and unstudied. But the procession has nevertheless been carefully orchestrated. The whole Venetian polity, from the lowliest member of the citizen-dominated confraternities to the highest state officials, are present. Yet a strict equity prevails. No-one stands out more than the others, even the doge. Were it not for his golden mantle and the umbrella held above his head, it would be difficult to pick him out. Each person has their proper station, each their proper dignity, and each is as valuable and necessary as the rest. And to the painting's intended viewers, common citizens all, such harmony was doubtless a source of pride.

The final component was permanence or, rather, immortality. To counter the natural tendency to think of polities and offices on a human scale, as instruments capable of being turned to private interests, care was taken to present both Venice and its institutions as greater and more durable than any individual. Just as Contarini memorably suggested that Venice's founders had established a Republic that would live in perpetuity, so even the most exalted magistrates were held up as mere custodians, whose powers and prerogatives would far outlive their mortal span, and whose efforts were hence naturally devoted to the greater good. A glimpse of this can be caught in Titian's portrait of Doge Andrea Gritti (c.1548–50). Painted some years after Gritti's death, Titian's portrait captures the extraordinary forcefulness of his personality, yet it is overshadowed by the abstract authority of his role. Gritti's robes, heavy with brocade, outweigh his bulky frame; his stance, perhaps modelled on Michelangelo's *Moses*, is monumental; and his gaze reaches far beyond the viewer's ken.

The greatness of the man is apparent but the transcendence of his office – and the Republic itself – even more so.

Myths and lessons

This was all myth-making, too, of course, just like the idea of Venice as the 'true home of liberty'; and, to an extent, even Venetians seem to have recognised it as such. It was as much an attempt to constitute as it was to celebrate, if not more so.

But the advantages were palpable. Rather than trying to change human nature – to make bad men good, as it were – this image of Venice provided a model of society into which the efforts of even the most imperfect citizen could be subsumed, in which all had a defined place, and in whose benefits all could share. It idealised the curtailment of private interests, while still allowing for the pursuit of private ambitions; it celebrated individual merit, while reinforcing the supremacy of the whole; and it placed all beneath the overarching good of the Republic. As such, it allowed people to identify themselves with the ideals of equity and the common good without making any specific demands of them. And in doing so, it made liberty appear not so much a remote and perfect end, but as a tangible, immediate way of living for flawed human beings.

The effects of this myth of Venice's political history are hard, if not impossible, to gauge, and we should perhaps be suspicious of any attempt to find in it an explanation for the Republic's extraordinary durability. Yet its impact on wider perceptions of liberty is hard to underestimate. For many contemporaries, the mere fact that Venice had preserved its liberty, when all other Italian republics had failed, seemed proof that in the myth lay a profound truth – and that the illusion had become a reality. Within a little over a century of Petrarca's death, Venice had come to be regarded as the very archetype of Renaissance republicanism, a living ideal of liberty, worthy not just of praise, but of emulation. When Florence expelled the Medici in 1494, it was upon Venice that Girolamo Savonarola modelled his 'New Jerusalem'. And it was in the hope of making England more like 'La Serenissima' that James Harrington dedicated *The Commonwealth of Oceanea* (1656) to Oliver Cromwell.

And perhaps this myth has lessons to teach us today, as well. Though the circumstances of the Renaissance state are far removed from those of our own, and the Venetian system of government bears little relation to its modern heirs, its outlines resonate still. As Edward Muir has memorably noted, it speaks to 'Rousseau's warning in the *Contrat Sociale* that a state, if it is to endure, must enlist not only the interests of men, but their passions as well'. It illustrates that, at root, liberty resides in the imagination of the imperfect, and that its future relies less on the virtues of citizenship than on a sense of pride, structure, and belonging.

Portrait of Benjamin Constant,
by Hercule de Roche, 1820.

LIBERTY IN THE SHADOW OF BONAPARTE

Jeremy Jennings

One recurring theme in eighteenth-century discourse in Europe was the idea that society was moving away from an age of war to an age of commerce, an age where trade would replace war as the way in which both individuals and societies would interact with each other. This was perhaps most famously articulated by Adam Smith in his four-stage stadial conception of history, beginning with the Age of Hunters and followed by the Age of Shepherds and the Age of Agriculture, before finally reaching the Age of Commerce. Here, in his words, people 'would exchange with one another what they produced' and receive in turn the commodities they could not themselves produce. Crucially, in such a society, individuals were allowed and encouraged to pursue their own route to prosperity. If Smith recognised that the 'first duty of the sovereign' was that of protecting society from 'the violence and invasion of other independent societies', he also saw that in modern societies the expense of fighting wars was 'out of all proportion greater than the necessary expense of civil government' and, moreover, that the fighting of wars encouraged what Smith termed 'the profusion of government'.

There are many other examples of this type of reasoning that could be cited but one in particular merits attention: namely, the argument confidently advanced by Montesquieu in 1748 in *The Spirit of the Laws* that as 'an almost general rule' commerce cured 'destructive prejudices' and 'the natural effect of commerce was to lead to peace'. As Montesquieu explained, 'two nations that trade with each other become reciprocally dependent; if one has an interest in buying, the other has an interest in selling, and all unions are founded on mutual needs'.

Smith's own argument was framed in the context of what he referred to as 'the late war', namely the Seven Years' War that had ended in 1763, and the subsequent war in America: wars, in his view, fought in support of the monopoly of colonial trade. Nevertheless, the persistence of wars and of their negative consequences did little to diminish Smith's faith in his grand narrative of the progress of commercial society and in the 'revolution of the greatest importance to the publick happiness' that it would bring.

Adam Smith died in 1790. In the years that immediately followed, Europe would be engulfed, first, in the French Revolutionary Wars of the 1790s and, then, the Napoleonic Wars, wars that not only revolutionised the manner in which war was fought but also introduced the world to wars fought on a previously unimagined scale. In such circumstances, was it still possible to believe in progress towards a commercial society and, no less importantly, in the possibility of an extension of our individual liberties?

One writer who retained his faith in the emergence and benefits of commercial society was Benjamin Constant. As he was to write in what is now his famous lecture comparing the liberty of the ancients with that of the moderns, if war preceded commerce, so too it followed that 'an age must come in which commerce replaces war'. That age, Constant asserted, had now been reached. Today, he proclaimed in 1819, commerce is 'the normal state of things, the only aim, the universal tendency, the true life of nations'. In such an age, Constant further argued, people wanted 'repose, and with repose comfort, and, as a source of comfort, industry'.

Constant is without doubt a curious figure. Born in Lausanne in 1767 into a Protestant family, he received an education of sorts at the University of Edinburgh. Having initially greeted the French Revolution with enthusiasm (like most at the time), he first arrived in Paris in 1795 and there started to write about politics, fearing the likelihood of both a royalist counter-revolution and a new seizure of power by the remaining followers of Robespierre and the Jacobins. What followed is too complicated to be described here but, suffice it to say, that Constant spent much of the period of the First Empire of Napoleon Bonaparte in internal or external exile. Unfortunately, Constant's complicated love life and predilection for gambling did little to enhance his reputation as a serious thinker, with the result that, if in later decades he was remembered at all, it was for his novel *Adolphe*, a *roman à clef* detailing the love of a disaffected young man for an older woman. Nonetheless, it was during these years that Constant produced a body of writing that provided a coherent liberal programme for successive generations of French writers.

In particular, the question that Constant sought to answer was how and why it had been possible for a revolution that had set out to emancipate people in the name of the rights of man to descend into the Reign of Terror, and then the military dictatorship of Napoleon Bonaparte. Constant's clearest answer came in a lecture delivered in Paris in February 1819, entitled 'The Liberty of the Ancients Compared with that of the Moderns'. His thesis, in brief, was that the revolutionaries had mistaken the character of modern liberty, with disastrous consequences. This confusion, Constant announced, had been 'the cause of many an evil'.

When Constant talked of ancient liberty, he had in mind the liberty that had prevailed in classical Greece and Rome. It consisted in the right to participate in the decision-making processes of society, to decide on questions of war and peace, and in voting on laws. It was, Constant argued, a form of 'collective freedom', but it was also a form of freedom that countenanced the 'complete subjection of the individual to the authority of the community'. All private actions were subjected to surveillance. No importance was attached to individual independence. There was no liberty of thought and, in particular, no 'right to choose one's own religious affiliation'. As a private individual, the citizen was 'constrained, watched and repressed in all his movements'. One example was the practice of ostracism, where society had 'complete authority' over its members, and where the individual was subject to arbitrary and discretionary power with no right of redress.

Constant further observed that such a conception of liberty was appropriate to societies that possessed three distinctive characteristics: ancient republics were restricted to a narrow territory; as a consequence of their small size, they were inevitably bellicose and obliged to preserve their independence and security 'at the price of war'; and, finally, 'by an equally necessary result of this way of being, all these states had slaves'.

By contrast, the foundations of modern states, and therefore of modern liberty, were very different. As moderns, we lived in large states, causing 'a corresponding decrease of the political importance allotted to each individual'. Second, slavery had been abolished among European nations, thereby depriving individuals of the time to devote themselves to public affairs. Third, the activity of commerce left individuals with little opportunity to devote themselves to 'the constant exercise of political rights'. Two things had followed from this. As moderns living in an age of commerce we had developed 'a vivid love of independence'. We had also learned that, when governments sought to act on our behalf, they often did things incompetently and expensively.

What then was the nature of modern liberty? It consisted, Constant told his audience, of the right 'to be neither arrested, detained, put to death, or maltreated in any way by the arbitrary will of one or more individuals'. It was, he continued, 'the right of everyone to express their opinion, choose a profession and practise it, to dispose of property, and even to abuse it, to come and go without permission, and without having to account for our undertakings'. To this, Constant added the right to associate with other individuals and, most importantly, the right to profess a religion of one's choosing. Henceforth, Constant therefore concluded, 'our freedom must consist of peaceful enjoyment and quiet independence'. It also followed that we could no longer enjoy the liberty of the ancients.

How did this analysis enable Constant to answer the questions that most troubled him? First, he did not doubt that the aims of those who had initially led the French Revolution were 'noble and generous'. 'Who among us did not feel his heart beat with hope at the outset of the course which they seemed to open up?' he said. However, those same men failed to recognise the changes brought about over 2,000 years in the 'dispositions of mankind'. By the nature of the education the revolutionaries had received, they were 'steeped in ancient views which [were] no longer valid', and this, Constant believed, 'furnished deadly pretexts for more than one kind of tyranny'. They had believed that everything should give way before the public will and that, in the name of an austere republican and classical virtue, 'the individual should be enslaved for the people to be free'. In short, they had attempted to turn free men into Spartans and when this failed, as it was inevitably destined to do, they had had no alternative but to resort to coercion and terror. 'It follows that none of the numerous and too highly praised institutions which in the ancient republics hindered individual liberty is any longer admissible in modern times,' Constant wrote.

What conclusions followed from this? The first was that, as moderns, we needed to learn that limits had to be placed upon the extent of social power and collective sovereignty over the individual. This included a recognition that unlimited sovereignty, whether it be in the hands of one person, or several, or all the people, was bound to constitute an evil. It was then not a matter of attacking those who held power but of attacking the nature of power itself. As Constant wrote in one of his earlier essays on the principles of politics, there was 'a part of human existence, which by necessity remains individual and independent, and which is, by right, outside any social competence'. It also followed, as Constant expressed it in his 1819 lecture, that he wanted 'a liberty suited to modern times' and, in line with what he had argued, that 'individual liberty is the true modern liberty'.

Was that the end of Constant's story? Many – including those who have never quite managed to read through to the end of the lecture – have often thought so. Yet he had another lesson to teach us. If the danger of ancient liberty was that men would attach too little value to their individual rights and enjoyments, the danger in modern liberty was that those very individuals might be so absorbed in the enjoyment of their 'private independence' and the pursuit of their 'particular interests' that they would all too easily be willing to give up their share in the exercise of political power. Moreover, those who held political authority were only too eager to encourage us to do this. They are, Constant argued, 'so ready to spare us all sort of troubles, except those of paying and obeying'.

It is at this point in the argument that the shadow of Napoleon Bonaparte became all too evident. Constant thought long and hard about what to make of this remarkable man and what he had visited upon Europe. What Napoleon embodied was the spirit of conquest and, in its name, he had scarred Europe with the brutality of barbarism and the excesses of violence. Constant also saw that to force Europe into a general war of such a massive scale was 'to commit a gross and disastrous anachronism'.

It was, however, the internal repercussions for France of Bonaparte's regime that interested Constant. The First Empire, he argued, was a novel form of usurpation, a form of arbitrary and illegal power exercised by one man who had slithered onto the throne 'through mud and blood'. Its guiding principle was the centralisation of all power. The ambition was to impose uniformity and unanimity. To that end, it employed spies and informers, and sought to silence all opposition and freedom of thought, subjecting all it touched to 'moral degradation and ever-growing ignorance'. More than this, this regime had sought to destroy all the institutions of civil society, with the express intention of rendering individuals 'strangers in the place of their birth', casting them 'like atoms upon an immense flat plain', and forcing them to live in a state of isolation and indifference towards their fellows.

But there was a further novel dimension to this regime of usurpation, a dimension that, in Constant's opinion, made it more to be feared than the traditional forms of absolute despotism that had preceded it. 'Despotism rules by means of silence, and leaves man the right to be silent; usurpation condemns him to speak, it pursues him to the most intimate sanctuary of his thoughts, and by forcing him to lie to his own conscience, deprives the oppressed of his last remaining consolation.' The usurper, in short, demanded public approval from those he had enslaved.

And, so, it was with this experience in mind that Constant concluded his lecture with the assertion that, rather than abandoning one or other of the two forms of liberty, we had to learn of necessity 'to combine the two together'. This was because the individual and civil liberty we now treasured could only be guaranteed through the continued existence of political liberty. It was not to happiness alone but to our self-development that we were called, and political liberty was the most effective means of achieving that end. Political liberty, Constant told his audience, 'by submitting to all citizens, without exception, the care and assessment of their most sacred interests, enlarges their spirit, ennobles their thoughts, and establishes among them a kind of intellectual equality which forms the glory and power of a people'. Fortunately, the mechanisms of representative democracy now made possible such political engagement in modern, large-scale societies.

Here then was Constant's considered response not only to the mass murder inflicted by the French Revolution, but to the attempt to reduce the whole French population to the condition of willing slaves under Bonaparte's First Empire. As already indicated, in setting out these ideas, Constant provided the foundations for a liberal programme that was to be developed by later writers in France and elsewhere. As importantly, he provided, with great insight, a diagnosis of the character of a distinctively modern form of usurpation or dictatorship that can be applied to our analysis of many subsequent totalitarian regimes, warning us, in the process, that we should not allow the power of government to substitute itself for society or allow the authority of society to substitute itself for the rights of the individual. Moreover, in an age where governments in liberal democracies increasingly have resort to the language of crisis, emergency and war to justify the surrendering of the legislative function to executive power, these are arguments that need to be heard clearly. If not, we will most likely see the ever greater infiltration of the power of the state into the lives of individuals.

Declaration of the Rights of the Man and of the Citizen of 1793. Coloured engraving by French school, 18th century.

STICKING TO THE FREEDOM SCRIPT

Christopher Coker

The earliest surviving inscription on a monument to the fallen in battle was published in the summer of 2010. It commends the Athenians who fell in the battle of Marathon fighting the Persians, 2,500 years ago:

ERECHTHEIS
Fame, as it reaches the furthest limits of the
...sunlit earth
Shall learn the valour of these men: how
They died
In battle with the Medes, and how they
Garlanded Athens
The few who undertook the war of many
Drakontides
Antiphon
Aphsephes
Xenon
Glaukiades

The survival of the casualty list is due entirely to the interests of an Athenian millionaire, Herodes Atticus, who lived in the second century AD and was tutor to the young Marcus Aurelius. He had the monument installed in his country house in the eastern Peloponnese.

What is striking about the monument is that as far as we know it is a first: the first monument to enumerate the death of ordinary men, not only aristocrats, who died fighting side-by-side for the right to live their own life. We have grown so used to such inscriptions from the commemoration of the fallen in two world wars that we might be forgiven for missing the novelty of this approach. The Athenians thought it was worth recording the names of the lowliest as well as the highest. They were

celebrating the sacrifice by men who, being equal in the eyes of their enemies, the Persians, were equal in their own eyes in battle. Although unequal in status, wealth and class back at home, they were targeted indis-
criminately by the enemy. In this case, the 'few' really did mean few. No
one knows how many Persians died at Marathon, but we do know how
many Athenians – only 192.

These days when we remember the Greco-Persian wars, we don't think
of Marathon so much as Thermopylae, the most famous battle to be
fought during the second Persian invasion of the Greek mainland. The
novelist William Golding, after visiting the battlefield, wrote that 'a little
of Leonidas lives in the fact that I can go where I like and write what I like.
He contributed to set us free.' Leonidas, of course, was the Spartan king
who held the pass at Thermopylae against a vast army that he couldn't
hope to defeat. My students know it from Zack Snyder's film *300,* which
was panned by the critics even though it was a great box office success.
The Greek government formally complained that its homoerotic content
might mislead audiences into thinking that Sparta was the gay superpower of the age. And the Iranian government lodged a formal complaint
with UNESCO against the depiction of the Persian king as a sexually
ambivalent, cross-dressing freak of nature. But Marathon continues to
remain the touchstone of Western liberty in the narrative the Western
world has crafted through the ages. Montaigne's friend, Étienne Le
Boétie, was the first European writer to see the Greco-Persian wars as a
historically significant fight for liberty against tyranny. The English
writer Edward Creasey chose it 300 years later as the first decisive battle
in history. For liberty, both writers tell us, doesn't come without
sacrifice.

Thomas Hobbes, cynical as ever, would have none of it. In the *Leviathan*
he expressed surprise that human beings would want to sacrifice their
lives for a cause, or a country or a noble ideal. Sacrifice, he wrote, was 'the
privilege of absurdity to which no living creature is subject, but Man
only'. So, it behoves us to ask whether the sacrifices we have made for liberty through the ages are to be found in our biological or cultural DNA?

The Greeks were the first to ask the question. Unlike Darwin, they
were unable to grasp the 'science' of altruism. Darwin recognised that if
natural selection works at the level of individuals genetically (we fight to
survive), society works at the level of the collective. Society can turn self-
ish genes into selfless people. The Greeks, however, did recognise that

culture is the key. As Pericles notes in his famous funeral oration – or at least in the speech that Thucydides gives him – the sacrifices made by the Spartans and Athenians differed significantly.

The Spartans' willingness to die for one another was firmly rooted in family. Armies were organised by clan and kin; sometimes grandfathers, fathers and sons might all fight in sight of one another; the extended family was privileged over the nuclear family – boys were removed from their parents at the age of seven. In other words, Leonidas's band of brothers was the product of a rare social experiment in the ancient world. For the Athenians, the situation was quite different. For them, citizenship was the key to the sacrifices they were willing to make for each other. They had translated *philia* (love) of country into something much greater – *eros*. *Eros*, writes Paul Ludwig, can be translated as lust, and lust can be applied to other abstract concepts, such as learning and knowledge. The love of liberty, as the Greeks knew perfectly well, was not unique to the West but the 'lust' for liberty probably was.

Hardwired into our biological DNA, there does seem to be a need to value ourselves, our customs and our ancestral gods. Another English seventeenth-century philosopher, John Locke, told the story of a city of Tatars that had surrendered their persons, wives, children and wealth to the Chinese conquerors. But when ordered to cut off the plait of hair which, by custom, they wore on their heads, they took up arms and were slaughtered to a man. What Locke believed the story demonstrated was that we all prize liberty – the freedom to be ourselves. A lust for liberty, however, would suggest something more. And in the eighteenth century, the Western world began to see liberty, not in terms of human being, but human becoming. And that required something more: the ideational idea of liberty as a natural right.

We can, of course, question whether any values are in any sense 'objectively' true. Another Western philosopher, David Hume, didn't believe any values were universally true, or even innately so. Our judgements of what is right and wrong are just matters of sentiment which we project into the world and imagine constitute part of the fabric of reality. But those who take the opposite view (as most of us do) accept that values do exist and that they are real enough if they reflect our individual interests and concerns, even if they differ from culture to culture. What is undoubtedly universal is the idea of value itself. We all demand fair treatment and a measure of self-esteem. Both are pro-social values for we are social animals, which is why in every culture people dislike betrayal and disloy-alty. As James Q Wilson argued in *The Moral Sense* (1993), just as children are equipped to learn language, so we come into the world equipped with a specific set of moral prejudices that make us social beings fit for society; sociopaths don't have them. And we have those values for a reason; it is one of the central ways we coordinate our lives with those of others; we appeal to them whenever we are trying to get things done together. The key insight of modern philosophical reflection is that language has been hardwired into us – it provides an evaluative tool that helps us work with each other more effectively. It allows us to value someone for being 'a hard worker' or a 'good mother' and to devalue those we find to be anti-so-cial. Unfortunately, most values, including liberty, are inherently judge-mental. What one culture may value, another may not.

Western civilisation just happened to take a specific path. For Montesquieu, in *The Spirit of the Laws*, 'the love of liberty is natural to mankind'. Several decades later, liberty had become a human 'right' rooted in social contract theory, one of the great just-so-stories of Western political philosophy. In his *Lectures on the Philosophy of History,* Hegel spun another story: history as the story of freedom becoming conscious of itself. It begins with the freedom of one man – the pharaoh or emperor of China; then the freedom of a collective, such as the Greek city state. Later Christianity preached that all men would be free in the next life. In the final phase of history, Hegel wrote, freedom would be achieved through humanity's own efforts. This vision was inspired by the French Revolution and its founding document: the *Declaration of the Rights of Man*. History would now be powered by liberation wars and revolutions. 'Give me lib-erty or death' was Patrick Henry's famous cry at the beginning of the American revolutionary war. On the scaffold, the English revolutionary Henry Thistlewood, one of the Cato Street conspirators, declared that it was better to die a free man than live in servitude. 'What did he mean by that?' asked the Russian ambassador's wife at the time. She was an intelli-gent woman, and her husband cosmopolitan, but culture usually trumps biology. A Russian's DNA is different from an Englishman's. We have far more cultural instincts, as it happens, than we do biological ones, as William James reminded us. The fact that human beings are willing to die for an abstraction such as 'liberty' (however they define the word or understand the concept – a fact which so mystified Hobbes, the great materialist) is what makes our species unique.

The Western idea of liberty is rooted in the idea that we cannot be truly human without it – either in the sense of 'being' (our individual self-worth), or in the sense of 'becoming' – we allow the quest for freedom to pull us towards a future in which we will become, hopefully, better people. Fast forward to 2003 and we find G W Bush claiming that in Afghanistan the West was fighting for the 'non-negotiable demands of human dignity'. We have made liberty into a human right which we are willing to export, whether people want it or not. Liberty can demand nation-building and regime change, and cost a great deal in blood and treasure. A great many – among the three billion coming into the world between now and 2050 – may choose not to embrace our own idea of freedom. But that is no reason for abandoning our script. We don't know how universal the wish for liberty is; we don't stand at the end of history, from where we can look back and see the 'inevitable triumph' of freedom. It's even impossible from a reading of history to prove that human beings have rights. But from a passing knowledge of the twentieth century, we know the appalling consequences of believing that they don't.

BREAKING FREE

Illustration of the Gustave Flaubert novel
Madame Bovary, by Albert Fourie,
19th century.

THE TRUTH SHALL SET US FREE

Marie Daouda

What do you really want? This question calls for a level of disclosure with which few are comfortable, because it opens a field of possibilities one might fear to face. To ask oneself 'What do I really want?' is to ask 'What would I do if all the limitations to my liberties were suddenly removed?' In the series *Lucifer*, hosted by Netflix, the eponymous character – the devil roaming free on Earth – gains control over his victims by reading into their souls to discover their most secret desires. This excursion into the realm of possibilities seems exhilarating until it becomes scary. We have the impression that facing our desires is like looking at an unforgiving mirror, and that our desires reveal something about our deep true self.

Most of the self-help books you would find on the shelves – especially the ones targeting a female audience – put forward the idea that following one's desires is the way to happiness, and that the liberty to follow any desire to reach your deep true self is the supreme good. In 2022, Amanda Trenfield wrote a memoir about how she left her husband and children after 12 years of marriage when she met her soulmate. And as the title of the book is *When a Soulmate Says No*, Trenfield unapologetically explains that this experience was worth the grief and pain it caused because she had been genuinely following her desires all along. Trenfield writes that her private consulting practice (as a life coach) embraces her two passions: 'guiding women to embrace their true self, and businesses to embrace the uniqueness of their employees'. Fashionable as it seems, there is nothing obvious about the idea that the freedom to be true to yourself is a *sine qua non* to your liberty.

Our desires are not our own, we don't have a deep true self, and it is not the freedom to follow our desires that makes us free, but the commitment to truth that grants us authentic liberty.

The French Revolution coined liberty as the key to individual happiness. Since the seventeenth century, libertines defended the freedom of thought and belief aside from Christian dogma. A century later, libertin-ism was deployed in defence of moral relativism: following Voltaire, Rousseau and the philosophers of the Enlightenment, mankind is inher-ently good, social norms are oppressive, and nothing bad can come from the pursuit of desire. If each individual is granted the liberty to do as they please, the community as a whole will be better. The humanist principles of 1789, however, ended in the bloodbath of the Terror in 1792. At the same time, Sade explored the consequences of absolute political freedom in erotic and pornographic dialogues such as *La Philosophie dans le boudoir,* reaching the position that the only logical conclusion of a revolution is permanent anarchy, since no power could ever claim to be legitimate fol-lowing the end of open hostilities. In the early Napoleonic era and during the restoration of the monarchy, a Romantic generation of politicians and novelists influenced by Kant and Goethe, among them Chateaubriand, Benjamin Constant and Victor Hugo, took as their chief purpose the dis-covery of the self through the pursuit of desire. After the failure of the 1848 revolution and the collapse of the Second French Republic, these ideas were held in suspicion by writers who stood against the Romantic narrative. When Gustave Flaubert published *Madame Bovary* in 1857, eight different political regimes had come and gone since the last years of the absolute monarchy. Needless to say, Flaubert had little to no patience with the Republican ideal of universal and mutually beneficial liberty, and even less for the notion of liberty as a key to happiness.

Madame Bovary was put on trial because of the licentiousness of the her-oine, and because of the scenes describing her adultery and her demise. The procurator, Ernest Pinard, accused the book of offending public and religious morality as it did not present any explicit condemnation of the heroine's deeds and made no attempt to stage her conversion. In response, Flaubert's lawyer, Sénart, argued that the novel was, in fact, a warning against libertinism and misguided education, as Emma Bovary's down-fall discloses with no ambiguity the dreadful consequences of poorly ordained freedom. Emma can be seen as the typical novel heroine, led by desire while stuck in a boring reality. When Emma first appears in the novel as the daughter of a Normandy farmer, what she really wants is a respectable, gentrified husband. She marries Charles Bovary, a doctor, but soon enough wants a Parisian luxury lifestyle, then lovers, then a life of adventures. Flaubert's skill is that he discloses the mechanics of desire. Emma did not wake up one day wanting a husband, a luxurious lifestyle, multiple affairs or a life of adventure. The reader sees her borrowing these desires from the romances, the novels and the newspapers she reads. And that is great news for us, because we are all like Emma: each one of us is ready to borrow and imitate desires, then to weave them into the way we live our life.

We want to be unique, we want to be original and unforgettable, because we are conscious of our inevitable death; and we seek singularity by duplicating what we perceive as being unique or original. René Girard, a French comparative literature specialist turned anthropologist, studied the origins of desire, and coined the phrase 'mimetic desire'. For Girard, Romanticism nurtures the idea that the individual is moved by singular, unique desires. Girard distinguishes the Romantic mindset from a Romanesque mindset, where one acknowledges that one's desires are imitative. In *Mensonge romantique et vérité romanesque,* Girard notes that imitative desire is at the core of modern fiction, from Cervantes to Proust, and in *Le Bouc émissaire*, he extends these reflections to anthropology. Something or someone can be completely insignificant to me until someone shows it to be desirable by owning it or by wanting it. According to Girard, what I want is not so much the object, as to be identical to the owner of the object. We usually think of desire in a linear way: A wants B. In Girard's theory, desire is triangular: it is the basic rom-com plot where A falls in love with B because high-status C has expressed interest in B. For Girard, A does not want B, A wants to be like C. A wants to live in C's world.

Marketing specialists know what strings to pull to make us good consumers. We want to own things that make us feel unique, but not so unique that it would single us out in society and turn us into scapegoats. We want to own things that would make us feel and look like we belong to a community. I am not casting any stones here. As a teenager, I was a goth. Many thought I was original, but I knew I was not. I wanted to be a character from an Edgar Allan Poe short story, an Anne Rice novel, a Tim Burton film; and dressing like I had just locked myself out of a ruined Gothic castle was simultaneously a way to filter out people who did not have the same artistic interests, and to send a signal to those who could see my style as a quotation, so that they would know we were part of the same tribe.

Most of the urban fashions tap into this idea that following a trend helps you discover and perform your deep true self. But it only results in creating endless copies of one same model, because what we really want is to be part of a community that acknowledges one set of norms as its standard. There is a reason why all the Romantic heroes look the same, and all the goths look the same, and all the punks look the same, and so on and so forth. These tribal codes are not about freedom in fashion, they are a matter of survival, as they show one belongs to a group that can offer shelter and protection, be it in the modern form of online validation.

This does not only apply to clothing cues, but to entire self-narratives. Think, for instance, of the trend to go on a 'soul-searching trip to Bali' after the publication and film adaptation of Elizabeth Gilbert's *Eat, Pray, Love* (2006). It is now a feature of modern Bovarysm that in case of crisis, one has to go to a remote, exotic country to 'rediscover oneself' in the same way thousands of others have done before. Under the guise of originality, a new shared narrative appeared and became a new norm in less than 10 years.

These networks of imitation are particularly explicit on social media, where there are so many influencers – but where no one would ever say he or she is 'influenced'. We don't talk about being 'influenced', but about being 'empowered', as influencers provide their tribe with a shared set of norms regarding clothes, food or speech, that help them distinguish themselves. 'Empowered' is a passive adjective and we must be honest about the consequence it implies: the power is never on the side of the empowered. Suppose I am empowered into thinking that my real self does not match my body. In order to shape my body in accordance with my real self, I would go on a diet, or get a new wardrobe, or undergo irreversible medical treatment, so that my outer shape finally matches my deep true self. But life happens. Five or 10 or 50 years later, new encounters, new experiences will shape me differently, and I will soon outgrow what I thought was my deep true self. 'It's just a phase' is quite an annoying grown-up sentence to hear; but there are many things in life that are just a phase, a temporary state as one moves towards something else.

The freedom to fulfil our desires at all costs will, at best, allow us to match an image of ourselves that is about to change, to be updated, or even outdated. If we only see liberty as a way to push further the limits of what we can do, we face two possibilities. Either boredom, because our desires are infinite, or monstrosity, because we would need to go further and further to stimulate our exhausted desires.

We change and truth does not. We live in a time where truth is subjective, but look at the public outrage when the media or a politician says something that is not true. We know that without truth, we expose ourselves to cognitive dissonance; yet we collaborate in a condition of subjective truth which leads to isolation, loneliness, even madness. There are not many steps from 'I am free to see the world as my own representation' to 'there is nothing real at all'. This explains most of the mental health crisis that teenagers and young adults are facing: extremely online, young people want to be free and unique in any set of norms, but need the constant validation and approval of onlookers to confirm 'their' truth.

And you know what sentence expresses this validation? 'You do you' – which is very sad because when someone says 'You do you', what we really want to hear is: 'I love you no matter what. Even if you are about to do something I consider absolutely stupid, I will not kick you out of my house, I will not block you on social media, I will not shame you publicly, because I want you to exist in my world too. I want us to exist in the same world.' That is what we yearn for: sharing the same understanding and knowledge of the world, partaking in the same understanding of reality. After Emma's death, her husband discovers the letters of her lovers and realises that they had been living in separate realities all along.

Truth shall make us free because when we acknowledge that our desires are borrowed, we can dissociate ourselves from our impulses by saying: 'I only want this because this person or that event made it look desirable.' It also enables us to be grateful for the amount of good things we borrow, instead of pretending to be original. Once we acknowledge that truth is extrinsic and objective, we can collaborate towards understanding it, no matter how divergent our starting points can be. And the truth shall set us free because when our freedom is constrained, limited, even destroyed, we would still have the inner liberty to say: 'This is wrong. This is a lie I do not wish to be part of.'

Resisting falsehood is a matter of public safety. In *The Origins of Totalitarianism*, Hannah Arendt states: 'Before mass leaders seize the power to fit reality to their lies, their propaganda is marked by its extreme contempt for facts as such, for in their opinion fact depends entirely on the power of man who can fabricate it.' Nowadays, subjectivity and feelings are deemed more important than facts. Yet it is precisely through accepting the same facts that we can get a grasp on reality. For Arendt, the only way we can stay free from shapeshifting totalitarian thought is to keep 'the distinction between fact and fiction' and 'the distinction between true and false'. Once these are blurred, no matter how free we think we are, we are still entangled in a web of lies and delusions.

Liberty is not a value. Values fluctuate on the stock market of ideas and we have seen recently that safety could literally kill liberty when these two values are opposed. And it goes the other way around, too.

We cannot use liberty as an empty word. Abraham Lincoln said: 'We all declare for Liberty, but in using the same word we do not all mean the same thing.' And in *Four Essays on Liberty*, Isaiah Berlin noted that 200 different meanings of the word have been recorded by historians of ideas. 'Liberty' can only be a relevant and meaningful concept if we root it in a shared understanding of reality. The only way to save liberty is to define it as part of the culture we hold on to. A culture is not just a matter of heritage and traditions. It is the set of norms people are willing to share. But in order to share these norms, we must first agree that truth is not subjective. We will never discover our magical inner self by following each and every desire we borrow; but provided we work together towards knowing and sharing the truth, we will enjoy priceless, unconditional liberty.

Jean Monnet, 1958.

THE ELATION OF LIBERATION

Agnès C. Poirier

In a conversation about liberty and freedom, there is often one crucial aspect missing, that of liberation, the moment one is being freed. It can be an act of emancipation, the end of tyranny; it is always a feeling of pure elation and a moment of foundation for the future. It is indeed difficult to understand what freedom is about without the memory and knowledge of this very particular moment and feeling. In France, *La Libération* is a defined moment in contemporary history that lasted weeks and months, starting one early morning on 6 June, 1944, also known as D-Day, when 150,000 magnificent allies came to the rescue.

La Libération

Friday, 25 August, 1944. At dawn, the young composer Maurice Jarre, then 19, suddenly woke up in the two-room flat he shared with his aunt on the Avenue d'Orléans, the large boulevard linking the south gate of Paris to Notre Dame. He could feel tremors. The whole building was shaking. Jarre, who later became the celebrated film composer of *Lawrence of Arabia* and *Doctor Zhivago,* confided to me in April 2006: 'We thought it was the German Armoured Division sent by Hitler to crush the Paris insurrection. We thought we were finished. We were petrified. The roaring sound became greater and greater. I opened the window and crawled onto the balcony. I looked. When I realised what it was, it took my breath away. Leclerc's 2nd Armoured Division was entering Paris. There were no words to describe what we felt at that instant in time.'

A few hours later that day, Jean-Paul Sartre, leaving his room at the Hôtel de la Louisiane on the Rue de Seine, ran towards the Boulevard Saint-Michel. The philosopher was one among hundreds of thousands of Parisians now crowding the pavements to get a glimpse of their liberators. The Free French and the Spanish Republicans enlisted with General Leclerc's 2nd Armoured Division started pouring into the boulevards, coming from the south, while American, British and Canadian soldiers from the US 4th Infantry Division were entering the city from the east. Sartre watched Leclerc's Free French on their tanks rolling down towards the Seine. 'They looked, screamed, smiled. They waved at us with their fingers forming the V of Victory, and we could all feel our hearts beating as one. There were no civilians, there were no soldiers, there was one free people,' wrote Sartre, a week later on 2 September, in an article for the resistant newspaper *Combat*.

The elation of liberation is not only in the feeling of emancipation but also in the myriad details that surround it. It is often those details that are the most moving because they are symbolic of the power of freedom. Every tank of Leclerc's 2nd Armoured Division bore the name of a Paris street, a *quartier* or a Napoleonic victory such as Austerlitz, Jena or Wagram. One tank, baptised simply PARIS, had a live snow-white rabbit proudly resting next to the driver's hatch. On another was a portrait of Hitler with the word *merde* written across it. As for the Spanish Republicans, they had named their tank *Guernica*.

Now, what to do with the *libération* and with this 'orgy of fraternity', as Simone de Beauvoir called it? Paris became, in the second half of the 1940s and early 50s, a laboratory of ideas to rebuild democracy, a beehive of utopian projects and initiatives. Many failed, others were more successful. Here are three.

Philosopher Jean-Paul Sartre as party leader

In March 1948, the prodigiously prolific Sartre was now ready to cross the Rubicon: he would make the ultimate radical pledge and found a political party. With two well-known *résistants,* David Rousset and Georges Altman, Sartre created the RDR, Rassemblement démocratique révolutionnaire (the Democratic and Revolutionary Alliance). In *La Force des choses*, Simone de Beauvoir described the idea behind the party: to 'unite the non-communist left under one banner and to promote an independent Europe' as a bridge between the two blocs, the United States and the USSR. And to present as many candidates as possible at the next elections. The press conference to launch it was attended by more than a thousand French and foreign journalists, and was followed, just a week later, by the party's first public meeting. The communists, sensing the danger, increased their attacks against Sartre and Beauvoir. Many communist newspapers, such as *Action* and *Les Lettres Françaises,* published salacious stories about their private lives, alluding to orgies. This did not prevent the RDR from gaining in popularity. Albert Camus gave his support. The black American writer Richard Wright became a member, so did André Breton, the pope of surrealism. Even the Gaullist and conservative daily newspaper *Le Figaro* wrote favourably about the RDR. *Le Monde* chose to support it too and called it 'L'alternative'.

Only the *New Yorker* correspondent in France, the great Janet Flanner, could not help being sarcastic: 'Two of the best-known literary figures, Jean-Paul Sartre and David Rousset, have founded a political party, heaven help us. Sartre's political ideas are less clear, if more optimistic, than his novels. His talent, his scholarly mind, his French essence, and his hypersensitivity to Europe's dilapidation give momentary importance to his political hopes. The Sartre party declares that it expects to collect, in the next six months, a hundred thousand followers. If words were all, its followers should number millions, from all over this earth.' (Janet Flanner, *Paris Journal, 1944–1955,* 14 June, 1948.)

She was right. Tensions were simmering within the RDR: for how long could they still occupy the political middle ground? Some in the party were ever more ardently anti-communist, while Sartre was passionately anti-Gaullist. At the end of April 1949, during the party's congress, members were asked to vote on what direction the RDR should take. The party was split up, the neutralist attempt had failed. There was no Third Way – at least in practical politics.

That night, Sartre wrote in his carnet: 'The RDR has imploded. Tough. New and definite lessons in realism. One doesn't give birth to a movement. It did correspond to an abstract necessity, defined by an objective situation; however, it didn't answer a real need in people. This is the reason why, in the end, they didn't support it.'

The end of the RDR was the end of a dream. Sartre would eventually take sides and embrace communism.

One government for one world
In November 1948, Garry Davis stormed the UN's first session in Paris to launch his movement, 'one government for one world'. The Paris correspondent Art Buchwald remembered him as 'a carrot-topped, pleasant, shrewd and slightly corny Air Force veteran'. At 27, Davis thought the

solution to the Cold War was to create a world government in order to dilute nationalism once and for all. The UN needed to have its power extended. To preserve the peace was not good enough a mandate; the UN needed to be able to impose peace. To dramatise this, he decided to become the first 'world citizen' by giving up his American passport in front of the Palais de Chaillot, where the UN was meeting for the first time. In 1948, an American passport was the most cherished document on earth. Anyone who would give one up was regarded as crazy. Davis wanted to prove that any sort of identification paper was ridiculous. After he tore up his passport, the police arrested him for not having proper identification. A star was born.

On 18 November, UN sessions were open to the public, and seats in the balcony were allocated to whoever made a request. Everything had been carefully plotted. When the Soviet Union's high representative took to the podium to speak, Davis got up and shouted 'one government for one world', while his young comrades threw leaflets on the UN delegates seated below. The military police arrived and the youngsters decamped, but three did not run fast enough and were arrested, among them, Albert Camus. A few days later, Camus, now freed and accompanied by André Breton, who delighted in the surrealism of Davis's concept, improvised a press conference in a café at the Trocadéro. It was followed by a public meeting attended by 20,000 people. Davis, Camus and Richard Wright spoke. The world media reported their every word in print and on the air-waves. There was no escaping this new Parisian utopia.

Albert Einstein sent a cablegram to 'Monsieur Davis'. It said: 'I am eager to express to the young war veteran Davis my recognition of the sacrifice he has made for the well-being of humanity, in voluntarily giving up his citizenship-rights. He has made out of himself a 'displaced person' in order to fight for the natural rights of those who are the mute evidence of the low moral level of our time. The worst kind of slavery which bur-dens the people of our time is the militarisation of the people, but this mil-itarisation results from the fear of new mass-destruction in threatening world war. The well-intentioned effort to master this situation by the cre-ation of the United Nations had shown itself to be regrettably insufficient. A supra-national institution must have enough powers and independence if it shall be able to solve the problems of international security. Neither can one nor has one the right to leave the taking of such a decisive step entirely to the initiative of the governments.'

A few days later, praising Davis's scheme, Eleanor Roosevelt wrote in her famous newspaper column: 'How very much better it would be if Mr Davis would set up his own governmental organisation and start then and there a worldwide international government.'

Letters from the whole world started pouring in, and soon Davis was renting 10 rooms in his Left Bank hotel on Boulevard du Montparnasse to accommodate his staff, all volunteers. Again, the utopia did not last. But Davis would dedicate his life to promoting the scheme. In January 1949, he opened an international registry of world citizens; 750,000 people from more than 150 countries registered. When he went back to the United States in 1950, he came back as an immigrant, without legal documents. Until his death in 2013, Davis kept issuing world citizens passports. In 2012, he issued and sent a world passport to Julian Assange, and then another to Edward Snowden, in the care of the Russian authorities.

An idea with a plan: a European Union

If there was no stopping Cold War politics, a new project for Europe would nonetheless soon take form. On a grey spring morning in 1950, the Paris-based US journalist Theodore H White had a meeting with a French senior civil servant called Jean Monnet. 'A full-chested, round-faced, acid Frenchman with a needle-pointed nose', as White described him, Monnet was among the statesmen he met in his career who impressed him the most.

'Jean Monnet introduced me to a craft which I have since come to consider the most important in the world: the brokerage of ideas. Monnet was a businessman by origin, cool, calculating, caustic; but he did love ideas and could sell ideas to almost anyone. Ideas were his private form of sport – threading an idea into the slipstream of politics, then into government, then into history. He talked about how and when to plant ideas like a gardener. He coaxed people in government to think. There were few counterparts to Monnet in other countries.' (Theodore H White, *In Search of History*, 1978).

White invented the phrase 'power broker' to describe Monnet, an expression that passed into general use.

Six weeks before the invasion of Korea, Monnet placed on the agenda of world politics the idea of a united Europe, an old idea but this time clothed with a plan. What Monnet was proposing was this: a new coal and steel community in which not only Frenchmen and Germans, but Italians, Belgians and Dutch, would share resources, facilities and markets. In other words, Monnet was suggesting the creation of a common market. He sold the idea to the French foreign minister, Robert Schuman, who in turn sold it to the US secretary of state, Dean Acheson.

White wrote: 'Washington recognised that Jean Monnet, this businessman turned dreamer, turned planner, was the most imposing, though officeless, leader in his country. Monnet's prestige in French politics was akin to that of George Marshall in American politics. He belonged to no political party and enjoyed the confidence of all (except the communists). Thus, only he had the temerity and prestige to present to both American and French governments the plan that would give flesh to an idea which, ultimately, both would have to accept as the substitute for a grand settlement of peace.'

The elation of liberation always generates crazy ideas, which often fail but sometimes succeed. Creativity and freedom are feeding each other. All we need to do is keep on trying.

Steve Jobs, co-founder of Apple, 1981.

THE REBIRTH OF AMERICAN POWER

Francis J. Gavin

America in the 1970s is an interesting puzzle. Within recent memory, the United States had been economically and geopolitically dominant. And it was to return to economic and geopolitical primacy soon after the decade ended. But the 1970s represented a trough, a low point, a period of pessimism and malaise. It was also a time of unexpected turbulence in world order once again, sandwiched between decades of relative peace, prosperity and stability.

In the midst of what seemed to be decline and even chaos in America's domestic and international politics, however, transformative new forces and factors were emerging. Many of them came from the largest state in the Union, facing the great Pacific Ocean: California. Some of these dynamics were technological and economic, such as the rise of Silicon Valley and its dominance in computing, or the emergence of the great California shipping ports, like Los Angeles and Long Beach, on the back of growing trade with Asia and new shipping container technology. Other examples were more in the realm of how people ate, laughed, and thought about their bodies and human sexuality. While the causal origins of many of these forces are mysterious and their consequences uncertain, something very important, if elusive, took place during the 1970s – in some of the most basic categories of human potential, expression and freedom – symbolised by changes emerging from the so-called Golden State.

The 1970s reconsidered

It is important to review the standard narrative of the United States and world order in the 1970s. The picture was bleak. Geopolitically, the Cold War competition had settled into an uncomfortable stalemate. While strategic arms control and détente lessened the possibility of a great power war, such stability had come at a cost: recognising the political and moral equivalence of a communist, authoritarian and often ruthless great power, the Soviet Union. The Helsinki Accords had accepted the post-war boundaries of Europe and implicitly acknowledged a pressing Soviet empire in the once independent states of Eastern Europe. Western Europe, mired in its own political and economic frustration, increasingly distrusted the policies of its transatlantic patron, the United States. While the threat of a great war receded, murderous interstate and intrastate conflict raged on every continent.

The international economic order was in even greater disarray. The Bretton Woods system of fixed exchange rates, backed by dollar-gold convertibility, was unilaterally suspended by the US in 1971 and abandoned in 1973. Resource shocks, especially in dramatic increases in the price of oil, acted like a cancer on growth. Currency volatility, debt crisis, inflation and stagnation were all worsened by a lack of global coordination, and protectionism and economic nationalism increasingly framed politics. Global institutions set up to manage these crises, such as the International Monetary Fund, the World Bank, and even the United Nations, were sidelined or seen as unimportant.

The challenges to order were greatest within the anchor and author of the post-war system, the United States. The disastrous US military intervention in Vietnam, which claimed more than 50,000 American lives and considerably more in Southeast Asia, undermined the post-war consensus on both America's role in the world and its supposed goodness. Richard Nixon's deep political corruption, most visibly revealed in the Watergate scandal, was less anomalous than representative of national, state and local politics throughout the country. A crime and drug epidemic was destroying America's largest cities. Racial, ethnic, gender and class divisions polarised and poisoned America's politics. America's economy suffered the twin plagues of inflation and unemployment, as traditional manufacturing collapsed. The technological innovation needed to increase productivity seemed far more likely to come from the booming economies of East Asia, led by Japan, or even Western Europe.

To contemporary observers, this grim narrative spelled a slow but inevitable death, both to the post-war liberal order and the leading role of its architect, the United States. Simultaneously, however, powerful, unseen, tectonic forces were at work that would dramatically upend this narrative. By the end of the 1970s, the outlines of a new and completely unanticipated way of living had begun to take shape.

California: technology, socioeconomics and culture

Perhaps the most consequential shift was the disruptive emergence of Silicon Valley as a hub for profound technological change. This was preceded and accelerated by a less well recognised development: the emergence of California as a defence and aerospace superpower. The 1960s and 1970s saw Southern California, in particular, become the centre for innovative companies and institutions in this field, ranging from CalTech and NASA's Jet Propulsion Laboratory to Northrop Grumman. This less noted but crucial development created the hardware engineering culture in places such as Pasadena that complemented the north. This not only drew technological talent to California, but highlighted the important, if often controversial, relationship between the national security state and the more libertarian, hippie culture that emerged in companies like Apple.

The digital revolution that so marks our world today began, expanded and intensified in an area that is part of the greater San Francisco area, around Santa Clara Valley. It did not simply do things such as increase computing power and capabilities, but – first, through Apple – began to put these tools in the hands of individuals, rather than at the service of larger organisations. It also connected these technologies to increased levels of access to information, unmediated through the state or other institutions, providing individual independence and communication. The Silicon Valley experience also transformed how innovation was encouraged and financed, with the rise of venture capital and the new start-up culture. A culture of entrepreneurship, which celebrated risk and tolerated failure, took hold. The consequences for America's power position in the world was undeniable. Many of these technologies were related to, and accelerated, a revolution in military affairs that provided the US with both strategic and battlefield advantages unforeseen in the 1970s. It also created both immeasurable wealth and soft power, as Silicon Valley's success became a model that cities and nations around the world attempted to emulate.

This is what the historian Margaret O'Mara calls the American Revolution, which combined 'entrepreneurship and government, new and old economies, far-thinking engineers and the many nontechnical thousands who made their innovation possible'. As she points out, few people had heard of Silicon Valley before 'a journalist decided to give it that snappy nickname in early 1971'. At that point, 'America's centres of manufacturing, of finance, of politics' were 3,000 miles away, and 'Boston outranked Northern California in money raised, markets ruled, and media attention attracted'. Ten years later, the situation had transformed, creating the foundation for the radically different world we live in today.

A year after the term Silicon Valley was coined, the firm Kleiner Perkins Caufield & Byers opened offices in Menlo Park, becoming the leading entity of a new way of financing emerging technology that avoided traditional and more conservative banks by pooling venture capital. The state also hosted the nation's first discount airline, Pacific Coast Airlines, whose cheap fares in the unregulated state market helped inspire the Carter administration's deregulation of the airline industry in 1978, transforming the cost and availability of air travel.

A more mundane, but perhaps equally important, example is the container shipping revolution, which emerged in several places but turned the ports of California and, in particular, the adjacent ports of Los Angeles and Long Beach into global trading powerhouses. Trade as a percentage of American GNP was low in 1970, but as the restrictions on capital and finance were lifted, and global economic interactions exploded, the ports of California – utilising the new, less labour-intensive technologies of containers and container ships – became the hub in the massively increased economic interaction between the United States and the rising economies of East Asia – first Japan, then the Pacific Tigers, and today, China.

A force that combined both economic power and American soft power was the Hollywood film and television industry. Hollywood had always made entertainment for the world. But in the mid-1970s, the American film industry began to produce blockbusters on a new scale, such as *Jaws* and *Star Wars*, with increased global reach. The post-1970s Hollywood powerfully influenced tastes, fashions and ideas around the world. And despite great efforts, no other national film industry has been able to approach Hollywood's power.

A similar conflation of economic and cultural power was the rise of the wine industry in the Napa and Sonoma valleys. Wine was first grown there in the eighteenth century, and by the late nineteenth century, a wine industry existed. Georges de Latour protégé Andre Tchelistcheff moved to Napa Valley in the late 1930s and introduced new techniques. But throughout most of the twentieth century, Americans were not heavy consumers of wine. Nor was American wine seen as comparable in quality to that made in Europe. In the 1960s and 1970s, a group of innovators, led by Robert Mondavi, transformed California winemaking. The quality of the Golden State wines was demonstrated during a 1976 wine test in Paris – captured in the book and film *Judgement at Paris* – when a group of California whites dominated the top rankings, and the gold medal for red wine was awarded to the 1973 Stag's Leap.

These are the obvious manifestations of the energy and innovation emerging from California during the 1970s, which upended American society and eventually large parts of the globe. But they are not the only ones. In 1969, then-Governor Ronald Reagan signed the nation's first no-fault divorce law, fundamentally altering American family dynamics forever. The state developed some of the first legal protections against discrimination in housing and employment, including an early law (1978) protecting pregnant women from contract termination. How humour was generated and employed changed in this period. When the popular late-night show host Johnny Carson moved his programme from New York City to Burbank California, the state became the capital for modern stand-up comedy, aimed at subjects ranging from gender and race relations to politics to routine observations. While much of this humour upended polite norms and challenged traditional authority and beliefs, it became enormously popular. The Comedy Store in Los Angeles trained a generation of comedians whose humour transformed how, and at what, people laughed.

Human bodies and identities were not immune to these Californian changes. San Francisco clothing store Levi Strauss went public in 1971, moving from providing blue jeans to cowboys to creating a global brand that has become part of a universal uniform of sorts. San Francisco also became the global epicentre for a gay culture and lifestyle that was no longer kept hidden. It developed as a nascent political force, with the election (and tragic assassination) of gay advocate Harvey Milk to the San Francisco Board of Supervisors. A fine meal in an American restaurant before the 1970s likely consisted of surf and turf. Alice Waters, using fresh ingredients (from places such as the Corti Brothers supermarket in Sacramento), transformed the American palette with her Berkeley restaurant, Chez Panisse. Its success spawned successors everywhere, and marked the birth of the modern 'foodie' restaurant. Before 1970, specific exercise regimens were rare, and exercise in public was even rarer. Professional athletes were warned off weightlifting, for fear it would damage their health. Gold's Gym, and the muscle pen of Venice Beach, became the model for the ubiquitous health clubs now seen throughout the world. The San Fernando Valley became the capital of a booming, global trade in pornography, films and photos showing human sexuality in ways that were unthinkable before 1970, a phenomenon captured in Paul Thomas Anderson's 1997 film, *Boogie Nights*. As a nation of immigrants, California's role in welcoming and refusing people from around the globe was crucial. The Latino influence throughout California was one that preceded but accelerated in the 1970s. Less recognised was the dramatic increase in immigration from East and Southeast Asia. California became home to America's largest diaspora of ethnic Chinese, Philippine and, after the end of the war in Vietnam, Southeast Asian refugees.

The 'California dreaming' story matters for at least three reasons. First, what happened in California in the 1970s played an outsized role in creating the world we live in today – both in the United States and in large parts of the globe – for better or worse. It is not an exaggeration to say this was a historical shift on a par with the changes wrought by the Industrial Revolution in the late eighteenth through to the nineteenth centuries. The means of producing wealth moved from a domestically based, mass industrialised economy to a more decentralised system focused on 'just in time manufacturing', sensitive and integrated global supply chains, complex finance, and, especially, revolutionary information and communication technology. Personal identify shifted away from fixed characteristics and affiliation with large, inflexible histories and organisations – ethnic origin, political parties, churches and synagogues, unions, corporations, communities – to curated, flexible, often autonomous conceptions of the self, based on individual preferences and tastes. Demographics were upended: where and how people lived, and with whom they cohabited, transformed, as the structure and composition of both family units and communities evolved dramatically. Politics became more micro-targeted and focused as much on cultural issues as on the socio-economic concerns that dominated the first three-quarters of the twentieth century. Everything from markets to culture to identity to politics became fluid, disaggregated and disintermediated from legacy institutions, shaped by historically unprecedented choice and impermanence.

Enormous amounts of wealth were generated. Tolerance of difference increasingly became the norm. Diversity was celebrated as a positive attribute. Global economic and cultural interaction intensified. Innovation exploded, and technology dramatically increased access to vast amounts of knowledge and information, and communication became much easier and cheaper. The choices available to the newly empowered individual – from travel, to what they ate or worshipped, to how they earned their living, to what they laughed at, or who, or even if, they married – was unparalleled.

The second reason the California dreaming story matters is because it highlights the existence and the importance of understanding competing histories. There is a textbook, conventional wisdom about the United States during the 1970s which concentrates on malaise, chaos and American decline. The focus of this history is on the failings of traditional economic and political institutions, largely on the eastern seaboard of the United States, particularly New York City and Washington D.C. The California dreaming story was not uniformly positive, as we continue to deal with the consequences of polarisation, inequality, climate change, disinformation, and other consequences from the 1970s. It is, however, a dynamic story of American growth, rebirth, and reimagination. In this historical retelling, culture and technology matter as much as politics and, over time, intersect. Change, though dramatic, was often hard to recognise in real time, unlike the more traditional domestic and international economic and political narrative of the 1970s. Time horizons are not measured as much by shifting presidential administrations or foreign wars, as by new technologies and popular mass entertainment events. To be clear, competing narratives can both be true, and are obviously inextricably linked. But by focusing our lens only on the most conventional political and economic history, we may risk missing the profoundly important tectonic forces shaping the world.

Which brings up the third reason this story is important: when assessing how political and economic order developed in the post-war world, both domestically and globally, California dreaming forces us to expand the aperture of 'what matters'. A history that focuses on legacy institutions, be it the United States Congress or the World Bank, will not suffice. The history of Apple Computer or the rising influence of Hollywood tells us as much, if not more, about the rise, fall and rebirth of this order as a micro analysis of any G-7 summit or annual World Bank meetings. California dreaming should force us to think in more creative ways about the actors and agents that matter, what time horizons shape our current world, how to locate complex historical causality, and, perhaps most importantly, how to reimagine how we understand power. Power in international relations has often been understood as fixed, kinetic and material, built upon mass-industrialised economies that could convert these assets into the capacity to build armies and navies and conquer territory. But the 1970s inaugurated the world we live in today, for better and worse.

People gather outside the New York Public
Library in support of author Salman Rushdie after
an attack. 19 August, 2022.

THE WRITER'S RIGHT TO SPEAK FREELY

Alexander McCall Smith

Are writers free to write what they want? That is a simple question, answered in the average Western society with an unambiguous yes. We believe in freedom of speech, one of the basic freedoms, and are quick to criticise restrictions on the ability of writers to express themselves artistically without fear of recrimination. When measures are taken – elsewhere – to silence writers, these are condemned as an unwarranted interference in literary freedom.

The battle for freedom of expression through the printed word has been a long one. State and religious authorities have in the past been unembarrassed about silencing writers who write in a way of which they disapprove. The banning of books by awkward authors was a fairly unexceptional activity even into the late twentieth century: Europe witnessed the public burning of books in the fascist period and the silencing and persecution of dissident authors under communism. Then came the Salman Rushdie affair, when we saw an author go into lengthy hiding to escape the attentions of religious zealots. And it was not all that long ago, of course, that D. H. Lawrence's *Lady Chatterley's Lover*, a novel that is, by today's standards, completely incapable of raising an eyebrow, was the focus of a *cause celèbre* in the London courts. How things have changed, one might be tempted to say. And yet, have they? Has all that moral energy devoted to preventing the publication of seditious or obscene material simply been transferred to other targets?

In one view, writers even in those countries that ostensibly protect freedom of expression are, in fact, increasingly subject to restrictions on what they can say. These restrictions may be subtle, and yet are just as powerful for their indirect nature, having a strong inhibiting effect on artistic freedom. In what follows, I should like to identify ways in which artistic liberty is today threatened by illiberal attempts to tell authors what they can or cannot say, and to threaten those who do not comply with isolation, embargo and, in some cases, with police investigation and prosecution.

Of course, not everything about our current cultural climate is bleak. Sensitivity to the feelings of others, and awareness of the extent to which many voices have been silenced in the past by exclusion, is indicative of greatly enhanced moral understanding and is to be welcomed. That represents progress, and few would argue for its reversal. Against that background, restrictions on the expression of extremist opinions intended to cause social unrest are an important part in the defences of liberal societies. Freedom of expression does not include the right to threaten social peace by inflaming divisive sentiment or encouraging the unjust treatment of others. There is every justification for criminalising writing that sets out to inflame others to feel hatred for another section of the community. Some writing is clearly intended to encourage acts of violence and should not be allowed to shelter behind any protection provided by the principle of freedom of speech.

Yet acknowledgement of that principle does not end the debate. Even if we accept that public order provisions will necessarily restrict artistic liberty, the proper boundaries of these restrictions may be difficult to identify. This is particularly so in the contested areas of children's literature, the offence principle, and authorial identity. In all of these areas, there is clear tension between freedom of expression and the pursuit of social and political goals. It is here that literature has become something of a battleground between liberalism and tolerance in one corner, and illiberalism and intolerance in another.

Children's literature
Children's literature may seem an unlikely locus of disagreement, and yet it has long been a sensitive area. The notion that children's books are a powerful way of transmitting values to the next generation is hardly new, and any glance at children's books from the Victorian era onwards will reveal the high moral tone adopted by authors of such works. There are some who will remember from their youth *The Struwwelpeter*, a German collection of cautionary tales that terrified generations of children with stories of the fate awaiting those who behaved badly. That robust tradition continued in the twentieth century with more modern practitioners revealing their inner moralist, dealing out much anticipated and appreciated comeuppance to deserving recipients. Hilaire Belloc was one such writer; his characters met with strikingly unpleasant ends,

usually brought about by some failing or bad habit on their part. Children are never slow to get the point: behave badly and something unpleasant will happen to you. Roald Dahl also comes to mind here, with his recognition that children like to see the proud laid low and the underdog rewarded.

The moralising tendency of children's literature today has taken a different trajectory, moving beyond the encouragement of the traditional virtues – kindness, respect for others, and so on – to the pursuit of a broader agenda in which children's literature becomes part of what is perhaps a more politicised project. One focus of this project has been to stress gender equality, a laudable goal. If girls played a subservient role in children's books in the past – and there is no doubt that they did – then this is certainly no longer the case. The bookshelves of any children's bookshop are groaning under the weight of books about little girls whose ambition it is to be an engineer or a pilot, or any of the other callings to which boys have traditionally aspired. But those same shelves now seem barer of encouragement for boys, who seem to be somewhat relegated from the front bench. That might be necessary in a period of correction, when old-fashioned sexist assumptions are – rightly – challenged, but even welcome and much needed corrections can go too far if they then marginalise or exclude others on class or gender grounds. In particular, the sense of self-worth of boys needs to be taken into account. And there is always a danger that encouraging a particular view of society will lead to the exclusion of authors themselves because they do not fit the profile that editors wish to project. No author should be silenced because he or she comes from a particular class or is of a particular gender. To do so is to recreate the sort of discrimination that existed in the Soviet era, when bourgeois writers were penalised for accidents of birth.

Children's literature should be moral; it should be sensitive. But it must not exclude those whose faces do not fit, nor should it be monolithic, portraying only one section of society and ignoring others.

Taking offence
The offence issue provides perhaps the most vivid example of the threat that cancel culture holds for freedom of artistic expression, because its objectives have been and continue to be pursued illiberally and, in some cases, in a way that threatens important aspects of our cultural heritage.

Offence most frequently rears its head in an academic context. Typically, it arises where objection is raised to elements of the curriculum that are seen to be in some way disturbing to students. It is an inevitable concomitant of literature that there will be books that are a harrowing or upsetting read for certain readers. It would be surprising if things were otherwise, as there is always something that will offend somebody – if one looks hard enough for a potential victim. This is because the world is a harrowing and upsetting place, and if literature reflects that, then some degree of distress is inevitable. If literature is to have any pretence of reflecting the world in which we live, then it will inevitably have to deal with matters that are uncomfortable in the eyes of those who do not want discomfort. The poet T. S. Eliot once remarked that humankind cannot bear much reality. He was absolutely right. There are many who do not want to be reminded of the harsh truths of our existence. There is war; there is suffering; there are numerous small tragedies, countless disappointments and failures, in the lives of just about everybody. Being offended is part of being human. A life without offence would be an artificial one, removing one from the world of emotions in which any reasonably aware life is lived.

There is, of course, much at which offence might be taken. Charles Dickens, for example, is an upsetting read in so far as he portrays the brutal social conditions of his time. That was the whole point of Dickens's work, as it was of many writers who have sought to expose suffering, deprivation and injustice. Sometimes, books of that nature have a major impact on the way in which society is ordered, and a novelist may find himself or herself creating an entire climate of reformist opinion. It is important, then, that there should be novels and short stories that portray unequal and exploitative social conditions, or depict societies in which blatant wrongs, such as slavery, were tolerated. Reading about this may be upsetting, but is it grounds for the suppression of major works that reflect that particular reality? Unfortunately, there are those who take exactly that view and argue for the exclusion from the academic curriculum of those works that cause them offence. The argument is that the portrayal of social or individual injustice may be just too painful for sensitive students who are entitled not to be upset by such things. The unacceptability of this form of censorship is obvious but, increasingly, universities are yielding to such pressure and removing from the literary canon those works which are identified by pressure groups as being offensive to contemporary students. One would think that the whole point of university education is to encourage exposure to ideas that may make one feel uncomfortable, but that is not the way these objectors see it. They wish to decolonise the curriculum, which means the removal of those works to which they take ideological objection. The offence principle is invoked as a means of achieving this objective.

The unacceptability of this approach to literature hardly needs to be spelled out. If one were to apply this to the study of the classics, for example, it would mean the removal of many major elements of Western literature. For example, it is doubtful whether Homer would survive such scrutiny for long. The *Iliad* is, of course, deeply distressing to anybody who finds gory accounts of fighting one another unpalatable. And while the *Odyssey*, that matchless account of the universal human theme of the journey, is less bloody overall, there is still much in it that is capable of shocking modern sensibilities. When I read it, as I take great pleasure in doing, I must confess that I find myself appalled by the way in which Odysseus behaves when he eventually arrives back in Ithaca and deals with the suitors and with those who, in various ways, accommodated them. It is very unpleasant, but it is ancient Greece, after all, and what do we expect? A modern attitude towards the rights of others? The concept of anachronism seems to be something the defenders of the sensitive do not fully understand.

It is easy to find in some of these instances of protection of students a risible hyper-sensitivity. Yet even the absurd demands – often taken seriously by university authorities – may have a concealed agenda of the discrediting of an existing cultural inheritance. If people are made to feel bad about their cultural inheritance, then they will be inclined to feel bad about themselves – and in this way, the sway of a culture may be weakened. The homogeneity of culture may be undesirable and may rightly be challenged to include other cultural influences and claims, but its complete suppression could involve abandoning aspects of a heritage that have value and are worth preserving. The Homeric epics could be abandoned because they are blood-thirsty, but if we pruned our cultural heritage in that way, we would end up with nothing worth keeping and with a landscape that was bland and arid. We need to be shocked; we need to be saddened; we may even need, at times, to be disgusted. By all of these reactions we assert the range of our humanity and remind ourselves of who we are and how we got where we are.

Identity and authenticity

One of the potentially most limiting restrictions on authorial freedom is a product of the emphasis on identity in a whole range of spheres, including literature. The argument of the censorious is, in essence, that authors should only write from the perspective of one who shares their particular identity. In that view, an author who attempts to write about those who have had a different historical experience from his or her own is, effectively, appropriating an experience he or she has not had. If this argument is followed to its logical conclusion, then a male author should not be able to write about the experience of a female protagonist – and vice versa – nor should a straight author write of the experience of a gay character, or a gay author write about those who do not share his or her sexuality. The limiting nature of this position is self-evident and indeed it goes against the grain of the very essence of being a writer. A writer is almost by definition an outsider – an outsider who looks in on the lives and experiences of others. And it is this externality that gives the author insights worth expressing. It is often the outsider who will see things that the insider does not see. The outsider's perspective should, therefore, be welcomed, rather than discouraged.

Think of the great travel writers – usually complete outsiders – who open a window on another culture, and often in a way that leads to an increase in understanding of and sympathy for that other culture. How narrow and arid would literature be if publishers and other literary gate-keepers were to say that the only thing anybody should write about was what has happened to that particular person, with his or her particular historical experience. That would kill imagination stone dead – and it is imagination, above all else, that enables literature to do its task of bringing home to us what it is to be human.

Literature cannot thrive if the deciding factors in a book's reception is going to be the identity of the author. What matters is the content – its insights, its sympathy, its vision. The identity of the author may be a significant factor in our understanding of how the work came to be written, and of the perspective that the work adopts, but it is not the work itself. A perceptive author should be able to rise above the constraint of his or her own identity and to write, with freedom, about the full range of humanity and human experience. In dealing with this particular assault on authorial freedom, we might do well to remember those benighted times when female authors might have felt obliged to adopt a male pseudonym to secure publication and an audience. Do we seriously want to return to silencing people because they are, quite simply, the wrong shape or come from the wrong place?

If it is the case – and it appears to be so – that authors today feel intimidated by those who would have them conform to a current consensus, a received truth, in all respects, and who are, in addition, prepared to use social media to hound those who deviate in any way from that consensus, then literature is in a dark place. Lights need to be switched on in that dark place so that authors can follow their artistic inclinations and write about whatever they want to write about, subject only to certain clearly defined limits, intended to maintain social order and prevent real harm and real distress.

THE MEANING OF LIBERTY

Donald Trump and Steve Bannon, 2022.

A DECADE ON THE CULTURE WAR'S FRONTLINE

Fraser Nelson

I t's impossible to date the start of the current round of the culture wars, but I can date my first losing battle. I had become editor of *The Spectator* in September 2009 and inherited a debate about the nature of HIV. There had been a group of filmmakers who quoted Luc Montagnier, a Nobel laureate, saying that the virus could be shrugged off with a healthy immune system – the implication being that many African Aids deaths may be a function of malnutrition. It was a fringe argument. But it was interesting that their film was then banned. This was odd: if the claim is false, isn't it better to expose it through open debate?

So that's what we did: lined up some academic experts to discuss the film in front of a live audience. It was all booked by the time I took the editor's seat. I wrote a short blog outlining the debate. 'A good, but suicidal move,' someone said in the comments. 'Prepare to meet the Aids denialist online community who'll be showing up in 5, 4, 3, 2...' said another. I was baffled, until the trolls struck. Within minutes, I was labelled an 'Aids denialist' for 'platforming' weirdos. 'Aids denialism at *The Spectator*,' wrote a Guardian columnist.

The trolls then took formation for what I now recognise as the classic Twitter attack. Those who had agreed to come on the panel, if they were on social media, were targeted and asked why they 'shared a platform' with an Aids denialist. If they didn't respond, the trolls worked out who their employers were and targeted them: are they 'okay with' their employee being involved in 'promoting Aids denialism'? Pretty soon, all of the panellists pulled out and we had no debate. That evening I went to see Paul Johnson, then a *The Spectator* writer, and told him about this. 'It's war,' he said. 'You need to pick your battles – and never fight one you're unsure you can win.'

It has been war ever since. Journalism, if done properly, ought to be about picking fights. The magazine I edit, the world's oldest weekly, has been promoting minority opinion since its inception. We have always been for free speech and sharing ideas, championing causes found to be outrageous. We alone in the British media backed the north against the slave-owning south in the American Civil War, and almost went bust as even our own readers were appalled. We backed the decriminalisation of homosexuality in 1955, a decade before it happened, and were attacked as the 'bugger's bugle'. We backed Brexit in the 1975 referendum. We backed Thatcher in her first leadership battle.

So, if as editor I could not make sure *The Spectator* kept publishing minority – often incendiary – opinion articles, I'd have failed. I made it my business to study the art of digital war, the methods by which trolls attack, and the pressure points they use. From this came a new strategy, so all of our (small) staff know precisely what they are up against and how to fight. The battles change, so what follows is a contemporary state of play. But it's a snapshot of the vulnerabilities and paranoia that has had some of the most venerable titles in the world cowing before a Twitter mob.

In her resignation letter, the writer Bari Weiss argued: 'Twitter is not on the masthead of *The New York Times*. But Twitter has become its ultimate editor.' She was precisely right, and its power extends over a great many more titles. But how could this be? How could the world's greatest newspaper end up cowering in front of trolls? As an editor, I felt this acutely – and watched, amazed, at how digital mobs started to claim scalp after scalp.

As editor of *The Sun* from 1981 to 1993, Kelvin MacKenzie fought the world, and won. It doesn't matter, he argued, if our non-readers don't like us. But digital changed this dynamic. Most of the complaints that editors now face are from non-readers, who pass articles around online and then protest, sharing quotes that they dislike. This has become standard behaviour. But it changes the editing game. We're publishing copy not just for our readers, but for the world.

And that world packs a punch, as MacKenzie found out when he was forced to resign for a column in which he referred to Ross Barkley, then an Everton midfielder, as a 'gorilla'. He meant it as a general term of abuse, but it later turns out that Barkley had a Nigerian grandfather so qualified as an ethnic minority. This meant MacKenzie's term could be seen as racist – cue a Twitterstorm – and MacKenzie was sacked. A man who survived the worst the 1980s had to throw at him fell at the first shot in today's culture wars.

He was an unusually right-wing victim. When Ian Buruma was elevated to the editorship of *The New York Review of Books*, he came with impeccable progressive credentials. An academic and an author, one of his early commissions was an article from someone acquitted of a sex crime. The aim of the piece was simple: to describe a journey to 'public toxicity' from a perspective seldom seen in print – that of a man accused of a sexual assault. As was expected, outrage quickly ensued.

At first, Buruma was unapologetic. Yes, the #MeToo movement had been a necessary corrective, he said, but 'like all well-intentioned and good things, there can be undesirable consequences' – such as a 'general climate of denunciation'. This further enraged the mob, who went after the advertisers, who started to threaten to pull out. 'The owner of the magazine thought that the way to deal with the panic was to let me go,' Buruma later observed, noting that he had been 'convicted on Twitter, without any due process'.

The New Yorker's David Remnick is perhaps the world's most successful editor. But when he proposed an on-stage interview with Steve Bannon, Donald Trump's chief strategist, he also suffered a staff rebellion. They complained on Twitter that Bannon was being given a platform, advertisers were then targeted, and Remnick was eventually forced to back down. It was quite a sight: a journalistic event, an interview with a former White House chief of staff, cancelled due to journalists – journalists! – complaining about too much free speech.

There are all too many other such examples. The Glasgow *Herald* columnist Iain Macwhirter was fired after making an ironic comment on Twitter, wrongly represented as racist. The formula is the same: the Twitter mob identifies the pressure points, then goes after them. Senior staff, advertisers, even family members of staff or contributors, and their employers. They are not used to taking heat, and succumb. In this way, the defences of newspapers – built over decades to protect free expression – were penetrated by the Twitter mob.

Journalists are in no position to whinge about digital media. Journalists cannot lament social media. It generates a third of *The Spectator*'s traffic and new subscriptions, it brings in millions of new readers. There is good there, as well as deranged evil. But being exposed to the good means learning the nature of the evil. How it's wired. How it works. How to outwit it.

Social media feeds on outrage, with algorithms designed to infuriate. The 'what's happening' section of Twitter is not news at all, but tweets which the algorithm thinks will solicit a reaction from you. 'Look!' it says to you. 'Here is something appalling!' It is begging for your condemnation. 'Don't let them get away with it! Do a quote-tweet, a reaction, anything to express your anger! Show the world that you oppose it! Anonymously, if you will.'

The anger machine needs to be fed, which is why now every publication is scoured for potentially outrageous content. A sentence or a joke, to be taken out of context. There are technical aspects to this: you can post a picture of a headline, rather than a link to the article. This allows for misinterpretation, as readers never get to explore further. An article exposing the return of eugenic science entitled 'eugenics is back' can, in this way, be presented as a jubilant paean to eugenics and the author can then be pilloried. I know, as I was the author of that particular piece. I've ended up being denounced by the Chancellor of the Exchequer as a result of screen grabs, with my resignation then demanded.

But I have survived. Just. For a few reasons. The main one is that at the magazine I edit we have learnt from every skirmish and have built defences. It has been a dilemma. If you ask writers to self-censor, to worry about whether their every sentence is going to be ratioed on Twitter, they cease to become a writer. The right to write for your readers – not for a world of anonymous braying critics – solicits the kind of candour and honesty that *The Spectator* has had for 190 years. Ask writers to keep writing as if only our readers will see. We worry, so they don't have to.

And we have seen the price of being careless. The Aids fight could have been won, had we prepared for what was to come. Had Remnick anticipated the uproar over a Steve Bannon interview, he could have prepared the ground better and faced it down (as *The Economist* later did). To be naive about these battles is to guarantee defeat.

So, you prepare for battle. Every article in *The Spectator* is sent for legal checks, to make sure it doesn't violate libel law. That was, once, the great threat. But what costs editors and writers their job these days is having their work misrepresented – and then being fired, because no one is willing to stand up to the digital mob. I call this 'risk', and our articles are now read for risk by a team who ask of every article: is any of it open to misrepresentation?

Anything on trans issues, race, jihadis, climate science or satire of any kind is in the highest category of risk. Any jokes are in the middle category. Most copy is in a third category. Everything is thoroughly fact-checked, but this is (now) standard. Our reputation depends upon readers being able to trust everything they read. The new test is to look for words which could be maliciously misinterpreted. Usually, careful editing can defuse any potential IEDs. So, the sense and meaning of the article is preserved exactly. If I'm doing my job, then every week there will be a list of articles, or turns of phrases, likely to anger the trolls. As editor, I ask: have we weighed it up? Are we sure the article is accurate, and defensible? If so, we publish.

It is a paradox. The braver that you wish to be as a publication, the surer you need to be about what you publish. The era of hyper-scrutiny is, in many ways, pushing up standards. The aim is to keep picking fights but to do so knowingly, rather than stumble into them. Our 'red team' analysis makes sure controversial articles are read from the perspective of a crazed campaigner itching to find tiny grounds for complaint. Where is the weakness in the argument? Is there a lazily worded sentence that can be twisted or screen-grabbed with malign intent?

The Spectator's red team, or fact-checkers, are now the praetorians, the people who safeguard the nature and character of the magazine in the age of cancel culture and politicised correction.

The battles still come. For example, some of our writers – Matthew Parris and Debbie Hayton for instance – are uneasy about the language of the trans lobby and the notion of gender self-identification. Their work caught the attention of a left-wing group called Stop Funding Hate, which seeks to organise campaigns against publications, encouraging people on Twitter to target their advertisers. 'Hey @Acme,' the trolls will say, 'Are you okay with your adverts being published next to transphobic content?' The hope is that @Acme panics.

Normally, the advertiser does not know where their adverts are placed. It's all done via agencies. If the target company then says they won't be advertising in the offending publication again, the trolls have their hit. If one advertiser pulls out, then others are prevailed upon to follow. This tactic is intended to terrify the more easily scared commercial people at a publication, who complain to the editors. The aim is for a message to go out: no more articles questioning trans orthodoxy, or from 'problematic' writers.

In our case, it was a British supermarket chain, the Co-op, that took the trolls' bait and said it would not advertise with us anymore. Twitter was delighted. Andrew Neil less so. A former *Sunday Times* editor and a veteran of the Battle of Wapping, he now runs the business side of *The Spectator*. Having received death threats and arrangements for his funeral, he is not one to run scared from Twitter. Nor are our proprietors, the Barclay family. In fact, they'd rather lose money than give an inch to advertisers who threaten editorial independence.

After about ten seconds' consideration, Neil announced that the Co-op was banned from ever advertising in *The Spectator* again. He then said he was looking for 'other woke advertisers ready to follow Co-op's example' but found none. It was the first time, in all of these years of madness, that a publication has turned the tables on the trolls. Who, of course, scarpered. The Co-op backed down, apologised, and sent us a case of its in-house champagne to apologise. The original decision, it turned out, had been taken by a junior Twitter account holder. Such people now have the world's greatest newspapers running scared.

The Spectator is a tiny magazine: I'd hesitate to say we have created a model for anyone other than ourselves. But the mob is there to be defied. The extra scrutiny we apply anyway makes articles stronger, while giving our writers all the protection they need in an era where their reputations can be targeted. Careers can be ended over one stray word. If all newspapers got together and banned advertisers whose threats amount to editorial pressure, we could reapply the commercial-to-editorial boundaries that have protected free speech until now.

When I became editor, I expected to be fired within a year. There were too many bullets flying around, I thought, and I was bound to be hit sooner rather than later. I'm now in my 14th year editing a magazine whose sales have doubled in a market that fell by two-thirds – and I survived due to a team that protects all of our writers. Readers do want variety of argument, a respite from the demented domain of the internet's self-appointed censors. To keep the fanatics at bay, you need a team willing to go out with the bayonets. It's exhausting, and a battle that no one in publishing wants. But if freedom of thought and expression is to be protected in this digital age, there really is no option other than to fight.

Scottish economist Adam Smith, 18th century.

SHARE POWER

Merryn Somerset Webb

The story of shareholder democracy is really the story of the invention of the limited company – one of the greatest conceptual innovations of all time, and one that also shifted the economic power base in ways it was hard for its early adopters to imagine. Your losses as a shareholder became limited to the amount you originally invested. You would, of course, not want the company to fail – and would keep a close eye on those hired to run it (namely, the directors). But if it were to fail, as a shareholder your only problem would be the loss of your stake. That its debts might not be paid back in full would be a problem for those who had lent to it (a risk they understood when they made the loan). This might sound like a small change, but it wasn't.

With losses capped, investors could take on more overall risk – investing in more companies and creating economic growth along the way. This changed everything. Without the structure and the organisational capacities of companies, notes *Financial Times* columnist Martin Wolf, 'the unprecedented economic development seen since the middle of the nineteenth century would have been impossible.' Who would have put up the money for, say, the then-crazy sounding ideas of the original railway entrepreneurs, the internet start-ups and companies such as Tesla, if they thought they could lose their house in the process? No one. But knowing only the original stake could be lost made it much more attractive. If you are looking for the key invention that created the modern world, the limited liability company might be the one to go for.

Not everyone was enthusiastic about the limited liability idea. Early observers thought it scandalous that investors might be able to walk away from losses as well as being protected from any negative consequences of the activities they had facilitated. They also worried the structure would cause conflict between shareholders and company managers: if they were to want different things, who would prevail? Adam Smith, in his wonderful book *The Wealth of Nations*, published in 1790 (and a bestseller at the time), did not seem completely convinced.

The directors of such [joint-stock] companies, however, being the managers rather of other people's money than of their own, it cannot well be expected, that they should watch over it with the same anxious vigilance with which the partners in a private copartnery frequently watch over their own…Negligence and profusion, therefore, must always prevail, more or less, in the management of the affairs of such a company.

Smith was right to worry about what became known as 'managerial capitalism'. He would, I think, have approved, then, of the shift in the 1970s to what we now know as 'shareholder capitalism', the idea that companies should be run less to humour the whims of their employed managers and more to make money for their shareholders, and the creation of incentive systems to make sure this happened. He may not have been so keen on the latest shift in the dynamics of listed company ownership.

We live today in a world not so much of managerial capitalism, but of money manager capitalism. This is a type of shareholder capitalism in that control over corporates is still wielded by big shareholders. But the shareholders who matter are not the beneficial owners of companies – the world's investors – but huge institutional fund managers. Forty years ago not many people owned shares (in the UK about 3% of the population). But those who did owned them directly (they had share certificates that gave them all the rights shareholders should have). Today, the majority of people in most developed countries own some shares – in the UK, for example, nearly 80% of those employed are auto-enrolled into a pension scheme. However they rarely hold them directly – rather, they are in a collective fund (often a passive one) managed by a big fund management company. And when I say big, I mean big.

Fund management is an industry increasingly dominated by giants. In the US, the three largest asset management firms, BlackRock, Vanguard and State Street, together manage around $20 trillion of assets. That's one-third of all the assets managed worldwide, and 80% of all assets under management in the US. Even 30 years ago, it would have been unusual for any one firm to hold more than 1% of shares in a big company. Today in the US, one of the 'Big Three' is the top shareholder in 495 of the companies in the S&P 500 – the benchmark index of America's biggest firms. All in all, they control, on average, a staggering 20% of 495 companies in the index. How is that for an oligopoly? And this pattern is not unique to the US – BlackRock, run by long-term chief executive Larry Fink, is now the largest asset manager in the UK. The Big Three held an average of 7% of the average FTSE 100 company ten years ago. Today, it's 12%. BlackRock and Vanguard control over 10% of more than two-thirds of the 100 largest listed UK companies. BlackRock is the number one shareholder in 41 of those firms. Vanguard is a top ten shareholder in 98 of them.

Given the general lack of interest when it comes to voting among other shareholders, this situation gives the big fund managers enough clout and voting rights to demand a company does pretty much anything it fancies. This is a huge change from the past. Shareholder capitalism should be, and is in theory, hugely democratic: one share equals one vote. But if the majority of these votes rest with fund managers rather than individuals, that changes. In the days of managerial capitalism, the worry was that one person would have too much control over one company. Today, the issue is similar yet in very different form: a small group of people have close to effective control over pretty much every large listed company in the world.

'We have a new bunch of emperors,' said Charlie Munger, the vice chair of Berkshire Hathaway, in the summer of 2022, 'and they're the people who vote the shares in the index funds. I think the world of Larry Fink, but I'm not sure I want him to be my emperor.' Herein lies the problem. If a group of powerful asset management chief executives can ask companies to do whatever it is they want, we must pay attention to what it is that they want. For the last six to seven years they have been interpreting the phrase environmental, social and governance (ESG) investment – and the rise in interest in it – as a mandate to reshape the world as they see fit, to make sure the companies they own parts of (the vast majority of firms) take responsibility for the wellbeing of not just their shareholders, but their customers, employees, suppliers, communities, and the environment. This, these top three men tell us, is a win-win. ESG investing makes the world a better place. It also makes investors more money – well run companies with an eye to the future and the welfare of the world do better than others. 'Good' companies (as defined by ESG criteria) do better than 'bad' ones. Between May 2005 and May 2018, ESG was mentioned in fewer than 1% of earnings calls according to analysis by asset manager Pimco, reported in the *Financial Times*. By May 2021, it was mentioned in almost a fifth of earnings calls – and had become one of the main topics in conversations between fund managers and companies. Fink has been

ESG's chief evangelist. He has barely been off stage (at any stage) in the last five years, and his annual letter to the companies in which BlackRock invests have made it very clear what he expects from them.

You might think this sounds like a good thing. And it could be. It does however come with a lot of problems. The first is that half of ESG's promise is based on inadequate data. ESG portfolios did outperform non-ESG portfolios up until the end of 2021. But that turned out to have little to do with ethical actions and everything to do with the fact that most ESG portfolios were heavily weighted to growth stocks. When the growth story collapsed in late 2021 and 2022, so did ESG outperformance.

The second issue is that while ESG looks easy to define, it is actually very difficult. There was a reason we used to use long-term profits to judge companies – it was easy. Judge them using moral or ethical considerations, subjective by definition, and we can only fail. Consider defence – a key area that is beginning to make clear why ESG, as it stands, is meaningless. Investing in defence has long been an absolute no-no for full-on ESG funds. It's also been mainly verboten for most funds with a bit of an ESG overlay (almost all funds). After all, jets and tanks have a significant carbon footprint – and anything designed to frighten and kill is surely impossible to classify as a 'good' thing.

But think a bit more carefully and it isn't so simple. If you are only selling goods to so-called nasty dictators, it's hard to see how you could fit under E, S, or G. And investors wouldn't want to buy shares in such firms anyway, as they would likely worry about governance issues for the firm's client base, meaning the fund manager would never get paid. War is nasty, the weapons that facilitate war are nasty, and buyers of those weapons aren't always particularly steady clients. But if you supply weapons to the invaded underdog in an unprovoked fight, or to the countries backing said underdog, could we not file your activity under 'S', as a social good? As the Latvian deputy prime minister said this year: 'Is national defence not ethical?'

You can make similar arguments for fossil fuels. Sure, they are a minus environmentally, but what about socially? All progress, and in particular great leaps forward, has been driven by cheap energy. Fossil fuels remain the driver of almost all economic activity globally – and, whether we like it or not, will be for decades to come. Rating them as 'bad' and divesting from them (as ESG funds tend to) limits exploration and production, and, it could be argued, is part of what has got us to where we are today, a place where ordinary people's living standards are being affected by high energy prices.

It is also worth pointing out that Western fund managers not investing in oil companies does not mean less oil is produced or used. It is still produced, but the profits are received by different groups – and not always ones that give a fig for the environment. Thus, divesting can make things worse, not better. That's not good socially or for governance. There is also an absurdity inherent in renewable energy investment. For example, ESG considers wind turbines a 'good' thing and an ESG fund will happily invest in these – but it might not invest in the producers of rare earth metals vital for energy transition (mining is dirty), and it certainly will not invest in coal mines, yet steelmaking mostly needs coal and turbines need steel. And what of governance in general? Our new emperors are very keen on environmental issues, but there was a point in late March when Russian-listed oil companies had higher ESG scores than some North Sea ones. I can't be sure which companies were the most environmentally responsible at the time. But one would have thought North Sea firms should have won, at least on the governance part of the equation.

Almost all our financial troubles today stem from the great financial crisis in 2008. ESG is no exception. Fund managers know they got off very lightly then (remember they were the shareholders who never asked the hard questions). This has been part of their attempt at rehabilitation – or deflection, depending on how you look at it. The worry is that in their efforts to look good – and take the easy route to doing so – they have sown the seeds of the next crisis. Investing in what is well-meaning – rather than in what is useful and productive – comes at a long-term price. By raising the cost of capital for fossil fuel firms for example, the big fund management companies have played a part in forcing them to cut back on exploration and production. The resultant supply crunch has contributed to the sharp rise in the price of fuel, and hence to the inflation crisis today engulfing the global economy.

There is good news however. The war in Ukraine has begun to show ESG up as the nonsense that it can be. There is a new awareness that environmental, social and governance issues can be in conflict with each other, that something that is something to everyone is also nothing – and crucially that profits and going concerns do matter. Money is flowing from the usual ESG-approved sectors to the sectors we need to finance (even if we must hold our noses as we do so). Vanguard has now said it will not stop new investments in fossil fuel projects. BlackRock has announced it is likely to vote against some of the shareholder resolutions brought by climate lobbyists pursuing a ban on new oil and gas production. And at the same time there are hints that power will soon begin to shift from money managers to end owner. Individual investors are looking for ways to grab back some of the power they mistakenly (and unknowingly) delegated to fund managers – and fund managers are increasingly keen to let them do so (it turns out that being emperor isn't always easy). Vanguard has, for example, said it is committed to 'working with clients, policy makers, and others to help ensure long-term investor voices are heard', while BlackRock is, it says, keen to work 'with members of Congress and others on ways to help every investor – including individual investors – participate in proxy voting if they choose'.

If things keep moving in this direction there is every chance a more rational form of ESG will emerge alongside a new form of shareholder democracy – something I suspect Adam Smith would very much have approved of.

Rishi Sunak, the United Kingdom's first
Indian-origin prime minister. November 2022.

THE NEW AUTHORITARIANS

Kemi Badenoch

I had an epiphany after speaking at a conference in the summer of 2018. The panel on which I appeared was titled 'Beyond Black and White' and addressed whether a post-racial society had already been achieved or if it is an impossible goal. As a black woman serving in the British parliament, and a first-generation immigrant, the answer seemed so obvious to me: of course, the UK is a post-racial society. With ethnic minorities represented at all levels of public life, the colour of one's skin does not determine success.

Yet, I was met with hostility by a group of young people in the audience. All white, mostly female, they tut-tutted, hissed and shook their heads vigorously at almost everything I said. I was intrigued by the manner in which they dismissed my 'lived experience'. After the panel ended, I went over to them and we had a lengthy conversation. It was eye-opening. It was the first time I had encountered the young people in the front line of contemporary identity politics. What I found was that the adherents to this modern creed do not think in terms of individuality and personal responsibility, freedom of association or expression and shared experiences, but separated, segregated identities of victims and oppressors. They were baffled that I, an oppressed black woman, was not angrier about racism and couldn't see that they had 'white privilege'. It was clear that they had never spoken at length to anyone who disagreed with them. They were bemused by me but by the end of the conversation, I knew I'd had an impact as I watched them begin to question some of their own assumptions and argue among themselves. It was refreshing for me to see that if you make an argument, you can challenge – and even change – assumptions that at first seem quite unalterable.

In the course of the conversation, I asked them why they held such strong views when they clearly hadn't spent much time thinking about what they really believed. One of the girls looked at me and said, 'Because I need to feel like I'm a part of something important'. And that gets to the heart of it. They didn't see themselves as simply holding views about which reasonable people can disagree, but as warriors for their understanding of social justice, crusaders in a movement that provided meaning and security for them. That is why this phenomenon, which I call authoritarian progressivism, is both so powerful and why the 'new authoritarians' who practise it are so dangerous. It is powerful because it gives these new authoritarians a sense of meaning and purpose in their lives. And it is dangerous because it creates a justification for coercion and undermines values that we have, until now, taken for granted and which form the foundations of British society.

I dislike the term 'woke'. It mocks this sentiment. It may sound pithy, but it fails to capture the deep logic that drives this movement. Calling things woke masks the destructiveness of an ideology that presents itself simply as an interpretative tool which highlights social justice issues but, in fact, aims to polarise society along fractured lines. As the equalities minister, I saw first-hand how these new authoritarian views are destabilising the positive norms we use to govern society. We see it in the increased politicisation of the workplace and a proliferation of workplace political activism masquerading as ethical campaigning. Unlike traditional trade union activism, it has a coercive element to it. The ideology is more concerned with controlling the thoughts and behaviour of co-workers and customers than improving the economic lot of the workers as a collective. It is also based on subjective morality rather than economic improvement. So instead of workers asking for better pay and conditions, they take part in days, weeks and months of awareness raising and reflection on various identity issues in a manner redolent of a religious calendar. The focus is on issues that are frequently disconnected from the fundamental corporate purpose of an organisation, such as producing goods or making profits. Every year a new cohort of young people begin their working lives with no memory of the traditional workplace typical to those of us born in the 1980s, 1970s and earlier. They believe the workplace is there not to provide a livelihood, but affirmation and self-actualisation. This turns the office into an arena of competitive virtue signalling and leads to the dampening of free thought.

In *The Coddling of the American Mind*, author and academic Jonathan Haidt explains what is making younger generations more susceptible to authoritarian progressivism. His essay 'Why the past 10 years of American life have been uniquely stupid' explains the pernicious influence of social media. We may not be able to tame the worst excesses of social media, but we can stop making elementary mistakes that hamper our ability to tackle this new problem. Centre-right political thought has been on a downward trajectory since the mid-1990s, winning elections but not the broader argument at stake. It has failed both to understand the new territory of contemporary politics and the changed character of its opponents. Centre-right values were not an abstract concept in the Reagan-Thatcher era of the 1980s. They could clearly be contrasted with a dirigiste ideology and, most vividly, you could see the economic damage caused in places in which the principles of free thought, tolerating difference, equality before the law, and even limited government had been suppressed.

Unfortunately, too many of my contemporaries across the political spectrum do not understand that we are living in the post-modern era – in an age of entitlement and of identity politics. It is not 1995 or even 2005 anymore. Managerialism and more technocrats, however competent, are not going to be enough to solve today's problems. A conscious effort to understand the intellectual and ideological preferences of the opponents of a free society is crucial to defeating their ideas. In a world where people can get their own alternative facts online, reject the authority of experts they believe are manipulative, politically motivated or frauds, it is not enough to simply do better with the same failed bromides. People must *see* visible improvements in the quality of debate and real outcomes. They will not settle for just being told by politicians they no longer respect that all is well and their fears are unfounded.

To make itself heard to the public at large, the centre-right needs to rediscover the lost art of political argument. Today, centre-right politicians tend to assert, rather than explain. When the centre-right addresses deregulation in supportive terms, people don't interpret it as a call for freedom from bureaucracy, but as the loss of the regulatory safety net that protects them from exploitation. When taxes are cut for business, it is interpreted as a favouritism to wealthy business owners. When the argument is made for strong family structures, they feel that their lives, lifestyles and past mistakes are being judged. We don't require forcefully enough that our opponents use precise language. We must force new authoritarians to say what they really mean. Appearing at a select committee in the Houses of Parliament recently, I was asked a contentious question by the committee chairman. Her aim was not to shed light on government policy but to force me into making a statement that would look like I was against transgender people. Rather than trying to argue my case, I simply asked her, 'What do you mean by trans?'. She claimed that I was asking an unfair question. Like the young people I met at the conference four years ago, she could not define or explain a concept despite lobbying and arguing for particular policy positions based upon it. By providing a definition before responding, her posturing options were immediately limited and we could begin to have a real discussion rooted in the truth of the issue at large. In this way, I avoided the trap and highlighted the absurdity of her stance.

A new activist class has arisen, buttressed by legal and economic power in many of our societies. Contrary to popular opinion, it is not the elected government but this activist class that uses the power of the state to impose its views. It is at the forefront of identity politics and the culture wars. The growth of this class presents a huge challenge to conservatives and liberals. The activist class is not afraid to use its power to impose an agenda that says identity group X is good and identity group Y is bad. This, in turn, makes a mockery of the rule of law, because everything is politicised, including our traditional mechanisms for procuring justice for individuals and society. Liberals and conservatives are expending a lot of energy looking for areas of compromise with activists who refuse to acknowledge progress where it really has taken hold. They sincerely want a revolution and will continue to shift the threshold for political action as soon as their demands are met. For instance, after frequent campaigns to improve ethnic diversity in government over several decades, the current Conservative government is notable in having the most ethnically diverse cabinet in UK history. Three of the four great offices of state, the Treasury, the Home Office and the Foreign Office, are held by ethnic minorities. Yet, rather than being seen as a cause for celebration, new authoritarians attack ethnic minorities in government. They accuse them of being tools of white supremacy, dismiss their achievements and move the goalposts in claiming that representation has no bearing on the government's position on racial issues.

Another common mistake is to accept the presentation of certain problems as issues of injustice requiring the state to get involved. This reinforces the belief that state action can solve everything when, realistically, it cannot do so. More troubling is that new authoritarians have no fundamental concept of the meaning of liberty. They see it as the freedom to do bad things, whether they are offensive or exploitative. This is where reasserting the meaning and importance of liberty into discourse becomes relevant. Liberty is a practical necessity for a flourishing society, not just a philosophical 'nice to have'. The more state power grows, the more we curtail what people can and should do for themselves. Worse, we reduce people's ability to think for themselves. We begin to forget what the state's purpose is in national life, no longer asking, what should the state do, and what should it not do. If we fail to answer those fundamental questions and instead use state power to continue tinkering with every aspect of life in order to achieve social justice, we sleepwalk into a planned economy far more oppressive and stagnant than liberal thinkers of the twentieth century could have envisaged. The state should be used judiciously to avoid both authoritarianism and arbitrariness in its exercise of power. Time and again, those who seek to control others, and to take away liberty, always find a good cause to justify the state's encroachment on fundamental liberties. In seeking to use the law to force others to be nice, rather than to *respect* the liberty of the individual, we are asked by the new authoritarians to *affirm* their lifestyle and choices.

Much of what is referred to as 'woke' thinking seeks to replace the old view of an oppressed working class with a series of oppressed groups who are defined by gender, sexuality and race. The assumption being that these groups are constantly being oppressed by others – by men, heterosexuals, white people, and so on. To defeat new authoritarian thinking, it is essential to acknowledge that there are problems which need addressing. But we must also emphasise that so-called woke solutions based on discredited theories are not the answer. Indeed, they rob the individual of agency and dignity and treat people as groups to be manipulated and set against each other. In the reality of a new authoritarian, everyday life is treated as an oppressive structure which must be met with aggression in turn. To tolerate existing structures is to endorse this oppression. The slogan 'white silence is violence' is a perfect summary of this view, in which the idea that the liberty of others should be tolerated is represented as intolerant. A vicious circle of increasing hostility and polarisation is created as a result. New authoritarians see liberty as a sham which allows the oppression of marginalised groups by dominant groups. Individual freedom is portrayed as an illusion. We must refute this view. Liberty is the right of all individuals to choose their life and to make their own way in this world. It is the most fundamental right of all, without which almost no other rights are worth having.

Part of the problem is that, for the centre-right, liberty has come to mean a laissez-faire attitude – that we should sit back and do nothing. Those of us on the centre-right are told we must not take sides or fight culture wars. That this shift underway is the operation of a free society in action, that this is progress, or even liberty in action. This 'do nothing' attitude is deeply misguided. In reality, liberty must be protected and nurtured with reference to important broader principles. People should always be treated as individuals. Due process must always be ensured. A limited state should operate in a neutral fashion to all who live in our society. The rule of law must be protected, under which all are equal. All of these principles are anathema to the growth of this activist class which is dominating so many of our institutions. Whatever you choose to call it, this new ideology is successfully masking itself as liberalism. It proclaims itself as a liberation movement and that is why classical liberals struggle to attack the premise of many of its arguments. At every opportunity, we must expose how the ideology seeks to deny autonomy, corral choice, remove responsibility and impose the conformity of external rules decided by cadres of new authoritarians, instead of allowing individuals to draw on their own sense of conscience.

We cannot reverse time, but we can build a new future. This requires a more muscular liberalism that is strong, confident in itself and not overly fixated on the past. We must not bash or ban things without making a case for a better way. All this attitude does is create new opponents, but few, if any, new allies. A positive alternative is needed, not just harking back to an earlier picture of the good society. This project also requires the case to be made for small government. The unnecessary growth of the state beyond providing essential public services has created multiple opportunities for activists to spread their ideology. We need to make the case for leaner government. And yet, too much rhetoric speaks of a smaller state as an end in itself. A smaller state is a means to secure a better way of doing things, allowing bureaucracy to focus and prioritise its resources. The best governments do a few things well, not many things badly. We need to start from first principles and investigate what liberal frameworks already provide, rather than trying to reinvent the wheel. And we can apply it in new ways. For example, as a minister, having to deliver a racial equality strategy from scratch would have been impossible if I did not have a framework to draw on. I did not just go back to basics but repurposed classic liberal values for the work I was doing, and the strategy relied on three principles: disparities are not always due to discrimination; institutions should not be damaged by making the perfect the enemy of the good; and universalism rather than specific targeting of identity groups should be promoted.

Even when problems are discovered within them, we must be creative in finding ways to strengthen institutions rather than to tear them down. And this means not inviting people who do not care about our institutions to advise us on how to please them. That leads to activists marking our homework – we will never pass their tests. There will always be new hoops to jump through. Activists must also be distinguished from genuine victims. Too often there is a conflation between vulnerable or disadvantaged groups and those who claim to speak on their behalf. Recognising the difference between activists and those in genuine need is critical, and also sidelines those who are interested in bringing down the system. Deference in Western society is dead. The most difficult thing we will need to do is restore trust in authority and in the knowledge and information which society relies on. There are no easy answers to how we do this. People no longer assume that what the government or officialdom say is true, let alone what they hear in church or at university. This requires reform of authority itself and how it communicates. In an age when scrutiny is high and tolerance of mistakes and personal failure is low, those who provide a comforting narrative are able to exploit cynicism and create more polarisation.

The logical conclusion of coercive post-modernism is the unravelling of liberal democracy itself. The narrative of the culture wars obscures what is really at stake. Arguments over pronouns and gender-neutral toilets or statues and white privilege seem trivial when compared to solving climate change and the demographic timebomb of an ageing population. But they are inextricably linked. You can't encourage the rest of the world to make sacrifices to achieve net zero if you've told them Western civilisation prospered only by exploiting them. Why on earth would they trust our intentions on everything from technology to public health? And what do we expect will happen to social cohesion if younger immigrants, on whom our migration policy relies, are immediately told that the majority population has privilege over them based on their skin colour? What else can you expect except an inbuilt hostility, to the elderly in particular?

We will pay a heavy price if we fail to defend our beliefs merely to avoid difficult conversations. If the West, supposedly, is only prosperous due to slavery and colonialism, if all its success is down to the patriarchy, white supremacy and hetero-normative oppression, there is a price to be paid. That price is that our beliefs, democracy, equality before the law, meritocracy, free markets and so many other liberal values are mere fiction. Fairy tales we tell ourselves to cover up a dark and murky past. There can be no resolution of the big problems of our age if we lose confidence in our history and the story of Western liberalism. Should we fail to defend it, there are many competitor states who will happily allow the new authoritarians and their post-modernism to do the heavy lifting in undermining all we hold dear, and will then replace whatever noble intent drove their progressivism with something far more sinister.

CREATING
THE FREE WORLD

Portrait of Edmund Burke. Original painting by
Joshua Reynolds, 18th century.

THE GERMAN KEY TO EUROPEAN LIBERTY

Brendan Simms

Liberty always exists in a particular geopolitical context. Many seventeenth and eighteenth-century Britons saw a deep connection between their own parliamentary and religious freedoms, German liberty – that is, the constitution of the Holy Roman Empire – and the liberties of Europe, which was a contemporary synonym for the balance of power on their continent. The nature of the link shifted over time, but its importance remained undiminished. It is part of the wider history of Western liberty and grand strategy whose legacy remains with us today.

These connections developed during the early seventeenth century and the English Civil War. Most Puritans and parliamentarians (the two groups overlapped but were by no means identical) saw the defence of the Protestant cause in Europe against 'popery' and 'universal monarchy' – a rough synonym for dictatorship – as essential for the protection of their own rights from domestic or foreign encroachment. If the forces of counter-Reformation Catholicism and Habsburg hegemony managed to dominate, so the argument ran, they would then over-run the Low Countries – the 'counterscarp' or outworks of England – and it would not be long before they landed on its southern shores. In order to prevent this, many Englishmen supported the traditional rights of the princes of the Holy Roman Empire – German liberty, as it was termed – against the power of the emperor.

This was not just an English concern. Towards the end of the Thirty Years' War in Germany, the Swedish chancellor, Axel Oxenstierna, announced that his aim was 'to restore German liberties...and in this manner to conserve the equilibrium on Europe'. For this reason, the treaties of Westphalia which brought the war to an end not only (re-)established a system of power-sharing within the Holy Roman Empire, but also a system of external guarantors (Sweden and France). The emperor remained at the apex of this order, but he had to recognise the rights of the various imperial 'estates', the electors (who chose him), the princes, the ecclesiastical principalities and many other smaller territories. The intricate German imperial constitution – the *Reichsverfassung* – was thus an integral part of the European balance of power.

During the late seventeenth century, the emphasis shifted from opposing the Habsburgs towards confronting a new European hegemon: the France of the Sun King, Louis XIV. Many in England feared he would dominate the continent and then turn his attention to them. They also suspected, not without reason, that their own monarchs, Charles II and James II, were conspiring with the French king to undermine their parliamentary liberties. Soon, the Austrian Habsburgs – the sworn enemy of Louis' designs – became England's favoured partner in defence of the Holy Roman Empire and the European balance of power more generally. But the fundamental connection made between English – and after the Union with Scotland in 1707, British – freedoms and the frustration of tyranny on the continent remained unchanged.

This understanding was explicitly articulated by the House of Commons at the start of the War of the Spanish Succession in June 1701. It undertook to support William of Orange's efforts in conjunction with the emperor and the Estates General (the Dutch Republic) for 'the preservation of the liberties of Europe, the prosperity and peace of England, and for reducing the exorbitant power of France', as explained in my book, *Three Victories and a Defeat: the Rise and Fall of the First British Empire.* After the war, the three powers established a 'barrier' system of fortresses to keep the French out of the Low Countries. This alliance with the Austrian Habsburgs and the Dutch Republic was so routinised that it became known as the Old System.

British understandings of their own liberty were thus always tied up with the liberties of others. This link was not based on the assumption that they needed to export their own system in order to defend themselves. Most Britons did not want to establish mini Westminsters or Churches of England across the Channel. Theirs was a much more diffuse, or nuanced, sense of concern, not only for European Protestants and anti-absolutist forces, but also with the constitutional and geopolitical framework which protected them. Over time, this sentiment largely emancipated itself from its religious origins and became more purely political and geopolitical. The Habsburgs might be Catholics, but in geopolitical terms they were Protestant, in so far as they defended the liberties of Europe and, therefore, British freedoms. In that sense, eighteenth-century Britons believed they could not long remain free if others were subjected to tyranny. To them, liberty in Europe was not divisible.

In the early 1740s, Britain worried about the weakness of the Habsburgs after the death of Emperor Charles VI without a male heir. It was feared that France, which had just bested Austria in the War of the Polish Succession, would try to take advantage of its new ruler, Maria Theresa, in order to partition the Habsburg lands. These anxieties were greatly increased by Frederick the Great's invasion of the Habsburg province of Silesia. The London government and many Britons feared that if France succeeded in subverting Germany, the 'barrier' would be compromised and, with it, the security of the home island. Then the French would join up with the Jacobites and destroy parliament, Protestantism and British freedoms as they knew them.

This connection between British and European liberty was repeatedly articulated by protagonists. For example, Henry Pelham, later prime minister, remarked in early 1740 that, 'The [German] Empire may be considered as the bulwark of Great Britain which if it be thrown down leaves us naked and defenceless.' In December 1741, Lord Carteret (then a foreign secretary and soon to be prime minister) announced that, 'The liberty and repose of Europe is almost lost after which we shall not keep ours for long.' Summing all this up, the Scottish peer Lord Hyndford remarked, not long before becoming ambassador to Prussia, that the death of Charles VI rendered 'the German Body [the Holy Roman Empire]...lifeless and inactive'. This mattered, he continued, because it 'threatened the liberties of Europe and thus Britain'.

Across the Atlantic, many American colonists agreed. Despite the distance separating them from the mother country, they saw their cause and freedoms as inextricably linked to that of the European balance of power. It was axiomatic to them that if France gained the upper hand in Flanders or Germany, Britain itself would be in danger and, with it, the security of the 13 colonies. For this reason, the colonists were content to sacrifice hard-won lands in America to prevent this from happening, for example when London returned the Canadian fortress of Louisburg to the French in order to secure their withdrawal from the Low Countries.

Similar concerns surfaced after 1792-1793, with the outbreak of the French Revolutionary Wars. The principles of the revolution of 1789 challenged ancient regime Europe not merely ideologically, which was manageable, but strategically, which was not. Many revolutionaries were convinced that they could only survive if they exported their principles to the rest of Europe, or at least to the states neighbouring France. When the French advanced into Germany and the Low Countries, this was immediately perceived by many Britons as a threat to the European balance and thus to their security and liberty. The *liberté* of 1789, in other words, clashed with German liberties and the liberties of Europe.

No one articulated this view better than the great Anglo-Irish politician and political philosopher Edmund Burke. He saw a 'great Revolution...preparing in Germany' which would be 'more decisive upon the general fate of nations than that of France itself'. Burke believed this mattered because the past 200 years of European history had shown 'the independence and the equilibrium of the [German] Empire to be the very essence of the system of balanced power in Europe, and the scheme of public law or mass of laws, upon which that independence and equilibrium are founded'. This would be threatened if the French attacked the smaller territories because 'it is on the side of the ecclesiastical electorates that the dykes raised to support the German liberty will first give way'.

If that happened, then – and here Burke was, of course, channeling an eighteenth-century commonplace – the barrier system in the Low Countries would be in jeopardy. 'Those outworks,' he warned, 'which ever till now that we so strenuously maintained as the strong frontier of our own dignity and safety, no less than the liberties of Europe.' There it was again, the link between British freedoms, German liberty and the European balance of power. It remained a very important, though by no means the only, element of the strategic rationale behind British strategy until the final defeat of Napoleon in 1815.

Of course, this Whig understanding of liberty and strategy was contentious in British policy and politics. There were many who believed that Britain's destiny lay on the oceans and in the colonies. Tories such as Jonathan Swift or Viscount Bolingbroke abjured continental commitments and they largely rejected the religious and political affinities rehearsed above. Over time, they were joined by radical Whigs and other 'blue water' enthusiasts who thought the 'wooden walls' of the Royal Navy protection enough, and wanted a primarily maritime orientation and strategy. For a time after 1760, this sentiment gained the upper hand, but the disaster in America and the revival of the French ensured a return to old orthodoxies.

It is worth adding that the eighteenth-century preoccupation with liberty did not extend to the black slaves being trafficked across the Atlantic, or to the non-Protestant populations of the British Isles, especially in Ireland. To that extent, the freedom of some involved, and perhaps even required, the lack of freedom for others. This began to change in the late eighteenth and early nineteenth centuries, with the rise of abolitionism and the demand for Catholic emancipation, both of which had been achieved by the mid-1830s.

The connection between British and European (especially German) freedoms was to have a fateful afterlife and resonates to this day. In the early and mid nineteenth century, maintaining the integrity of the new German Confederation – which replaced the old Reich shattered by the French onslaught – was central to upholding the Vienna Settlement. When Bismarck unified Germany, London was initially supportive on the grounds that the new empire would help contain France and Russia. But when the Second Reich developed, or was perceived to develop, hegemonic tendencies, Britain not only fought a world war to contain her but also looked to a combination of external constraints and internal political transformations to keep Germany under control. The trick was to make Germany strong enough to deter outside predators but not so strong that it would threaten its neighbours and the overall balance. Critics might say, though, that London did not do enough to secure liberty there, thus allowing the rise of Hitler.

Be that as it may, the operation was repeated during and after the Second World War. There could no longer be any doubt that tyranny in Germany, whether that took the form of German revanchism or a Soviet takeover, would threaten Britain. This was reflected even in the structure of the New German Federal Republic. Look at photographs of the founding moments of the Länder of Schleswig-Holstein, Lower Saxony and North-Rhine Westphalia, and you will see a general of the British army of occupation nearby. The 'dykes' and 'barriers' of the eighteenth century were re-erected. After 1945, saving Germany from tyranny was once again seen as central to preserving British freedoms.

Meanwhile, the torch which Britain had held since the early eighteenth century had passed to the descendants of their formerly junior partners, the American colonists. The old debates about Europe and Germany were replicated across the Atlantic and were a staple of American Cold War discourse, but the majority cleaved more to a 'Whig' than to a 'Tory' understanding of the issue. US strategists generally accepted that Germany was the central battleground in the contest with the Soviet Union, and that the defence of their own liberty required the protection of German liberty, that is the democratic order of the Federal Republic, as well.

Today, in the era of Ukraine and the fragmentation of German politics, the link is once again clearly visible. The Russia of Vladimir Putin represents a mortal threat to the European order, both strategically and ideologically. His irredentist projects menace the territorial integrity of NATO and the European Union. His claim to defend Christian and conservative values, and those of 'sovereign democracy' against the 'soulless' West, hits at the heart of our societal coherence. By February 2022, at the very latest, when Putin launched his second invasion of Ukraine, the challenge was clear to most.

In the face of this, the Federal Republic of Germany appears to be failing one half of the task set for it by history. To be sure, it has not threatened Europe militarily (though some see it as an economic hegemon), but equally Germany has not mobilised in the common cause either, or at least not to the degree required. Where the Habsburgs and their imperial allies were once the mainstay of coalition efforts against France, Germany today struggles to muster a serious military response to the Russian challenge. It now matters more than ever, not only to Britain but to the entire Western world, that Germany appears, to borrow Lord Hyndford's phrase, 'inert and lifeless'.

Ukrainian president Volodymyr Zelensky
participated digitally at the World Economic
Forum in Davos, May 2022.

BENEVOLENT HYPOCRISY? IN DEFENCE OF THE WEST'S DEMOCRATIC MORALISM

John Bew

The Russian invasion of Ukraine, which began in February 2022, is far from over at the time of writing. Yet it has already had many consequences in the strategic and political mind of the West. The display of Russian aggression against a sovereign democratic European state has led to a strong display of unity among the nations of Europe and North America, the expansion of NATO to include Finland and Sweden, the rapid mobilisation of military support to Ukraine to help it defend itself, and an unprecedented slew of sanctions against those instruments of the Russian economy that enable its war machine. Alongside this, we have seen a commitment to increase defence spending in several NATO nations and the scrubbing or revisiting of fundamental assumptions about the strategic environment, with energy security and supply chains at the forefront of the agenda.

Crises, as they present themselves to Western capitals, begin to look increasingly intertwined. And so the unfolding of events in Europe has simultaneously led to a growing focus on the future of the Indo-Pacific, as the nations of the liberal democratic world look at the prospect of authoritarian aggression or revanchism challenging the entire edifice of the international order.

Inevitably, then, this is a time of heightened intellectual activity – to go alongside the renewal of political and popular focus on international relations and the affairs of state. Foreign policy is front page news once again. The democratic imperative demands that leaders do more to stand up for democratic values against those that would harm or undermine them. At the same time, populations expect action to deal with the consequences of rising food and energy prices, accentuated by conflict and the disruption caused by war.

Intellectuals have rushed to the ramparts (or, at least, the ramparts of the commentariat) to make sense of Russian intentions, assess Ukrainian fortitude, and to venture theories about the new world order that seems to be unfolding before our eyes. This helps provide a frame through which to make sense of events, as we identify with the different camps in the debate. And yet the war in Ukraine has not necessarily been kind to scholars, academics and theorists of war and international relations. Few can be credited for predicting the coming crisis in a way that the intelligence services of the United States and United Kingdom did. Fewer still estimated the ability of Ukraine to defend itself so effectively in the teeth of a full-scale Russian assault designed to go all the way to the capital, Kyiv, or the deftness of President Zelensky as a war leader able to mobilise Western support. Different schools of thinking soon fell back into their familiar trenches. The American scholar of realism, John Mearsheimer, has courted controversy and a bitter backlash by laying the blame for Russia's invasion on the actions of the West.

Those who have begun to venture an idea as to what theoretical 'end state' may emerge at the conclusion of the war have found it a thankless task. The leap of imagination this requires leads to a sense that the scholarly mind has somehow diluted the principle that justice must prevail. Thus, the views of Henry Kissinger, in which he speculated in remarks at Davos that Ukraine may have to accept some loss of its territory, prompted a barbed response from Zelensky himself as being unfit for the era in which we find ourselves. 'You get the impression that Mr Kissinger doesn't have 2022 on his calendar, but 1938,' he said, 'and that he thinks he is talking to an audience not in Davos, but in Munich.'

The task of transferring academic knowledge into policy making and national security is not easy even in periods of relative tranquillity. When events such as war disrupt the geographic, ideological and emotional equilibrium, that task becomes even more difficult. The US national security strategy has been delayed by what has happened in Ukraine; the new NATO Strategic Concept was adapted in its final months to reflect a new era of Euro-Atlantic security caused by Russian aggression; in Germany and France, work is underway to set out a new framework for national security; while in the UK, the assessments made in the 2021 Integrated Review: Global Britain and Competitive Age are being tested once more, just a year into its existence.

At its best, the academic style of knowledge should bring a coolness, disinterestedness and long-sightedness to such processes. A degree of detachment from the heat of the moment can be an aide to more effective strategic thinking. And yet the experience of government in times of crisis suggest it is not always up to the moment. More accurately, the academic form of knowledge can lack a true appreciation of the zeitgeist as the single most important determinant in shaping affairs of state. At worst, the academic form of knowledge can appear out of touch with the gravity of contemporary events and the importance of the emotional in modern political life. Too often, its mistake is to regard emotion (outrage, a sense of justice, a simplistic notion of right versus wrong) as somehow irrational. It is this blind spot in the thinking of sophisticated people (theorists, analysts or empiricists) that means the gap between the academic form of knowledge and the political way of thinking can never be entirely bridged.

While the war in Ukraine has highlighted these tensions between academic detachment and the sense of morality that underscores democratic life, this story goes much further back. The dialectic between these two ways of thinking has been a profoundly important feature of statecraft in the Western world for more than a hundred years.

As such, I will focus on the emergence of the Anglo-American worldview and its expression through foreign policy across the course of the twentieth century. Within that, I will identify a form of democratic simplicity that remains a hugely consequential fact of political life today. At times, this democratic simplicity can be contrasted with a more sceptical and rationalist way of thinking more common to academic scholarship – sometimes understood as deriving from 'continental' European ideas of enlightenment and statecraft, that railed against moralism and cant. It will argue that ideas of the West have often been naive, delusional and hypocritical, but they nonetheless represented a profoundly important historical force. I will conclude that the academic answer to foreign policy dilemmas is sometimes, if not always, the wrong one.

The starting point for this story is what President Woodrow Wilson called 'open diplomacy', as captured in his famous 'Fourteen Points', introduced in a speech to Congress in 1918. Open diplomacy means foreign policy shaped in the glare of democratic scrutiny, open to the scrutiny of a free media, and created in a cacophony of political noise. Wilson thought this, on balance, would be a good thing in improving the relations between states and the quality of decision making on matters of peace and war. Treaties should be opened up to more eyes rather than secretly agreed upon among elites. The public would get to analyse and determine their contents, or insist they were stuck to if their governments began to walk away from commitments.

And yet, Woodrow Wilson's noble project began to collapse in the period after the end of the First World War. Many of his critics, often those with sophisticated and scholarly minds, thought open diplomacy was an encumbrance to clear-eyed thinking and *raison d'état*. It is a debate that rumbles on to this day. What chance would Castlereagh and Metternich have had at the Congress of Vienna if every move on the diplomatic chessboard was subject to intense democratic scrutiny? A certain brand of diplomat will always remain wistful about the pre-Wilsonian world. If only our diplomacy could be a little more closed, it could be more nuanced and less hot-headed, so the argument goes.

While there is a grudging recognition of the reality of democratic life, it is often seen by scholars as creating a hazy fog that can get in the way of insightful assessment in aid of realpolitik. Tocqueville, in his study of democracy in America, thought a degree of secrecy an imperative for effective foreign relations. The same concerns loomed increasingly large over British policy makers in the second half of the nineteenth century, balancing between the maintenance of a vast empire and the growing demands of a polity that was gradually democratising. 'We know no spectacle so ridiculous as the British public in one of its periodical fits of morality', as the English liberal scholar and historian Thomas Macaulay famously said. Nonetheless, it was a powerful force. Macaulay and his contemporaries faced this reality on debates about British foreign policy in parts of the crumbling Ottoman Empire – where the British national interest, defined by commerce, security and rivalry, would periodically collide with public concerns about the fate of Christians in places such as Greece and Bulgaria.

Yet rather than seeing this habit of democratic moralism as a drag on sophisticated policy making, I want to argue in its defence – as providing a coherence and sense of direction and vision to statecraft that is otherwise lacking. There is, of course, a balance to be struck here. To be clear, the instincts of scholars looking at foreign policy, to find nuance and subtlety away from the noise, are laudable and correct. They are the necessary palliative to the excesses of open diplomacy. But, ultimately, there is a virtue (both strategic and ethical) in the simplicity that democratic politics demands.

This becomes apparent by taking a closer look at the Atlantic (or Anglo-American) worldview and its expression through foreign policy across the course of the twentieth century. To this day, the driving assumptions that underlay it were (and are) often naive, delusional and hypocritical; but rather than 'fits of morality', they represent an irreducible core, a centre of gravity and identity. Indeed, rather than creating a fog of vision, they clear the fog and get to the core of a problem. This was what Anthony Eden, Churchill's foreign secretary, meant when he said that the lesson of the 1930s was that intellectual fatalism had clouded the strategic mind. The West cannot 'content ourselves with a passive recognition of unpleasant facts...Realism so defined becomes indistinguishable from defeatism.'

Of course, much of this is about strategic context and historical circumstance. The reason why fits of morality are often more common in Anglo-American/Atlantic foreign policy is because of the vantage point from which the world is viewed. This is both from the historical vantage point – from a position on the continuum of relatively advanced growth and comparative political, technological and economic development – and also the geographic vantage point, where there is comparative safety in the northern and western Atlantic sphere. In the Atlantic world, as opposed to the continental world of the Eurasia landmass, are countries that more commonly fight wars of choice rather than wars of state formation or national defence.

In this vein, the Swiss-American scholar Arnold Wolfers, in a 1956 collection of essays, drew an important distinction between the most prominent Anglo-American (English language) scholars of statecraft – from Thomas More to Woodrow Wilson with Hobbes, Burke, Hamilton, Jefferson, Mill, Mahan and Hobson in between – and the leading continental theorists of state – such as Machiavelli, Grotius, Spinoza and Kant. His goal was to 'explain some of the peculiarities of the contemporary British and American approach to world affairs, which often puzzle the foreign observer and lead him either to praise the special virtues of Anglo-Saxon policy or condemn what he considers its hypocritical wrappings'. This would also help to 'promote critical self-understanding within the English-speaking world, making for more awareness of its moral presuppositions and of the deeply ingrained traditional habits of thought which inevitably color conduct in a field where emotion and value judgement play an important role'.

Wolfers's argument was that the relative insularity and security of the Atlantic world had led to a foreign policy philosophy based on ethics and choice. This contrasted starkly with a continental tradition, in which sovereignty and territory was always contested, and which therefore prioritised necessity and *raison d'état*. In the continental world, there was ever present a feeling that nations were 'puppets in the hands of demonic forces, with little leeway if any to rescue moral values from a sea of tragic necessity'. Meanwhile, English and American experience travelled a different path. Even the concepts of 'necessity of state' or 'reason of state' seemed alien to those engaged in a debate about 'the best way of applying accepted principles of morality to the field of foreign policy'.

Where morality is found in statecraft, hypocrisy was never far away. When the continental theorists looked at the Anglo-Saxons – with their vast commercial empires – they saw 'cant', evangelism and preachiness. The British, said the German nationalist writers of the late Victorian era, were the original pirates who took resources by force and then, as someone tried to take them back, fell in behind a construct of international law that was crafted entirely around their self-interest. They bullied the weak and then said 'you are breaking the rules' (or 'that's not cricket!') when confronted with the strong.

Wolfers's contemporary, the Chicago international relations scholar Quincy Wright, described this as a dialectic between the 'sentiment of humanity' and 'reason of state'. And in Anglo-American or Atlantic strategic thinking, to this day, one can see a series of dialectics in which contending and contradictory ideas are held at the same time: the unsentimental promotion of national interests versus a sense of universalist humanitarianism; commercial self-aggrandisement versus belief in the shared beneficence that comes from economic growth. As Kissinger put it, there was inherent in this a convenient form of ethical egotism that insists that what is good for us was good for you. It is, one could argue, reflective of the tension between the idea of universal Christian virtue and Machiavelli's *virtù*. Virtue suggests beneficence and generous intention. *Virtù* embraces vigorous action – pride, toughness, energy and action.

In some respects, Churchill was the best emblem of this hypocrisy in the Western strategic mind, between fierce protection of the national interest and defence of empire and a genuinely held civilisational conscience that transcended narrow bounds. He was fighting to the death for British survival yet seeing this as a story of world historical struggle between barbarism and civilisation. As George Orwell argued, reflecting on the moral purpose in British policy in the Second World War:

'Hypocrisy is a power safeguard...a symbol of the strange mix of reality and illusion, democracy and privilege, humbug and decency – the subject network of compromises by which the nation keeps itself in familiar shape.'

Ultimately, the experience of the war in Ukraine should remind us that open diplomacy (or 'rowdy democracy') is a massive asset to the making of a clear and coherent foreign policy. It is the Atlantic nations where the resistance to a narrow form of realpolitik has been most pronounced. And it is that sense of simplistic right and wrong that is the precondition to *virtù*. It is the thing that summons rigour, action, energy, a willingness to try to shape Fortuna, rather than simply adjust to the world as it is or, as Russian military doctrine would have it, 'the correlation of forces'. Virtue in foreign policy is sometimes simplistic; but there is a virtue in simplicity. And it is better, above all, to exercise *virtù* rather than to succumb to the 'passive recognition of unpleasant facts'.

The fall of the Berlin Wall, November 1989.

THE WEST HAS NOT WON YET

Katja Hoyer

In the last freezing moments of 1989, the 37-year-old American actor David Hasselhoff hovered in a bucket crane above half a million Berliners. On the first New Year's Eve that the people of the divided city were spending together in decades, he was performing a song that would make him a much-loved icon in Germany. The frenetic crowds knew the lyrics by heart. *Looking for Freedom* had been the best-performing single of the year in West Germany. It had become part of the soundtrack to the Peaceful Revolution that helped force the East German authorities to open their country's borders on 9 November, 1989. When Hasselhoff appeared in Berlin seven weeks later, it was as a messianic figure, embodying the imagined West dreamt up by a population that had been cut off from it for decades. Against the evocative backdrop of the Brandenburg Gate and the Berlin Wall, Hasselhoff was an apparition of Western consumerism – from his permed hair and keyboard-pattern scarf, to his flashing leather jacket.

As the images of jubilant Germans went around the world, the West breathed a collective sigh of relief. The Cold War was over. Western capitalism had emerged victorious against Eastern communism. The fact that the Soviet Union and its dependents collapsed suggested that their populations had jettisoned autocratic rule and opted for Western liberty.

But this reading of events is too simplistic. Western liberty is not inherently the obvious choice, as the 'end of history' narrative suggests. Those born and bred in Western societies take it for granted that everyone else in the world would naturally want to live in the same way as they do. And where they don't, it must be because autocratic rulers prevent them from doing so. Yet, there are ample examples to suggest that it is more complicated than that. Vladimir Putin still enjoys real consent from much of the Russian population, and many nations around the world elect illiberal governments even when given a genuine choice.

It is tempting to forget that it has taken the West itself millennia to arrive at the system and values we hold dear today. Neither democracy in its current form nor the degree of tolerance and liberalism we take for granted today are cast in stone, and there was a time when this was taken into account. When the world took full stock of Germany's Nazi crimes in 1945, none of the victorious powers assumed that the German people would return to democracy as their natural status quo. The country was occupied for decades to come and its democratisation carefully monitored. Eye-watering sums of money, as well as time and resources, were poured into stabilising democracies in all of Western Europe, not just Germany.

But the Cold War changed this adjustment. True, between 1945 and 1990, the West still invested in convincing those who lived under authoritarian rule that a democratically-run market economy promised a better way of life. But in contrast to the realpolitik with which Western European democracies were rebuilt and stabilised, the image of Western liberty that was projected across the Iron Curtain was iconised and had little to do with its messy reality. With the Cold War fought largely on ideological grounds, neither side wanted to admit to its own shortcomings, not to its own people and certainly not to the other side. Just as communism presented itself as a classless society, while glossing over the inherent lack of opportunity, the West, in turn, promised opportunity without admitting that one can fall in a world that allows one to rise.

The West simply assumed that the advantages of the Western system were obvious, and dangling them over the Berlin Wall would suffice. And they seemed proved right when thousands of people streamed West during the first border openings in the late summer of 1989, and many more followed later that year as the dams between East and West broke.

But the initial wave of euphoria that accompanied the collapse of Soviet communism in Eastern Europe and East Germany began to wane quickly. Former East Germans are still more likely to vote for extremist parties than former West Germans. Hungarian democracy has taken an illiberal turn since 2010, and the EU is fighting a bitter legal battle with Poland over the principle of the rule of law. The West should take illiberal tendencies in European democracies seriously. East Germans are still dismissed as 'lost to democracy' because of their 'dictatorial socialisation' – a theory promoted in 2021 by the German government's own commissioner for East German affairs. Equally, the choices made by Eastern

European voters are usually met with head-shaking in Brussels. But responses that assume an obvious superiority of one idea over another will fail to promote their case. The result is dangerous complacency that is likely to disaffect people further, as well as preventing the healthy self-criticism that underpins progress. Ultimately, the argument has to be won. By definition, freedom and democracy are difficult to force onto people who do not want them.

A constructive approach should therefore recognise that 'winning' the Cold War did not mark the end of system competition. Western democracy is not the last man standing; autocratic models continue to exist and rival it. Rather than writing off millions of people as unable to 'get' democracy, the West should make an effort to bring them on board. Empathy is a prerequisite to a process in which the wounds of the Cold War may be healed and, ultimately, Western liberty be strengthened.

It follows that it is worth asking what people expected from Western liberty and where they were disappointed. What did East Germans see when they gazed up at David Hasselhoff in his flashing leather jacket in 1989 and professed that they had been *Looking for Freedom*? Did the phrase mean the same to them as it did to the American actor? Probably not. Unlike their Western icon, who had soaked up consumerism and democracy from birth, they had caught mere glimpses of his world from behind the Iron Curtain.

This perspective is completely alien to those who have never known anything but the chances and risks that come with Western liberty. But it is worth trying to look at the West through the windows of the East. The wall afforded a distant and narrow view of the world that lay on the other side, and it left an awful lot to the imagination. The imagined West was a product of fears and desires, rather than information and experience. When the walls of communism fell, the sense of release and freedom thus quickly mingled with bewilderment and disillusionment. Old certainties had irrevocably gone, and those who had grown up with them were expected to cope in this brave new world that held freedoms as well as risks.

With their close geographical proximity to West Germany, as well as their familial, cultural and linguistic links to it, East Germans had had the closest contact with the world they chose to join in 1989/90. They were also immediately absorbed into the West when their East German state virtually disappeared on 3 October, 1990. Yet they provide the clearest example of lingering division, with voting patterns, attitudes and life-styles differing from their Western compatriots to this day. In other words, they are best placed to illustrate the discrepancies between the expectations and reality of Western liberty.

One window into the West, open to almost all citizens of the GDR, was television. According to the regime's own surveys, more than 70% of East Germans watched West German broadcasts. There were only two regions in the north and east where the signal was too weak to reach, but the inhabitants – sarcastically dubbed 'valley of the clueless' (*Tal der Ahnungslosen*) – only made up around 15% of the population. The authorities knew they had no way of stopping people watching the class enemy's programmes and they gave up trying. They even scheduled their own broadcasts carefully to avoid clashes with particularly popular shows on the Western channels. Generations of young East Germans grew up watching not only the same soap operas, cartoons and dubbed American sitcoms as their Western counterparts, but they also watched the same news programmes alongside their own.

Conscious of this fact, Western outlets often reported on the activities of East German opposition groups, as well as the repressive action taken against them. In this way, GDR citizens were not only comparatively well-informed about what was happening in their own country, despite the media monopoly the Socialist Unity Party held there, but they also began to learn that Western news, too, had to be taken with a pinch of salt, given that reports about the GDR didn't always match their lived reality. Still, a view of the West through television could only ever be a warped one. From cringe-worthy toothpaste adverts to the unlikely adventures of *MacGyver,* the image it projected gave few insights into the real lives of the people who lived there. Beyond the occasional news item, there was little evidence of the effects of the oil crises of the 1970s; the social, political and economic upheaval that led to strike action and unemployment across the West; the messy business of finding working majorities to govern divided countries. Instead, a world of scented shampoos, beautiful people and breath-taking car chases appeared on the screen.

Even the GDR's own television provided idealised visions of Western freedom by appealing to Germany's enduring love affair with the American West. In the nineteenth century, its association with liberty and opportunity had pulled millions of German emigrants to the US. But even those who stayed behind were fascinated. The author Karl May became one of the best-selling German writers of all time with his adventure stories of the Wild West, in which the native American hero Winnetou and his blood brother Old Shatterhand roamed a seemingly endless and untamed landscape, fighting corruption and cruelty. There was not only a Karl May Museum in the GDR, but a whole genre of so-called 'red westerns' (or *Osterns*), which spread across the entire Eastern Bloc. The 1966 film *The Sons of Great Bear* was watched by nine million of the GDR's 16 million citizens and catapulted its star, the German-Serbian actor Gojko Mitić, who would come to play Native American chieftains in many future productions, to legendary status behind the Iron Curtain. Just like Karl May, who had never set foot outside Germany when he wrote his novels, most East Germans based their ideas of Western freedom on fiction rather than fact.

However, the vast majority of East Germans also came into direct contact with real Western things and people. Many had relatives in West Germany, and in the 1980s visits both ways became somewhat easier to organise. More common, still, were parcels sent through the post. 'West parcels' were deeply evocative windows into consumerism. Many East Germans remember the excitement they felt when they carried them home from the post office, ready for the celebratory opening with the whole family. The intense mix of roast coffee and perfumed soaps carried strong connotations of wealth, indulgence and wonder, suggesting a world of plenty on the other side of the wall. Similarly, the so-called Intershops just 'smelled of freedom', as an East German interviewee once told me. Her eyes glazed over and she was back in 1981, in the little place in Zittau where they sold imported goods in exchange for hard currency – dreams made of scented washing powder and tinned pineapple. Intershops, too, were material windows into the West, with goods that were everyday items in Western supermarkets reaching quasi-magical qualities in the Eastern imagination.

Cravings for everyday Western culture were also hard to satisfy later. Blue jeans, particularly original Levi's, were highly sought after status symbols among the young. While the East German regime initially frowned upon them, this changed in 1971 when Erich Honecker became leader and decided that there was little harm in giving people their desired trousers. The General Secretary ordered one million original Levi's jeans from the US in 1978, not nearly enough to meet demand for this ultimate symbol of the West. So, the demand economy began producing replicas under their own evocatively named brands such as Wisent, Boxer and Shanty. But cotton procured from the Soviet Union was of a much lesser quality, rendering the East German products somewhat stiff and uncomfortable, and many East Germans continued to treasure original denim received from West German relatives.

Overall, there was no shortage of fleeting contact with Western output in the GDR. Alongside television, relatives and consumer products from the other side of the wall, there was also American and British pop and rock music, legally played on the radio and in clubs so long as a ratio of 40 to 60% in favour of East German output was adhered to. In the 1980s, the regime even allowed Western stars such as Bruce Springsteen and Joe Cocker to play in East Berlin. All of these windows into the West certainly played a part in fuelling a desire for Western freedoms but, crucially, they fell short of creating a real understanding of it.

This dynamic immediately unravelled when the Berlin Wall fell. Over the subsequent weekend, more than four million people visited West Germany, partially to satisfy their curiosity, partially to satisfy previously unfulfilled material desires. Clothing, toys, portable cassette players, coffee and exotic fruit were particularly popular spoils of these early trips. The first free elections of the GDR in March 1990 also revealed the deep longing for democracy. With a turnout of 93.4%, the conservative Christian Democrats came out as the strongest party, while the successor of the ruling GDR only received 16.3% of the vote share. Western accounts of the end of the Cold War tend to end at this point. After all, capitalism had triumphed over communism. The people of East Germany and Eastern Europe had made their choice.

It is certainly true that few of those who have lived under communist rule want to return to it. Yet many have found the collision of their imagined West with its lived reality sobering. Unemployment in East Germany soared to 20% after reunification. Many of the available jobs were insecure and low-paid. Disaffection with West German politicians, who seemed tone-deaf to East German concerns, rose. Turnout in every general election since 1990 has been lower in the former East than the former West Germany. At the general election in 2021, 27.1% of East Germans did not vote at all, while 15.7% voted for the far right party and 7.1% for the far left one. Taken together, this suggests nearly half of East Germans have turned their back on mainstream politics – more than three decades after choosing to join the system such politics seek to uphold.

To brush off the widespread disillusionment with the Western system as 'moaning', or a result of 'dictatorship socialisation', is dangerous. It is worth asking why people who once treasured images of Western freedom now find it difficult to live with the reality. Attempting to see our world through the narrow windows of those who lived outside of it is not a sign of Western weakness. It is a step towards finding ways to uphold, improve and promote Western liberty.

Portrait of John Locke, who articulated the
importance of liberty. Unknown artist, 1825.

THE POWER TO DO WHAT WE PLEASE

Peter Frankopan

reedom is fundamental to conceptualisations of the modern world – at least in the West, where freedoms of speech, of the press, of sexuality and gender, of religious conviction, and many more, are central bastions of the societies we live in. These freedoms, we are often told, have been fought for by our predecessors and need to be defended for this and for future generations.

As we usually think about them, these freedoms evolved from the Enlightenment in Europe, where thinkers such as John Locke, David Hume, John Stuart Mill and many others articulated the principles of what it meant to be 'free', how important liberty was and why it mattered. This says more about how we think about history in general than about freedom itself, which was the question that was pored over by scholars and philosophers in South Asia and in parts of China 2,000 years ago. They thought long and hard about if, how and why humans were able to be independent of nature, of each other and of higher powers.

The authors of the Upanishads, or scholars like Xunzi, writing more than 2,000 years ago, spent considerable energy investigating whether humans really acted freely and were able to control their own destiny – or whether they were constrained by divine will or by fate. In ancient Mesopotamian societies, astrologers and soothsayers looked for signs to help them understand meanings and portents, as well as for ways in which they (and contemporary rulers) could influence the future through making offerings.

Indeed, assessments of freedom were crucial even in Western societies more than a millennium before the Enlightenment: the law code assembled by the great Roman emperor Justinian (r. 527–565) took care to formulate a definition that could be applied in legislation. Freedom, says the code, is 'the natural power of doing what we please unless prevented by force or law'.

Of course, this sounds simple enough. But it raises many additional questions, perhaps most important of which concern the relative obligations between the individual and the state, and the ability of the latter to compel behaviour or make demands from the former. Much depends, in other words, on precisely what 'force' or 'law' mean and who is able to wield either or both.

Nevertheless, so heavily embedded are concepts of freedom within Western societies that during the Cold War, commentators often categorised the world as being divided into the Soviet bloc, on the one hand, and the Free World, on the other – a distinction that made more sense in the United States, Europe and former settler colonies such as Australia and New Zealand than it did in many parts of Africa, Asia and Central and South America.

Cynics might suggest that ideas about the 'free world' are a mirror of how Western societies not only like to present but also view themselves, namely as proponents of the most enlightened, progressive and sophisticated socio-economic and political model that is the benchmark to which other nations would want to aspire – perhaps best articulated in Francis Fukuyama's seminal article and book, *The End of History*.

Whether such cynicism might be merited is one thing; but another is that one of the most prominent themes in global geopolitics in the last decade has been the push-back against Western models, for which there are many and complex explanations. Taken as a whole, the idea that the international legal order is one that was set up by Western powers to protect their interests and exclude others has found widespread and increasing support in many countries around the world.

In the most extreme cases, this has been manifested by diminishing freedoms: across almost every index, societies have become less 'free' in recent years, with authoritarianism, restrictions and crackdowns not only increasingly common but also increasingly popular. Ironically, this is the case, too, in states with long traditions of democracy, where political debates have become measurably more polarised, institutions challenged, and media and social media have created antagonisms that present significant problems for centrist politics.

This, of course, creates ambiguities in high-income, liberal democracies in which freedom forms a central concept, not only of national identities, but of nationhood itself. The United States, after all, is the Land of the Free (as well as home of the brave); its constitution states that the purpose of the government is to 'establish justice, insure domestic tranquillity, provide for common defence [and] promote the general welfare', as well as 'secure the blessings of liberty'. If the simple rallying cry of France, 'Liberté, Egalité, Fraternité', leaves little to the imagination as to the importance of freedom, then the same can be said in Britain, where perhaps the most striking line in the patriotic *Rule Britannia* (composed in the eighteenth century) is that 'Britons never will be slaves'.

In the case of the latter, there is obvious and painful irony in the fact that the benefits of freedom from bondage owed much to the enslavement of peoples in other parts of the world, and from the requisitioning of raw materials, goods and labour that helped to build not only a fleet that ruled the waves, but an empire to boot.

That should serve as a reminder that freedom is usually in the eye of the beholder. Take, for instance, the constitution of one country that declares: 'Man, his rights and freedoms, shall be the supreme value. The recognition, observance and protection of human and civil rights and freedoms shall be an obligation of the State.' Few, other than Vladimir Putin and the circle around him, would seriously think that any of these protections were real or meaningful. And yet, such is how the Russian Federation presents itself to its own citizens, not only as an aspiration, but as a key duty of the state.

Likewise, guarantees that citizens of the People's Republic of China have the right to 'enjoy the freedom of speech, of the press, of assembly and of demonstration', show the mismatch between intention and reality – but also underline how states of all political persuasions and structures at least claim to defend freedoms as a central right for all citizens. In this case, too, that is further articulated by the constitutional commitment that 'the freedom of the citizens of the PRC is inviolable', something that might cause eyebrows to rise both in China itself and beyond.

The key question, then, is what freedom really is, and who gets to decide. In 2022, this was put into sharp focus by Putin, because of his actions in invading Ukraine in what he claimed was a 'special operation' rather than an invasion, and because he has often taken to mulling over his views in public about history, including in a series of turgid essays written in July 2021 and the summer of 2022.

States were either sovereign or they were not, he opined in June 2022 – 'There is no middle way between being a sovereign country and a colony.' In other words, one is either free or one is not free. Russia, by Putin's formulation, was a sovereign power, like the United States and China, that could act independently and, additionally, could not be coerced. This was not true, to judge from his statements, about other states – such as Ukraine, but also members of the European Union, which were dependent on energy, raw materials and more from Russia, and, as such, were vulnerable, dependent and effectively unfree.

While this throws up a great many questions, not least about Putin himself, for the current purposes of this essay, the most important one is whether or not he is right. In a world that has seen profound globalisation, accelerated over the last three decades, has the harmonisation of markets reduced independence and freedom because of the gamble that supplies of all kinds – energy, foods, materials and so on – would always be available? Or has globalisation served to increase risk by introducing points of failure that can be exploited intentionally (in the case of Russia, for example) or otherwise (such as in the case of the pandemic)? Has the international legal order become a cipher, in other words, for mutual dependencies that serve to create fewer 'sovereigns' and more 'colonies', to use Putin's formulation?

Economists might argue that markets solve problems better than political dogma, and provide sanguine reminders that what seem to be reckless actions (such as war) can also strengthen resilience and lead to supply-side gains, by triggering reforms that, in fact, can have positive long-term impacts.

A historian might look at this in a slightly different way and focus on the age of the Enlightenment, when liberty and freedom were topics of almost obsessive interest for scholars and philosophers in Western Europe. The concepts of freedom were set in a context not only of rationalism, scientific advancement and wider engagements with other parts of the world, but also that of sharply rising personal and public wealth.

It was important, too, that these ideas about liberty were framed in a specific set of assumptions and built on hard realities that enabled ideas about freedom to look better to those who talked about them than to the world at large. This was clear, for example, when it came to suffrage; it is easy to forget, or never learn, that women in what are now Uzbekistan and Azerbaijan were given the right to vote before women in Britain. And universal voting rights for all adults in what are now proud liberal democracies are still an extremely recent phenomenon in historical terms – in most cases, less than a century old.

That is because those who wrote about freedom and expressed strong opinions about how important it was were direct or indirect beneficiaries of the lack of freedom of others. That was evidently the case when it came to slavery, especially in the Caribbean and the Americas; but those freedoms were not limited to coerced labour and the fruits (and profits) it generated in lucrative industries, such as sugar, cotton and tobacco.

The key to staying free – or at least talking about it – was the acquisition and accumulation of resources from other parts of the world at the lowest cost. These did not just produce financial dividends, but calorie benefits too: sugar imports between 1600–1850 are estimated to have improved living standards in England by almost 10%, an astonishing amount, in other words.

The flow of benefits shifted in more recent centuries, with accusations being made 30 years ago, at the Earth Summit in Rio de Janeiro in 1992, that the parts of the world that had industrialised first were now guilty of neo-colonialism. Richer countries parked dirty industrial production on low-income countries, while taking advantage of the lower costs of labour and the lack of responsibility for land, air and water pollution that have significant knock-on effects on everything, from cognitive development to suicide rates.

In this sense, then, the single most important aspect of the meaning and practice of freedom is institutional development – that is to say, political structures that not only preserve independence, but prevent the accumulation of authority, power and decision making from what early modern scholars called tyrants.

As one Middle Eastern minister put it in the early twentieth century, freedom is never given, it is always taken. This is how liberal democracies evolved: not by the consensus that liberty was a good in itself, but because mercantile elites were able to take powers away from autocrats, and to build institutions that protected and enhanced their independence. The rewards of such developments owed little to conceptual ideas about whether freedom was good in itself – self-evidently the case, given how jealously participation in political life was guarded.

What elites did successfully in countries that later transitioned into fully functional democracies (at least in so far as all adults have a right to vote) was to force the introduction of controls on poor decisions that could lead to enhanced risks. One way that worked in Great Britain, for example, was for parliament to insist on meeting regularly, and, in doing so, restrict unilateral decisions made by the monarch. Curiously, it seems that a major part of the success in ensuring political stability, as well as sound investment in the army and the navy, was the insistence of parliament to raise taxes – and thus underline what lay at stake by making the population (including those not allowed to vote) at least partially invested in the success of the country abroad.

It is perhaps no coincidence, therefore, that while much attention is paid by commentators to individual countries and the threats that they pose, both real and imagined, the most significant development in the first two decades of the twenty-first century has been the degradation and undermining of global institutions, most notably the United Nations, but also the World Bank and the World Trade Organisation.

Despite appearances, this has not just been done by nefarious actors but by liberal democracies that have chosen to act unilaterally and, in some cases, even unlawfully. In doing so, it is not just the metaphysical pillars of freedom that have been weakened, but the international legal order too. The decision by the US and its coalition allies to effectively by-pass the United Nations over interventions in Afghanistan, Iraq and Syria has proved to have significant implications when others, too, have sought to take matters into their own hands through the use of force, most notably Russia.

The withdrawal of the United States from major climate agreements, from the Trans-Pacific Partnership as well as from UN agencies such as UNESCO, or the withdrawal of the UK from the European Union (and the intentional breaches of international law regarding the Northern Ireland agreement), all have their own logic – especially for the champions of such decisions. Nevertheless, taken individually and collectively, they represent cases of unilateral actions that benefit the few in the place of the many. As such, while they might offer additional freedoms for the beneficiaries, they limit those for others.

Not surprisingly, then, other actors have proved adept at exposing disunity, in playing on vulnerabilities that promise new solutions to old problems, and which further undermine local, regional and global institutions. We are living in a post-Enlightenment age, where powers are progressively being harvested by leaders with autocratic tendencies and authoritarian political structures, who present themselves as guardians of their citizens' interests, in much the same way as medieval kings did.

That is self-evident in countries such as Russia, China, Turkey, Hungary and others, where the apparatus of the state, as well as the media, is either in government or regime-friendly hands. It is increasingly true in liberal democracies, too, however, where chaotic domestic politics – from the prime ministerial merry-go-round in Britain to the 6 January 2021 storming of the Capitol in Washington – suggest there are serious problems in states that have long prided themselves on being stable, and able to avoid the personality cults that characterise autocratic rule.

It is hard to predict the impact on freedom of current economic pressures – with the financial implications of the pandemic dovetailing with inflationary headwinds, the exclusion of Russia from many international markets, sudden shifts by central banks to change money supply, and climatic stresses.

Historians, however, would point to the past to underline the strong correlation between downturns and reduced freedoms. What the coming years and decades have to offer is unclear. But few would bet that our world will be freer than it has been for the past 30 years, and a wiser gambler would put money on the chances that the opposite trend – of restrictions, exclusions, centralisation of power – will rise sharply. That prospect should concern us all.

ONE FOR ALL,
ALL FOR ONE

Finnish soldiers at Kuolemajärvi,
Karelian Isthmus, 1939.

WHY FINNS JOINED THE FIGHT

Charly Salonius-Pasternak

Only Finland – superb, nay, sublime in the jaws of peril – Finland
shows what free men can do.

PRIME MINISTER WINSTON CHURCHILL, 20 January, 1940

The Finnish nation is firm and united in the defence of her liberty
and of her democratic institutions.

MINISTER HJALMAR PROCOPÉ, Finland's envoy to the United States
1939–1944

The idea that the free sometimes have to sacrifice their personal liberty, or life, in order to defend collective liberty – in this case, the existence of Finland – was undoubtedly clear to both Prime Minister Churchill and Minister Procopé. It was also clear to many Finns on the eve of the Winter War in autumn 1939. It has remained clear to generations since, always with the added bittersweet expectation that now, like then, Finland would have to defend its freedom alone. This changed in 2022. Finland's path towards NATO may have been a long one, but as of now Finland is in no sense a reluctant ally.

In 2015, I wrote about how war may return to this part of the world, and, a year later, about how overlapping geopolitical zones were likely to increase conflict potential. Recent events, primarily Russia's expanded attack and attempt to destroy Ukraine, and Ukraine's brave defence, has galvanised multiple generations of citizens and politicians to talk about the importance of defending democracy and liberty. Here, liberty is both the freedom to do something and the freedom from having something imposed: the freedom to 'do your own thing' within broader constraints.

It is this that fundamentally explains Finland's – and I believe Sweden's – recent NATO membership applications: the desire to maintain for future generations a freedom from, and strengthen security against, those forces that seek to restrict the liberty of Finns. This desire for liberty is, of course, not new. In this volume, Mark Schiefsky's listing of the four freedoms Athenians wanted – not living under tyranny, ability to participate in society, being able to live largely as one wanted, and not being a slave

– could certainly be appreciated by Finns of any generation, in the sense that economic or social background does not shackle potential. In Finland, education is held in high esteem. It makes for better citizens but also, ultimately, citizens who feel there is a reason Finland must continue to exist as a country and society.

Throughout spring 2022, various commentators, upon discovering Finland's decades-long preparations for potential war if Russia chose to attack, sought to present Finland as the Sparta of the north. A far better historical analogy is ancient Athens, for the reasons indicated above but also because the Athenians had a clear sense that freedom required collective sacrifices, to defend the very liberties that they held dear. In Finland, more than four-fifths support this view, even with regard to the continuation of national military service, which obviously limits personal freedom, because without it there could be no effective collective action to defend Finland. The only real societal question is whether, in an age of equality, mandatory service should be expanded to everyone, not just men.

Because it has taken Finns (and Swedes) much longer to decide to seek NATO membership than to become a part of the EU, questions have been raised about whether Finland and Sweden are, in fact, reluctant allies – and what kind of allies they will be, and whether they can be relied upon to defend their allies and liberty more broadly. The latter concern must be dispensed with immediately: there is no doubt that Finland will fulfil its role in the defence of other NATO allies. I also have no doubt about this regarding Sweden.

Why have a majority of the Finnish public and political leadership consistently, since the end of the Cold War, been against Finnish NATO membership? Opposition to membership has been remarkably stable, despite an ever deepening cooperation with NATO that has progressed from the Partnership for Peace, through operations such as IFOR, SFOR and KFOR in the Balkans, and then ISAF in Afghanistan. This was followed by the signing of a Host Nation Support agreement in 2014, and even deeper cooperation as an Enhanced Opportunity Partner. From the late 1990s to late-2021, 60 to 70% of the population were against NATO membership, while 20 to 30% supported it.

This is at least partially explained through historical lessons to do with seeking to avoid becoming involved in great power competitions, and an almost fatalistic expectation that no one, in any event, would ever come to Finland's assistance.

A frequently quoted plaque by the King's Gate on Suomenlinna fortress, outside Helsinki, reminds the reader to 'stand here on your own ground and do not trust/expect foreign assistance'. Considering that before and even after the building of Suomenlinna, Russia had attacked the Finnish people between 30 and 40 times over the centuries – with the Finns effectively left to their own self-defensive devices – this was a reasonable reminder to make. This feeling of being left alone was strengthened by the Finnish national memory of being abandoned during the Winter War against the Soviet Union. This was not entirely true; Sweden did unofficially provide some assistance, but it was a far cry from what the international community has to date provided to Ukraine. This experience left many Finns doubting whether anyone would ever come to the aid of Finland – allied or not. In the one period when Finland was 'allied', it did receive important assistance. But in the post-Second World War international political environment, having been a co-belligerent with Nazi Germany against the Soviet Union didn't exactly fit the Finnish national story, even if, in the end, Finland had of course ended up fighting against Nazi Germany once an armistice with the Soviet Union was agreed.

The second historical lesson that impacted Finns' views on the idea of NATO is the sense that Finns have, throughout the centuries, been drawn into wars by the West (as part of the Swedish kingdom) or forced into wars by Russia. This contributed to the idea that it was best to avoid becoming party to great power competition; and, for many, NATO is still seen as a tool or reflection of great power competition. In academic international relations theory, the great powers are concerned about entanglement – the idea that a small ally might pull them into an unnecessary war. In Finland, quite the opposite has been the central concern, and an argument against NATO membership: that as a member, Finland would be forced into wars that others started, and which a non-allied Finland could have avoided.

To be clear, the Finnish population changed its view of the regional security situation quite dramatically in 2014, following Russia's annexation of Crimea. Until that point, the prospect of an actual large-scale war, one that could threaten Finland's freedom and thus the liberty of its citizens, seemed quite distant. Obviously, societal preparations for such a war continued, retaining national military service and an extensive system of shelters for civilians among them, but this had more to do with a concern for future generations – we were a link in the chain, not the link that would be tested.

This began to change after 2014, but even then the Finnish population did not see NATO membership as necessary. The motivation for this can be boiled down to four reasons: the aforementioned history; concerns about Russia's potential response (essentially an evaluation of whether the potential increase in defence assistance/deterrence would outweigh Russia's reactions); a belief in Finland's own robust national defence capability; and ever deeper defence cooperation, bilaterally, with Sweden and the United States, multilaterally through efforts such as the UK-led Joint Expeditionary Force and with NATO.

The sense among many Finns – including a majority of politicians – was that these factors, taken together, meant that NATO membership was not necessary. For most, membership was also not seen as necessary from the perspective of showing that Finland was part of 'the West'. Paraphrasing Churchill, Finland had, throughout its independence, shown the world what free men could do to defend not only their own liberty but democracy and the West.

Then, from the end of 2021, Finns began to change their views about what might be required in the future to safeguard their freedom. The opinion polls changed dramatically between December that year and April/May 2022, with the population supporting the idea of NATO membership soaring to 78%, from 25%.

Why did this happen? Over the coming years, research will give more definitive answers, but I have a few propositions:

1. Russian demands in December 2021 for spheres of influence, which would clearly limit Finnish freedom in the foreign and security policy sphere, and, over time, potentially in domestic politics.
2. Russia's clear willingness to use actual military force against a country much larger than Finland that was viewed by many as a brotherly state and people.
3. Proof of the clear difference between being a partner (such as Ukraine or Finland) as opposed to an ally, in terms of the material assistance given (including sanctions), while still being alone when it comes to the fighting.
4. A change in the Finns' belief that working relations with Russia would provide some protection from being attacked – at times going to great lengths to make clear that they were not a threat.
5. A reminder of what large-scale, mechanised war looks like, and what it does to civilians and cities.

These are some of the reasons why the population changed its mind, but I believe three more things were needed to re-forge, in a matter of months, the national security consensus to include NATO membership.

First, a deep societal pragmatism, especially regarding maximising Finnish security and freedom of manoeuvre – liberty on a national scale. If, during the Cold War, this required talk of 'brotherly love' and neutrality towards the Soviets – done. If, in 2022, this required seeking NATO membership – also done.

Second, Finland has had a lively debate about NATO membership for many decades. The societal conclusion had been, up until spring 2022, on balance, that membership was not needed or that its potential risks outweighed its benefits. In May 2022, President Niinistö made a call to Vladimir Putin to let him know that Finns had come to some new conclusions.

Third, and related to the previous one: the existence of a NATO option – the political idea that if the security situation changed, Finland could seek NATO membership. This idea has been enshrined in official government documents for the past two decades, covering every parliamentary party. This made it much easier for all parties and most politicians to change their views regarding NATO membership.

Before going into what kind of members Finland (and perhaps Sweden) are likely to be, a quick note about how the Finnish government motivated the need to seek NATO membership would be helpful. The report on the changed security environment that formed the basis for the parliamentary process and debate in Finland did not explicitly call for NATO membership, but when a second report proposing membership was published, it was foreign minister Pekka Haavisto and defence minister Antti Kaikkonen who, together, made the argument very clear.

The application was not about solving Finland's potential security issues in 2022, but rather about anticipating problems arising in the coming years and decades. Of particular concern was Russia's increased propensity to use military force; its ability to quickly mass hundreds of thousands of soldiers at a neighbour's border; and looser talk about the use of non-conventional/nuclear weapons. Due to the nature of these threats, Haavisto argued, Finland needed a stronger deterrence, including a nuclear component, and the potential for collective defence efforts – requirements that only NATO membership fulfils. Defence minister

Kaikkonen put it even more succinctly: Finnish NATO membership is about avoiding war and, failing that, to never again have to fight alone.

These words already give an indication of what kind of a member Finland intends to be. The talk in analytical bubbles in Finland has begun to shift from 'burden sharing' to 'responsibility sharing'. Looking at how Finland (and Sweden) behaves generally in international organisations, in the EU, and thus far with NATO (as a partner), will give some clues, as well as what has already been said about it – such as whether there will be any self-imposed limitations.

As Finnish politicians have made it clear that gaining nuclear deterrence is one of the reasons to seek membership, Finland is unlikely to place any additional nuclear weapons related restrictions on itself, except those imposed by the constitution. In short, no nukes in Finland during peace. This does leave quite a large door open to participating in 'nuclear missions' in other ways. It also seems unlikely that Finland would place Norway-like limits on NATO member forces or basing. Again, why pre-emptively limit the potential avenues of strengthening deterrence or defensive capabilities? That said, Finland is unlikely to ask for the permanent stationing of other NATO members' forces on its soil (such as the Enhanced Forward Presence battalions or soon-to-be brigades in the Baltics) – the exception being a NATO Force Integration Unit of some 20 to 30 people.

So, what kind of member will Finland be and how will it impact things? Finland and Sweden will contribute to strengthening the transatlantic relationship but not change some of the underlying dynamics regarding defence spending, and so on. Finland and Sweden are, together, going to change the political balance within the Alliance, in an opposite direction from that seen in the past few enlargements. Both are also likely to be quite 'Harmelian' in their approach, after the famous Belgian statesman, working to strengthen deterrence and defence, while also seeing the value and necessity of engaging in dialogue with Russia (at some future point). Unlike almost all post-Cold War expansions, Finland and Sweden also contribute significant military capabilities from day one. For NATO, Finland's and Sweden's robust military capabilities, long experience operating in a challenging regional environment and geographic location will contribute to the potential for collective defence. Ultimately, Finnish and Swedish membership makes it possible to reconceptualise the defence of the whole of northern Europe.

Finland will not change its fundamental approach to defence – that it is primarily in the hands of the Finns – nor its defence posture. At the same time, there is bound to be pressure to show that Finland is an active ally. The old 'partner-era' argument, that Finland's contribution is defending its own territory (NATO's flank), is no longer enough. The low-hanging fruit is: active participation in all NATO organisations and groups, requiring that it sends out not the minimum 80 or so civilians and soldiers but as many as possible, up to 200–220; taking on roles in Baltic and Icelandic air patrols/defence; contributing to an Enhanced Forward Presence unit in Estonia, perhaps with a combat engineering platoon initially and then a company; and allocating a ship to participate in a NATO Standing Maritime Group in the Mediterranean or Baltic Sea.

The practical and operational issues will be dealt with reasonably quickly. However, a far larger challenge awaits, what I think will be the biggest change that Finland and Sweden will have to undergo as NATO members. And that involves a process of changing national strategic cultures – in Finland's case, going from 'we alone' to being part of a collective defence family. This change in strategic cultural approach may take some years but it will happen. Finns' pragmatism and staunch belief in the importance of liberty – both individual and national – will ensure it.

A final historical anecdote may explain it better than any longer analytical treaties. In October 1939, a long train left the station at Vallila in Helsinki, heading towards *Kuolemanjärvi* (Death Lake). Aboard was the 2,900-soldier-strong JR 11, an infantry regiment composed of people from Kallio, Vallila and Sörnäis, all legendary workers' districts. Many were politically left leaning, and with fathers who had fought on the red side during the civil war some two decades earlier; the scars of that particularly nasty war were still in the process of healing. Nonetheless, while their fathers had fought for a worker's paradise, what these men abhorred was the idea that someone from the outside – namely Stalin – could come to tell them how Finnish society should be structured. To a man, all had seen and understood the importance of changes that were occurring in Finland. Changes that would in the coming decades – when Finland had maintained its freedom – contribute to the country becoming the most stable in the world (according to the Fund for Peace Fragile State Index), and the happiest too.

In the case of that JR 11 regiment, the human cost of defending Finland's liberty, and also their own, was high. After four months of conflict, of those 2,900 soldiers, only 850 would be left. While these men undoubtedly fought for each other in the foxholes, they also had a collective sense that Finland's existence and survival was important, that progress and safety were intimately tied to each other. A limitation on personal freedom – in the form of national service – was necessary to guarantee that national liberty. Because there needed to be a Finland and a Finnish political system that was free to make its own decisions, to build and maintain a social system with high quality schooling, from daycare through university, social services and health care, and so on, all the things that ultimately liberate the individual and allow them to flourish, irrespective of their social background. But only if Finland is free.

Ukranian soldiers in Kyiv, November 2022.

HOW A SECOND COLD WAR COULD HAVE
BEEN AVERTED

Mary E. Sarotte

Tragically, it became apparent in early 2022 that a major land war in Europe was no longer a thing of the past. Russian president Vladimir Putin's decision to launch new hostilities against Ukraine on 24 February signalled a renewed era of confrontation between an authoritarian regime in Moscow and democratic nations to its west. February 2022 was not the first time that Putin had used force against Ukrainians, of course, but the scale of the incursion in that month was an order of magnitude larger and more brutal than previous iterations. His gruesome actions made undeniably clear that he and the state that he controls are the biggest threats to democracy and liberty in Europe.

Among other consequences, these actions caused NATO to reassess its own strategy dramatically. Prior to the February 2022 invasion, the alliance had been focused on potential future threats from China. In July, however, NATO issued a new Strategic Concept emphasising the current threat from Russia instead, describing Moscow as 'the most significant and direct threat to Allies' security and to peace and stability in the Euro-Atlantic area'. NATO thereby once again found itself in the role of chief defender of that peace, stability and liberty.

NATO's return to confrontation with Russia means it has come full circle from the end of the Cold War, ending a period of cooperation and resuming confrontation and tension. How did the alliance once again find itself in this role? The answer to this question goes much further back than just February 2022. By re-examining a few key moments in the history of the Western fight with Russia over NATO's role in Europe, we can understand the origins of today's conflict – and how NATO might best deal with it.

Why, after a period of so much closeness and cooperation around the time of the Soviet collapse 30 years ago, did relations between Moscow and Washington deteriorate so badly? As much as we might wish for a simple answer, there is no denying that major events happen for multiple reasons. History is rarely, if ever, monocausal. American and Russian choices interacted cumulatively with each other, and with each country's domestic politics, to produce the decay. But it is hard to avoid the reality that one particular US policy call added to the burdens on Russia's fragile young democracy when it was most in need of friends: the post-Cold War decision to expand NATO.

Saying this is not the same thing as saying that expansion was a mistake. The choice to enlarge the Atlantic alliance was a justifiable response to the geopolitics of the 1990s. The problem was how it happened. To understand what went wrong, it is necessary to move beyond the familiar binary – either praising or condemning enlargement wholesale – and get into the weeds of the policy's implementation. Doing so shows how expansion carried both clear benefits and costs, and that the manner of enlargement increased the latter unnecessarily.

Put differently, the failure in US-Russian relations was not overdetermined, with both sides careening unavoidably toward renewed confrontation. Handling implementation differently could have meant both sides instead arriving, if not at a perpetually harmonious *modus vivendi*, then at a less toxic situation than today's. But in the 1990s, two American presidents were so focused on achieving the eastward extension of Article 5 that they did not sufficiently consider the consequences of how they achieved that goal. As President George H W Bush said in response to the idea that Washington might compromise with Moscow over NATO's future, 'to hell with that'. President Bill Clinton was certain that Russia could be 'bought off'. Along the way, a promising alternative mode of contingent enlargement that would have avoided drawing a new line across Europe fell to hardline opposition.

Given the space constraints on this essay it is not possible to delve into the full history in detail; rather, it is necessary to focus on a few key junctures, and the year 1999 was one of them. In that year, Clinton decided to have NATO's April 1999 summit in Washington publicly welcome the interest expressed by a host of Eastern European states, including the Baltics, in full NATO membership. This decision ultimately culminated in the so-called NATO Big Bang expansion in 2004.

Clinton made this 1999 decision at a time when the alliance was taking military action against Serbian forces in Kosovo, despite fierce Russian resistance to attacks on fellow Slavs. Clinton's promotion of Baltic membership in particular at this tricky moment in relations with Russia meant that the alliance would extend within what Moscow considered to be the former Soviet Union itself at a time of tensions. The United States could insist, correctly, that it had never recognised the Baltics' incorporation into the USSR, but that did not change the political import of the decision.

Nordic and Scandinavian countries privately tried to counsel caution. Because of their location in a neighbourhood that had long been Soviet-adjacent but not Soviet controlled, in earlier decades Norwegians and Danes had negotiated limits on their own NATO memberships. They had, in essence, developed a Scandinavian strategy for keeping long-term frictions with Moscow manageable. They would voluntarily refrain from hosting foreign troops and nuclear weapons on their territory in peacetime to reduce tensions. Something similar would be advisable for the Baltics, they felt, as those new states were now residing in a neighbour-hood that was also Russia-adjacent but not Russian controlled. Finns and Swedes emphasised this theme, warning of the need to keep frictions with Moscow manageable. But Washington was no longer interested in partial implementation of membership and proceeded with membership with-out any qualifications.

This fateful 1999 decision came not only at a time of tension over Kosovo. It also came at the same time that Russian president Boris Yeltsin, suffering both from heart disease and the health consequences of a drink-ing problem, decided to make his prime minister, Putin, acting president on the last day of 1999. Yeltsin informed Putin of this decision on 14 December, but said that Putin had to keep the news to himself until 31 December.

A week after this conversation with Yeltsin, Putin took part in an unveil-ing ceremony for the restored plaque of former long-time KGB head (and later Soviet leader) Yuri Andropov. The symbolism was obvious. Andropov's formative experience had been the 1956 uprising in Hungary. He had watched in horror from the window of the Soviet embassy in Budapest as an uprising threatened to topple the Communist government and remove Hungary from the Warsaw Pact. Andropov never forgot watching the bodies of executed Hungarian secret police swaying from the streetlights. The experience marked the birth of Andropov's so-called Hungarian complex, meaning a conviction that tolerance of even small protest movements could lead to serious challenges to Moscow's authority – a lesson Putin's attendance highlighted once again.

The significance of Putin's attendance at the plaque ceremony became apparent to all on New Year's Eve 1999. That morning, Yeltsin recorded a brief resignation video, to be broadcast nationwide at noon. Even though Washington knew Putin was Yeltsin's preferred successor, once it hit the airwaves, the hurried handover came as a shock. The US ambassador in Moscow awakened Strobe Talbott, the deputy secretary of state, at his home in Washington and told him to turn on a television. The two Americans stayed on the phone as they watched the Yeltsin era come to an end.

Yeltsin shocked the country with the news in his video. Promising that a new generation of leaders would do everything 'bigger and better', he disclosed that he had already signed a decree making Putin acting president. He bid farewell to his compatriots, expressing a last wish that they 'be happy'. After watching the broadcast of his own video in the Kremlin together with Putin, Yeltsin told his successor to 'take care of Russia'.

The legacy of these events for today is manifold and profound. For starters, tensions between Moscow and Washington in 1999 helped to close the window of opportunity for comprehensive US-Russian strategic nuclear disarmament – the most significant opening since the dawn of the atomic age. By the end of the 1990s, intelligence agencies reported on the beginnings of renewed nuclear competition.

Other forms of competition emerged soon thereafter, not least in the shredding of hard-won arms control accords. And today's permissive environment of a world almost wholly lacking such accords means both sides are reassessing the roles of not just nuclear but also conventional capabilities. In Europe in recent years, both the post-Cold War American drawdown of forces and the Russian shift of troops eastward have reversed.

Increasing tensions have also raised questions about security in cyber and economic domains. As the historian Adam Tooze has shown, renewed Russian aggression reveals that the post-Cold War 'disavowal of the obvious connection between trade and security policy' was a grievous error, one fully exposed by 'the resurgence of Putin's Russia'. Despite having a GDP not that much larger than Spain's, once the cooperative spirit died, Russia began leveraging 'its military assets to upend the geopolitical balance in Western Asia and the Middle East', and its cyber capabilities to wound governments and businesses around the globe.

Viewed in conceptual terms, it is clear that the world created by the 1990s did not fulfil the hopes of 1989 – meaning, among other things, the belief that the liberal international order had succeeded definitively, and that residents of *all* states between the Atlantic and the Pacific, not just the Western ones, could now cooperate within it. This outcome was not fore-ordained. Instead, both American and Russian leaders repeatedly made choices yielding outcomes that not only fell short of those hopes, but were explicitly at odds with their stated intentions. In the course of the 1990s, Bush talked about a Europe whole, free, and at peace; Clinton repeatedly proclaimed his wish to avoid drawing a line. Yet with their actions, both in the end promoted a dividing line across Europe. Gorbachev wanted to save the Soviet Union; Yeltsin wanted to democratise Russia; and both, in different ways, wanted to partner on equal footing with the West. Yet, in the longer term, both failed as well.

Residents of the former Warsaw Pact and Soviet states also experienced outcomes at odds with initial hopes. Although such states repeatedly said they did not want to end up in a grey zone, some did. The peoples of Belarus, Georgia and Ukraine all struggled to define their relations with Russia and, at times, defend their borders. Former Warsaw Pact states experienced their own uncertainties. While they succeeded in joining NATO (and eventually the European Union as well), they found that such memberships did not automatically lock in their democratic transformations and, like the rest of the continent, they suffered rising tensions with Moscow.

In the twenty-first century, what increasingly became apparent was that the pressures of simultaneously democratising and creating a market economy had produced fertile ground for latter-day, Soviet-trained authoritarians such as Putin. Once securely in power, Putin began gradually throttling back the democratic transformation while resuming old habits of competition with the West. And complaints about how NATO had moved military infrastructure to within former Soviet borders provided him with a useful rationale.

More public candour at the time from knowledgeable insiders about the options being foreclosed might have helped. Even as strong a supporter of NATO as then-senator Joseph Biden sensed that he lacked answers to key questions: enlargement, yes, but at what cost to relations with former Soviet republics, and to nuclear disarmament? Biden asked an expert witness – former US ambassador to the Soviet Union, Jack

Matlock – questions to this effect at a Senate hearing on NATO expansion on 30 October, 1997. Matlock responded that, despite the passing of the Cold War, 'the most serious potential security threat to the American people' remained 'weapons of mass destruction from Russian arsenals'. Biden replied: 'I agree with that concern.' One-size-fits-all expansion, Matlock continued, would not help to contain that threat and could even 'undermine the effort'. In reply, Biden concluded that 'continuing the Partnership for Peace [an alternative to giving out full Article 5 guarantees immediately], which turned out to be much more robust and much more successful than I think anyone thought it would be at the outset, may arguably have been a better way to go'.

The Partnership might also have helped its greatest critics, the Central and Eastern European countries, towards a more permanent democratisation. Social science researchers later established that it was not NATO membership that prompted these countries to complete civil and military reforms, it was the process of trying to join. Congressional investigators and others warned that countries were entering NATO before establishing strong democratic institutions. If the Partnership had survived as originally implemented, potential allies would – admittedly through clenched teeth – have had to earn alliance status over a longer period, presumably making them more resistant to subsequent attacks on democracy.

By the end of the pivotal decade of the 1990s, the Clinton administration had instead secured an open road for extending the alliance eastward. After Clinton and his advisors left office, they could only watch in alarm as Bush's son, George W Bush, took the keys to the NATO car and gunned it down that open road. Among other stops, the younger Bush attended the alliance's summits in 2006 in Latvia, the first such event on former Soviet territory, and in 2008 in Bucharest, where he pushed hard for the inclusion of Georgia and Ukraine. For Putin, that Bucharest summit – coming on top of Bush's 2003 invasion of Iraq and his 2007 decision to erect ballistic missile defences (in the form of ten ground-based interceptors in Poland and a radar facility in the Czech Republic), all around the time of 'colour revolutions' in post-Soviet states – proved to be the breaking point.

Since the alliance frowns on allies joining NATO to pursue pre-existing military disputes, Putin decided to escalate just such pre-existing conflicts with Georgia in 2008 and Ukraine in 2014 in violent fashion. The hope that such armed conflicts were gone for good had characterised much of the post-Cold War era. Russia's action signalled that the era was over. Putin also expanded Russia's conventional military budget, developed new missile defence and space capabilities, and began modernising Russia's nuclear arsenal. In response, the alliance's leaders suspended not only the NATO-Russia Council but 'all practical cooperation between NATO and Russia'.

Contrasting today's situation with other feasible outcomes to the process of reshaping order after the Cold War helps us to understand just how far short of better alternatives the current situation falls. As Russia expert Stephen Sestanovich presciently wrote in a 1993 op-ed in the *New York Times*, while real doubts could be raised about 'all the many' alternatives being proposed for cooperation with Russia, 'these doubts are nothing compared with the frustration and powerlessness we will feel once Russian democracy fails'. We are now living with that frustration – and the risks to liberty that it entails.

What has happened cannot be undone, but it is worth learning the lessons of the past as NATO once again expands. At the time of writing, Finland and Sweden are in the process of becoming members. They are fully justified in their desire to join the alliance, just as NATO is fully justified in accepting them, complaints from Moscow notwithstanding. But they should also proceed cautiously and learn from the history above.

Sadly, a situation of tension with Russia is once again the order of the day. Finns and Swedes should follow the example of Norwegians and Danes, and find ways to become NATO members while keeping tensions with Moscow manageable. The coming conflict with Russia – a second Cold War – appears set to last for some time. Finding ways to defend Western values and liberties, this time with the Finns and Swedes as allies, but without escalation, is the major challenge now facing policymakers. It will not be easy, but success is essential.

NATO Secretary General Jens Stoltenberg
speaks at NATO Foreign Ministers Meeting,
Bucharest, November 2022.

CAN EUROPE COME TO NATO'S DEFENCE?

Janne Haaland Matláry

When Western states use military force, they often do so without a clear strategy. Emile Simpson wrote a book that reflects on this, aptly named *War from the Ground Up: Twenty-first Century Combat as Politics* (2018). His military experience was mainly from the International Security Assistance Force operation in Afghanistan, but he also analyses the European use of force in more general terms. He argues that 'the tail wags the dog' – tactical military moves on the ground direct politics, not vice versa. This he calls 'armed politics', with the political implications of whatever is done at the operational level and below amounting to 'strategy', in induction-like fashion. This is the very opposite of strategy guiding the use of force in order to realise desired political effects.

There is no initial strategy for the use of force that guides it, Simpson argues. An operation happens because there is too much violence or trouble somewhere, and something has to be done about it. One throws in some military force in order to stabilise the situation, like a fire brigade that is sent to quell a fire. But once quelled, what then?

Is the use of force in NATO states in Europe – all liberal democracies – characterised by a lack of strategy? Does NATO do realpolitik, with a strategy to guide it in its major moves, such as enlargement? Or is NATO simply an international organisation like many others, with an openness to new members, as it declares that it is?

Is NATO based on values, not on strategic interests?
The preamble to the Washington treaty of April 4, 1949, reads that the member states are 'determined to safeguard the freedom, common heritage and civilisation of their peoples, founded on the principles of democracy, individual liberty and the rule of law'. This underlines the special character of NATO: it is indeed founded on these values, and obliged to

uphold them. In the short (and eminently readable) treaty, we also find that NATO is obliged to support the UN Pact, albeit not being a UN-associated organisation. Yet the *jus ad bellum* and *jus in bello* rules of international law are to be promoted and followed, and NATO will also seek the peaceful resolution of conflict. It is expressly a defensive alliance and has an 'open door' policy (paragraph 10), and demands that members are able to defend themselves as a first policy (article 3) before they seek help from others – the article 5 solidarity clause, the most famous paragraph in any international treaty.

Thus, NATO members are obliged to have a defence ability of their own as well as being democratic states. Both these criteria for membership are not entirely strict, as it were – there is no exclusion clause and Turkey today is far from a liberal democracy. Also, many members have relatively weak defence forces; the 'free rider' problem in NATO is infamous. Most members do not reach the agreed 2% of GDP spending on defence criterion, and the US carries a disproportionate burden and has always done so.

The question that is asked in this essay is whether NATO pursues a strategy of realpolitik in its moves, especially in terms of enlargement, or whether the values detailed above determine which states can become a member. In other words, is NATO a smart alliance that expands when its main adversary, Russia, is weak, or is NATO un-strategic as a whole?

The latter question is very important today as NATO faces Russia in the most serious confrontation since the Cold War. NATO's role is the good cop versus the bad cop played by the Ukraine Contact Group, some 50 states led by the US in close collaboration with the UK in Europe. The Contact Group delivers weapons to Ukraine and NATO intensifies deterrence at the border in Eastern Europe. NATO's recent summit agreed to much more deterrence capability in these members states, but not to any active role as such in weapon supply to Ukraine. Its military role vis-à-vis Ukraine, its partner state, is subdued and steers away from lethal aid. Yet NATO criticises Russia heavily with regard to values – the *ad bellum* rule in the UN Pact (para 2,3 and 2,4) is violated by this war of aggression, a very serious issue; and even more critical is the violation of humanitarian international law (the *in bello* rules of Geneva Conventions) in terms of war crimes of the worst kind.

NATO has been very vocal in accusing and condemning Russia on these themes, but has clearly acted as a defensive alliance with no military role in Ukraine. This would seem to indicate that NATO promotes values as an equally important part of its mandate as military defence. Yet this may not mean that NATO is un-strategic, only that it stays true to its defensive character. For it could have aided Ukraine with both weapons and soldiers had it so wished, in full compliance with international law; the UN Pact's para 51 allows any state that is unlawfully attacked to receive military assistance from other states. It is indeed this paragraph that is the basis for the weaponry aid from the Ukraine Contact Group.

Enlargement of NATO: values a necessary but not sufficient condition
Two theses about the role of principles versus realpolitik come to mind. One, democracies join but there is no strategy from NATO's side. Turkey joined early, in 1952, when it was a promising Muslim democracy, but it has experienced several military coups and was arguably well governed during this time. Yet Turkey's geopolitical position explains why it is a member, at the insistence of the US. Eastern Europe joined once it was democratic; Spain only after Franco's death; and the offers to Ukraine and Georgia were made with no calculations of any Russian reaction – what we can call the 'cheque that bounced' problem. The administration of George W Bush made this offer in 2008, against the warnings of European states. Once Russia reacted militarily in Georgia in August that year, the US retreated hastily, leaving the EU to negotiate something or other in Georgia, as Ron Asmus's excellent account in *A Little War that Shook the World* (2010) brings out. Thus, we see evidence of value-based enlargement efforts here.

Second, one can argue that realpolitik decides. Turkey joined because it was geopolitically important; Eastern Europe when it became possible (Russia was weak); the offers made to Georgia and Ukraine are evidence of strategic naivety, as events bore out. Neither Georgia nor Ukraine was ready for membership when the offer was made.

There is no evidence of a NATO strategy of enlargement, as I found in my book *NATO: the Power of Partnerships*, (with M Petersson, Macmillan, UK, 2011). Yet the lack of a clear policy or strategy on enlargement may also be strategic as it leaves room for ambiguity. NATO has no obligation towards the Ukraine beyond low-level non-lethal aid, but it could choose the same role (and risk) that the Ukraine Contact Group has chosen. Furthermore, NATO's lack of spelt-out strategy leaves room for treating each candidate state differently, depending on the risk situation.

If a Russian reaction is likely, why expand? Yet if one expands and nothing happens, NATO territory is larger, but that may not be advantageous as there is more to defend and more risk of having to defend it.

There is little evidence of this kind of strategic deliberation in NATO circles but, as stated, this ambiguity over NATO's enlargement policy can be strategically wise. Paradoxically, NATO does not seem to have a strategic design for its policy, yet may, for this very reason, enjoy a strategic advantage. To expand to a state that will need article 5 defence from NATO is hardly enhancing NATO security, whereas expanding democracy in states where no such Russian reaction occurs represents a security advantage for NATO.

After 2008, NATO put Georgian and Ukrainian membership on the back burner. This underlines the point that there was a lack of strategy behind the offer to expand. Moreover, the enlargement extended to Eastern Europe in the late 1990s and 2000s was largely risk-free, and the question of strategy did not present itself.

During the 1990-2010 period in Europe, the lack of strategy was perhaps understandable, as interventions into wars were 'optional'. But in the present situation of great power rivalry and state-to-state confrontation, strategy is again a must, as described in *Military Strategy in the 21st Century: the Challenge for NATO* (with Robert Johnson, 2020).

As a point of departure, let's assume that the use of force in Europe is like Simpson's 'fire brigade'. This may be so because few European states have a strategic/military culture with the ability to make decisions that are strategically relevant. Also, post-modern politics and the long, deep peace in the 1990-2010 period in Europe have meant that individual states' security interests have been thought of as a bygone concern, and domestic politics have replaced strategy as liberal democracies are prone to pay attention to public opinion, hence a tendency to risk-aversion in using force. Finally, the present political class has only known peaceful international politics in their own part of the world and is mostly unfamiliar with the use of military force, as Christopher Coker pointed out in his 2013 book *Warrior Geeks*.

Strategic deficit? The Europeans in NATO
Is there a military strategy in Europe? Some 23 authors try to answer this question in *Military Strategy in the 21st Century: the Challenge for NATO*, and

they find that there is little systematic strategic thinking in the political class – with some exceptions, such as France. But they argue that there is a clear need for nuclear strategy and for conventional and hybrid strategy. However, NATO adopted a military strategy in 2018, classified it, but adapted it to state-to-state competition.

The authors agree that there is little serious strategy making in Europe today, despite the surge in threats and risks. Perhaps this is because the long period of deep peace did not demand strategy. Now, however, the need is very obvious indeed. China and Russia stress the importance of military power in foreign and security policy, and terrorism and other non-state violence is rampant in Europe. In addition, there are cyber attacks across a range of targets.

What are the strategic needs for the various types of threat and risk? The war historian Robert Johnson presents a useful matrix of types of use of force: in *competition*, military base structures matter, trade 'wars' take place, cyber attacks, intelligence gathering. This is all familiar in Western states as well as in authoritarian states, and strategic planning certainly goes into it. *Confrontation* is marked by more risk taking, and can take the form of deployments, active measures, hacking, legal pressure, military signalling, false flag operations, threats and signalling. Here, military force matters more than before. If we move to *coercion*, sabotage, psychological warfare, blockade, covert operations, occupation of islands, political interference and manipulation, and so on, become the order of the day. And finally, in *armed conflict*, we see traditional uses of force in war fighting.

The point here is that the use of force is not only confined to clear war fighting modes or to humanitarian and stabilisation operations. On the contrary, there is a spectrum of possible uses of force, some clearly military; others where military force is used along with other tools. All this makes the use of force today more political, in the sense that the use of force must be closely calibrated to political intentions and its use must be flexible, prone to change. If the political goal is to secure the freedom of navigation, an armed escort to a supertanker may accomplish the goal, but should the situation escalate so that the escort is not sufficient, frigates may have to be deployed quickly – and perhaps frigates are able to deter escalation in the first place. If so, they should be deployed early.

Likewise, deterrence in general is back and needs risk willingness but also careful consideration of the danger of escalation. This requires political strategic ability of the first order, combined with a keen understanding of the military tool – and how it achieves goals.

Coercion and deterrence are the two main military strategies. Deterrence is more passive but rests on the political credibility of taking risk. If the adversary does not think that one will fight, one will not be able to deter. Coercion is riskier, being a specific action to put pressure on someone or some state, often in the form of an ultimatum. Coercion often fails when European states are behind it, as Rob de Wijk argues in *The Art of Military Coercion*, simply because the threat is not credible. Milosevic was threatened over Kosovo but did not believe in the threat until it was too late. Peter Viggo Jakobsen, professor at the Royal Danish Defence College and Center for War Studies, has studied the minimum requirements for successful coercion and finds that the massive threat of military attack is the key one, and one that Europe is not wont to make credibly.

In sum, the risk and threat that Europe faces requires a political strategy that is fine-tuned, risk-willing, and versatile, in the sense that situations change quickly. There is little indication that the Europeans are engaged to this end and that they will succeed, with the exception of states such as Britain and France.

Strategic culture: militarily able and risk-willing

Strategic culture is fairly well studied in the literature on defence and security policy, and has been a central variable in the scholarship since Glenn Snyder wrote his study about Soviet strategic culture in 1977. In their 2005 book, *Rethinking the Nature of War*, Isabelle Duyvesteyn and Jan Angstrom called for strategic thinking in Europe, arguing that it has been largely lost after the Cold War, and Sir Hew Strachan entitled his book on strategy *The Direction of War* (2013), in the tradition of Clausewitz, thus underlining that strategy's original purpose is exactly that – guiding the use of force, proving the rationale for using force – or not. Also, he laments the lack of strategic guidance for Europe's use of force.

Risk-taking is logically implicit in strategy because it involves hostile actors, in war, enemies. Strategy is therefore much more difficult than linear thinking and it requires unity of action and the ability to make decisions quickly, depending on the adversary's moves. Importantly, it involves risk to oneself, perhaps to one's life. It follows from this that strategy is a serious business, much more so than normal policy making.

France has perhaps the strongest strategic culture in Europe, followed by Britain. Germany is at the other end of the spectrum, with its clear choice of not wanting to lead militarily. In sum, there are major differences between states that are proud of their military and of its work, and states like Germany, where civilian terms replace military culture as a rule.

But how important is strategic culture for strategy itself? I have suggested that the former is a necessary but not sufficient variable for strategic use of force. By that, I mean that states without a strategic culture will not be engaged in deterrence, coercion, and operations in any risky and leading position. Their public opinion will have a much greater say in the use of force than any strategic elite around the executive. Such public opinion may call for the use of force in a humanitarian crisis – as happened with Germany in Kosovo in 1999 – but public opinion will not direct strategic action. Only states with a strategic culture for the use of force, including the professional military risk inherent in it, are able to take the risk of deterring, coercing, and fighting war on the ground. The risk is not only tactical, but also strategic: the adversary may attack your state; coercion may require brinkmanship, especially if nuclear weapons are involved. The strategic use of military force presumes a strategic culture which includes risk-willingness.

Indicators of strategy

Empirical indicators of a strategic mindset would include European interest in nuclear deterrence now that the Intermediate-Range Nuclear Forces (INF) treaty has been declared null and void. Intermediate-range missiles affect Europe, not the US, yet where is the alarm over this in Europe? The French urge the Germans to take an interest and perhaps promote a common European nuclear deterrent based on French and British missiles – something that is stonewalled in Germany. One does not want to discuss the need for nuclear deterrence, not discuss a European role in acquiring it, and not discuss how Russia can be deterred. It is as if the task of nuclear deterrence is America's, even when we speak about intermediate-range missiles and not strategic ones.

The lack of European interest in Europe's own deterrence is striking, and a clear indicator of a near total lack of strategic sense. Here, the UK and France are the exceptions.

Another indicator of a lack of strategy is the underfunding of defence, even if the 2% of GDP goal is self-imposed. Again, it is the Americans that demand more spending in Europe and Europe that refuses. Germany even broke ranks and proposed 1.5% GDP spending for itself, the richest country in Europe. The many quarrels between the Americans and the Europeans over this issue are another clear indicator of a lack of strategic sense in Europe. Given the US's high spending on defence, how relatively 'cheap' is the 2% to keep the Americans satisfied?

A third indicator is the paradoxical results of opinion polls that ask about article 5 in NATO – whether there is a willingness to defend allies that may be attacked. A Pew Research Center poll found that many more respondents said no to their own country's contributions than said yes to American assistance to themselves and others. They did not feel obliged by article 5, but were certain that the Americans would be. This was clear in the cases of Italy, Greece, Germany and others. This suggests that NATO solidarity is transatlantic only – if it exists at all.

This is also a clear indicator that many Europeans do not take defence very seriously and still think that the US will remain the one taking risks and fighting for them. Britain and France are the exceptions to this general European picture, both being nuclear deterrent states, spending 2.2% of GDP on defence, and leading military operations around the globe. France has also taken a lead in developing strategic thinking in Europe under President Macron.

It is clear that few states in Europe are willing and able with regard to military strategy and strategy in general, and this has grave implications for what NATO, and its 30 members, can accomplish. This has been the case for a long time, but this situation is critical today, with the Ukraine war and the concomitant Russian willingness to risk an invasion of a major state in the middle of Europe. Yet as we have seen in this conflict, it is not NATO that is the primary actor to support Ukraine, it is a coalition of the willing and able, led by the US. NATO has a secondary role.

FIGHTING FOR FREEDOM

Ernest Hemingway, 1959.

FIGHTING AGAINST THE ODDS

Rob Johnson

> The best people possess a feeling for beauty, the courage to take risks, the discipline to tell the truth, [&] the capacity for sacrifice. Ironically, their virtues make them vulnerable; they are often wounded, sometimes destroyed.
>
> ERNEST HEMINGWAY

One of the enduring paradoxes of the human condition is why, when success and survival appear impossible, men and women fight on for a liberty they will not live to see. It was recognised as early as 4BC in Sun Tzu's *The Art of War* and has reappeared throughout history, most recently in the Ukraine conflict. The odds are at their most extreme for irregular fighters and partisans when faced with the overwhelming strength of regular armies, intent on their destruction.

Yet, there are episodes when those who would support the apparently hopeless cause of liberty, outside the zone of conflict, wish to assist these desperate fighters. Sometimes, individuals set off to fight, inspired by a common cause, such as the young men and women from across Europe and America – including Ernest Hemingway – who chose to join the republicans in the Spanish Civil War (1936–39).

Despite the romantics and idealists, the most effective form of external assistance has been the full mobilisation of armed forces that come to fight alongside the partisans. But there have been other, more clandestine methods of support too. Special operational forces, backed by naval interdiction, the transmission of funds, equipment and munitions, have been used to balance the odds in favour of the partisans of liberty.

On 24 February, 2022, more than 200,000 Russian armed forces made an illegal and unprovoked invasion of Ukraine. Attempting to seize the capital, Kyiv, with an audacious air assault, the main body of ground forces were supposed to drive over the Ukrainian forces with speed and superior mass. But the initial assault failed for two reasons. Primarily, it was down to determined and astonishingly courageous Ukrainian resistance. But it was also, in part, due to the provision of Western intelligence on the direction, weight and timing of the Russian attack.

As the Russian offensive stalled, the Kremlin's original planning assumptions had to be revised. They had not expected such stiff resistance. We know this because there was a leak of the intended Russian victory announcement by the media company Ria Novosti, indicating that President Putin expected to have taken Kyiv in just three days. For a few weeks, Putin must have ordered his forces to press on, but the logistical chain, stretched as it was, began to break down. North of Kyiv, a vast column of vehicles and troops became stationary, ripe targets for bold Ukrainian Special Forces, who raided their fixed enemy with drones and Western-manufactured anti-tank weapons. Elsewhere, Ukrainian troops had been dispersed and fought from forested or suburban locations. They remained concealed, struck their adversaries and vanished quickly into the landscape, replicating the 'Motti' tactics used by Finland in the Winter War of 1939 against the Soviets. The Ukrainians' success in destroying columns of Russian armour with the West's anti-tank guided weapon systems soon made 'Javelin' and 'NLAW' familiar terms in the global media.

The Ukrainians also made extensive and adroit use of social media to capture footage of their tactical victories. Soon, video clips of exploding Russian tanks, burned-out armoured personnel carriers, abandoned or blasted trucks, all with that familiar 'Z' motif which the Russians used for identification purposes, became legion. Once again, the Russian reputation for using manipulative disinformation had been anticipated, and, amplified by the platforms of the media, the Kremlin's messaging was overwhelmed by the Ukrainian narrative of heroic self-defence.

Exasperated by the attacks from unseen enemies, and with contempt for the Ukrainian people, Russian troops began to inflict reprisals on civilians. The Russian authorities had spread the lie that Ukrainians were neo-Nazis, infected with unwholesome Western thinking which had, somehow, led them from the 'truth' that they were really Russians. The Kremlin's line was that the invasion was really a 'liberation'. Young Russian men, bewildered by the higher standard of living of those they now occupied, and by the resistance they faced, took to looting and vandalism. Empowered with weapons and the encouragement of their commanders, some tortured, raped, and murdered at will. When the Russians were driven back from settlements north of Kyiv and Kharkiv, evidence emerged of the abuse: random shootings of citizens in the street, a young woman branded on her back with a large 'Z', and individuals deliberately crushed under a tank.

Ukrainians, therefore, concluded that this was an existential war. Inspired by President Zelensky's resolve and willingness to be exposed to danger himself, Ukrainians found various ways to resist. Older women handed packets of sunflower seeds to Russian occupiers, with the assurance that, when they died, sunflowers – the national symbol of Ukraine – would grow where they fell. Householders threw Molotov cocktails from balconies and windows onto Russian armoured vehicles passing through the streets. Teenagers equipped Ukrainian soldiers with drones to provide tactical surveillance on Russian movements. This was a nation-wide resistance movement.

The Western countries had tried to deter Russia from the invasion. They had warned of unprecedented sanctions and made repeated diplomatic warnings. Putin ignored them. He had prepared thoroughly. He felt that, in time, the Europeans' dependence on Russian hydrocarbons would make the West compliant. He was confident in Russian military strength after years of building up his forces, of the prowess of his army following large scale exercises, and, as he liked to remind the West, of Russia's extensive nuclear arsenal. The Kremlin threatened nuclear retaliation if NATO intervened, it ridiculed Western leaders, appealed to the developing world as a champion of decent values against the West's overbearing decadence, and even claimed that NATO had expanded territorially at Russia's expense and so this 'special military operation' was no more than self-defence.

The West chose not to intervene directly. NATO could not invoke Article 5, the activation of collective defence, because no member state had been attacked. The risk of Putin's nuclear escalation had to be considered, too. Instead, the decision was taken to supply Ukraine with armaments, munitions and intelligence. The initial supply was a little haphazard. The UK and the United States were generous in packages of funding, and defensive weapon systems such as anti-tank missiles. In the first four months, the US sent 7,000 Javelin projectiles. Nevertheless, the Ukrainians estimated they were using up to 500 missiles a day. In time, as Russia refused to halt its offensive, the Western contributions grew into large consignments of more offensive munitions: artillery ammunition, howitzers, and, most significantly, HIMARS, the long-range rocket batteries. But European contributions were inconsistent. The German government of Olaf Scholz was anxious about breaking its established position of non-aggression, and tried to send only protective equipment, such as helmets and medical support. Eventually, Germany offered armoured vehicles. By contrast, countries that normally observed a neutral status, such as Sweden and Finland, sent war supplies.

The Kremlin believed that the West was, to quote Sergei Lavrov, the Russian foreign minister, 'engaged in a war with Russia through a proxy and is arming that proxy'. In fact, the West had not yet decided on such a course of 'war with Russia'. Its objective was to compel Russia to leave Ukraine through economic, financial and logistical pressure. 'Arming the proxy' was merely prudent. If Zelensky's administration received no aid, it was likely that Ukraine would be unable to sustain its resistance for more than a few weeks. The cost of the war to the Ukrainian economy was more than $5 billion per month, so financial backing was critical. Ukrainian soldiers had to be fed, supplied, armed and equipped. Every day, the Russians fired long-range missiles into urban centres, hoping to destroy transport nodes, depots and warehouses. Their destruction was also designed to demoralise the Ukrainian people, and thus stir the desire for peace at any price. Civilian apartment blocks, in particular, were targeted, torn open, and pulverised with depressing frequency. But the Ukrainian public picked up the pieces, wept for their losses, and continued to express their defiance of the 'Orcs', as they labelled the Russians, who were trying to take away their land and their liberty.

Those hoping to gain a glimpse of how arming a war of liberty externally would pan out looked to history. The results appear to be mixed. One of the most striking examples of success in the modern era is the American Revolution. For four years, there was limited progress militarily for the Americans, although politically the war for freedom became an established and accepted element for the public. Crucially, when France joined the war, the British were forced to divert sparse manpower and ships to protect both the UK and the lucrative Caribbean. Denuded of forces, the British suffered a humiliating defeat at Yorktown in 1781 and never recovered. The combination of military assistance, training and the presence of a French land and naval force, had undoubtedly turned the tide in America's fortunes.

External assistance did not always succeed, and could even end disastrously. General Charles Gordon had been despatched by the British government to assist the Egyptians in the administration of Sudan in the

1870s, and he was asked to return to evacuate Egyptian personnel in 1884 in the face of a Jihadist revolt. But when he arrived in Khartoum, he could not bring himself to abandon the city's inhabitants. Subsequently, besieged by a vast Jihadist force, he was at first convinced his government would come to the assistance of the people of Sudan. When it became evident the forces of liberation would not arrive in time, he chose not to escape but to fight to the end. A relief column arrived two days too late to change the course of events, and it was clear that Gordon had been killed along with his hungry and beleaguered garrison. The British government was brought down on the issue but Sudan was simply abandoned in an ignominious scuttle. It was only recovered 13 years later. Its second governor was Reginald Wingate, a keen supporter of the Arabs and Sudanese, who did much to rebuild a devastated region.

Wingate's distant cousin was Thomas Edward Lawrence, better known as Lawrence of Arabia, and his fortunes were just as hazardous. Lawrence was despatched willingly to Arabia in 1917 to act as a liaison officer to local leaders, as part of an Allied mission to assist the Bedouin to fight against the Ottoman authorities. Initially, Lawrence guided small bands of mounted Arab irregulars in raids against the Hejaz Railway, while the Royal Navy supplied the Arabs with munitions, rations and aircraft. Other British and French officers conducted training and led their own raids. Light artillery, with gunners from Egypt and North Africa, provided fire support, and, by the end of the campaign, bombers, fighter aircraft and armoured cars accompanied the increasingly regularised Arab armies.

Lawrence felt that British and French military assistance should be considered only as the enablers of a far more extensive campaign to liberate Arabs from Ottoman rule after the war. In this he was largely successful, although there were episodes of unrest in the region when local populations felt the Allies had stayed too long.

Lawrence was also aware of that dilemma of fighting for a liberty one might not live to enjoy. He was troubled by the expectation that others might have to die for the Allied war effort, but also the contradiction they might die for the cause of freedom itself and thus never experience it. In his desert campaign, he wrote that he was reluctant to put at risk his Arab fighters because 'only a man alive could taste liberty'. Yet, in his magisterial study of the war in Arabia in 1917–18, *Seven Pillars of Wisdom*, he encounters dilemmas that complicate such a neat economy of risks.

He was cornered south of Amman with his companions and they resolved they would sell their lives dearly. He witnessed the self-sacrificial charge of the headman of the village of Sheikh Sa'ad who had been incensed by Ottoman atrocities against civilians, and he himself gambled with his life when operations went awry in the Jordan Valley in November 1917. Lawrence's account, like so many memoirs of war, exposes an enduring paradox: why, when success and survival are so unlikely, men and women fight on for a liberty they will not live to 'taste'.

The decision to fight on when destruction is certain was recognised by Sun Tzu in *The Art of War*. He cautioned that one should avoid the complete envelopment of a cornered adversary to prevent his continued resistance 'from a position of despair'. It suggests desperate men, fighting without fear, could inflict disproportionate damage and perhaps even turn the tide of a battle. Those 'with their backs against the wall' have nothing to lose. The desperate nature of their situation produces its own energy and motivation. Some situations, therefore, create the circumstances where there is no choice but to fight to the death, although these tend to be short-lived.

Ukraine has a rich history of resistance. Partisans took on the Red Army in the Russian Civil War, using forests to conceal their communities. As the communists approached over the Steppes in 1920, early warning was given to small, mobile groups of fighters who progressively picked off the Red columns, then disappeared into the dense undergrowth. In the Second World War, Ukraine was overrun for a second time by Nazi occupation, but, once again, there was a strong desire to survive and resist, and some Ukrainians sided with Germany in the vain hope of assistance towards independence.

Polish and Jewish populations faced even greater odds. Here, the very existence of the people was under threat by the Nazi regime. While millions perished in concentration camps and slave labour conditions, some organised a last-ditch resistance from rural areas. In Warsaw, in 1944, the Polish Home Army, expecting imminent liberation by the Soviets, launched their bid for freedom. For weeks, they battled Nazi forces, but Stalin deliberately held back the Soviet forces that could have saved them. He calculated that the Nazis would wipe out the Polish leadership and he would then be able to impose his own occupation without resistance thereafter. More than 200,000 Polish personnel were killed during the failed rising. The Allies were simply too far away to offer any meaningful support, and the small number of Anglo-Polish relief flights that were mounted were even attacked by Soviet aircraft.

Elsewhere, the Allies were able to make a significant effort to support resistance movements in the Second World War, setting a precedent for the decades that followed. Specially trained personnel were first infiltrated by the British by land, sea and air into occupied Europe and Japanese-controlled parts of Asia, through the organisation known as Special Operations Executive (SOE). Established in July 1940, when invasion seemed imminent and there was a requirement for special commando units that could provide the nucleus of a resistance movement should Britain be occupied, the force was later redesigned to project force into Europe. Winston Churchill had demanded an organisation to 'set Europe ablaze'. He believed strongly that, if aided by Britain, Europeans would be willing to form their own resistance organisations. He imagined that, in time, British and American forces would land in Europe and link up with these well-equipped partisans to liberate the continent. A similar campaign would sweep the Japanese out of eastern Asia.

A range of operations were conducted, from small scale sabotage in the Netherlands to the mobilisation of guerrilla armies in Yugoslavia. But it all proved much harder to implement than anyone had anticipated. In France alone, before 1944, some 104 agents were killed in action, caught and executed, or died of their injuries. The numbers lost, across Europe, were proportionately high, but, shrouded in secrecy at the time, the fate of some is still unknown. An estimated total of 13,000 personnel served in SOE, of whom approximately 3,000 were women.

But the result of SOE operations, from Albania to China, was that the Allies enabled the liberation of Europe and Asia and ensured that sovereignty was restored after 1945. Only in the Soviet sphere were national and liberal resistance movements subsequently suppressed. This suggests that democracies are far more likely to aim for genuine liberation through their support of proxies, while authoritarian regimes may use them for the advancement of their own cynical interests, but they are unlikely to be tolerated after they have served their purpose. The history of external support to local forces, both regular and irregular, therefore produces some important considerations.

What are the deductions? The chief requirement for the exogenous supporting power is legitimacy. Offering external support to a polity, a movement, or a resistance organisation that lacks public support or legitimacy is doomed to failure. Even if military successes can be achieved, the lack of political consent will mean there will be no lasting foundations of support. This was the case with the Islamic Republic of Afghanistan between 2002 and 2021. Its repeated failures, endemic corruption, and the evident fact that it only existed because of the backing of the American-led coalition, eroded its legitimacy to the point where few Afghans supported it. Its enemies, the Taliban and other anti-government factions, enjoyed more support because of their discipline, Islamist credentials, and reputation for enforcing security at a local level.

The second insight is that only highly trained personnel, familiar with the terrain, the people, and the skills required for special operations can be deployed with any expectation of success. Each operation has to adhere to a well-crafted plan, accompanied by adroit messaging to the public, since indiscriminate violence, and reprisals, will alienate the people. These trained personnel are also the most appropriate to utilise remotely operated munitions such as mines, electronic warfare, satellite communications, and uncrewed aerial vehicles. Close quarter assassinations are high risk and would be rare, not only to reduce the risk to limited numbers of operatives, but also to protect the people from vindictive occupation forces. Trained personnel will know the importance of changing tactics and targets on a frequent basis to avoid setting patterns. Given the degree of surveillance available to states, the number of attacks in any given period has to be calculated against the increased profile, and therefore risk of detection, they produce. If the area of operations is too limited, it would not take an occupation force long to cordon and comb out a small area.

Hoaxes and deception measures are vital for the survival of operators, and they can elicit a large volume of data on the practices of any occupation force. These patterns can be studied and exploited by partisans with great effect, specifically to avoid detection or to mount attacks. To avoid compromise, the recruitment of local partisans also requires certain skills. Recruits have to be selected, usually by trusted authorities, and tested and inoculated with missions progressively, only proceeding to the most challenging and high-risk tasks once they are proven on those that are easier. Cells of partisans have to be unknown to each other, to avoid hostile intelligence or captured partisans giving away details of other groups under torture. Operators and partisan leaders have to spend as much time on education and planning as they can spare, and far more than on actual missions, probably at a ratio of 3:1. A counter-intelligence team is also crucial, with tests, surveillance and frequent changes of identity, passwords and codes to avoid penetration and betrayal. Specialists are needed for explosives, medical treatment, and communications. All these lessons were learned the hard way, often through bitter experience, by SOE and the Office of Strategic Services, the organisation set up by the Americans.

Historical cases also indicate that external authorities need a clear objective and a strong sense of local needs. At the government level, there has to be international recognition of the resistance. In the Second World War, governments in exile were supported by the United Kingdom in order to maintain their legitimacy. Their VIPs were accorded high levels of security, provided with intelligence, and invited to work as equals in Allied planning. With the Polish government, this worked well, but relations with the French, under Charles de Gaulle, were more fractious because of his insistence on independent decisions. Nevertheless, this joint planning proved vital, from the coordination of refugees and their welfare, to the acquisition of local intelligence and the positioning of Allied resources. The British enabled the governments in exile to maintain communications with their occupied populations through radio broadcasts. The widespread use of the 'V' symbol, in sound and in physical form, acted as an encouragement to those living under the Nazis, and it allowed everyone to participate. Rapping out the 'V' in Morse code, or daubing walls with the letter, let others know the allegiance to resistance. Radio also provided coded messages which could be picked up and used by resistance operators.

The resistance demands for armaments and munitions, and the means of covert transportation, require high levels of organisation and security. Western military and financial support to Ukraine in 2022 was significant. Before the conflict, Ukrainians had received military training teams, financial packages and some military equipment. Between the Russian invasion in February 2022 and August, the United States had sent $8.2bn, over half of which was in the form of military assistance, the rest humanitarian. The UK had committed $1bn of military and civil aid, and the EU six billion euros, mainly as financial assistance.

The sheer volume of munitions required came as a surprise to the Western states, as they had grown used to relatively low expenditures of ammunition against insurgents and a long period of peace. The sudden demands of large-scale industrialised warfare meant a rapid increase in production. The United States nevertheless rose to the occasion as the 'arsenal of democracy'. In the spring of 2022, it had sent 1,400 Stinger anti-aircraft systems, 11,600 anti-tank weapons, 100 Tactical Unmanned Aerial Systems or 'drones', more than 300 grenade launchers, 5,000 rifles, 1,000 pistols, and 600 machine guns with 60 million rounds of small arms ammunition, grenades and mortar rounds. It sent over one million rounds of artillery ammunition. The US also provided five Mi-17 helicopters, three patrol boats, and 70 High Mobility Multipurpose Wheeled Vehicles (HMMWVs, better known as 'Humvees'). To protect Ukrainian personnel, the Americans despatched counter-artillery and counter-unmanned aerial system tracking radars, counter-mortar radar systems, 25,000 sets of body armour and 25,000 helmets. They sent medical equipment to support treatment and combat evacuation, explosive ordnance disposal and demining equipment, and satellite imagery and analysis tools. The private sector joined in too. Elon Musk, the American entrepreneur, established a secure satellite communication system, known as Starlink, for the Ukrainians to use.

As the conflict in Ukraine has continued, there are inevitably consequences for the West. Russia imposed limitations on the supply of oil and gas, before cutting them off entirely. It blockaded Ukrainian ports, denying millions access to grain supplies, until Russia suffered a heavy loss in warships to missile strikes. Some in the West questioned the economic cost of the war, although the majority believed the cause justified the expense.

The case for supporting resistance in another state is ultimately a moral one. There is something deeply inspirational about humans struggling for liberty. The desire to be free of oppression and servitude is strong, even where the sacrifice it requires can be morally troubling. To willingly die in the service of the freedom of others is an ultimate act. It is moving, poignant and final. Yet, paradoxically, it is not quite so final as it seems. A sacrifice, such as the last-ditch defence of Snake Island and Mariupol by Ukrainian soldiers and reservists, gives direction, leadership and a measure to the depth of the cause. Those who cannot 'taste liberty' by their sacrifice have, in fact, laid the path that enables others to do so.

Not all agree. Sir John Keegan criticised the legacy of SOE, arguing that it had spawned modern terrorism. The justification for SOE operations at the time and since, he stated, are exactly those used by terrorist organisations. But this cannot be true. There is a significant moral difference in sustaining resistance against an illegal and immoral invasion or existential attack, such as Russia's or Nazi Germany's, and the ideological wars of choice pursued by terrorists. Most terror organisations do not seek liberation, and care little for public consent, except to serve their claims to legitimacy. Many terror groups will claim to be acting 'on behalf of' the people, or, as in the case of Jihadist groups, in the name of God. Their real objective is usually far more limited.

These claims are in contrast to true moral causes, such as that of Gordon of Khartoum, who was motivated by genuine altruism and expected moral support against slavery and oppression. Those who fight for national survival might equally expect empathy, and see a moral obligation to weaken an oppressive power, where the means exist and where their values are founded on principles of liberty of the people, the characteristics of Lawrence of Arabia and Winston Churchill. In 2022, that was also true of Volodymyr Zelensky.

An examination of the liberation leaders, and the nameless fighters who sacrifice themselves, or those who choose to support the cause of liberty as external agents, gives us a glimpse of the sacrifices that are required for liberty. Those who serve that purpose are, ultimately, 'the best people', just as Hemingway suggested.

The Kherson region liberated after Russian
retreat, 28 November 2022.

BEWARE THE ENEMY AT THE TABLE

Iuliia Osmolovska

The Russian invasion of Ukraine in February 2022 was preceded by an arduous series of negotiations lasting more than five years, in the Normandy and Minsk formats, which sought to end the war in Donbas. In autumn 2021, the Russians seemingly lost their patience and confronted NATO, and the US in particular, with ultimatums on European security, based on Russian terms. The way they presented their demands clearly indicated that they were not interested in negotiations as such but wanted to use them as a pretext for invasion.

Failed negotiations have become a justification for the current war, but it will still be negotiations that finish it. It is, of course, worth considering now when these negotiations should happen, who should be the main players and what might be key issues at the negotiating table. Yet, one important element is obviously missing from this approach. It concerns understanding the approach of the Russians. Before entering negotiations, it is crucial to be able to read the behaviour of the Russian negotiators, to understand their strategy and tricks. Winning on the battlefield will not be enough for Ukraine and the collective West. We should also be equipped to surpass Russia at the negotiation table.

Still, there is a knowledge gap we have to close before negotiations begin. Ukraine's Western partners seem to be not fully aware of the paradigm, methodology and overall mindset which govern the Russians in negotiations. This ignorance leads to a painful misreading and, consequently, misguided strategies in handling the Russians. But there is a particular style and culture with which Russian negotiators operate. All these elements – mindset, culture, style, strategies, and the various tools and tricks – comprise a whole matrix which we have to be able to decipher: the Kremlin Matrix of Negotiations. Let us study closely what that is.

On the fourth day of their invasion of Ukraine, the Russians generously offered to negotiate a peace deal. After almost two years of denying any proper communication with key decision makers, the gesture was met with great enthusiasm from the Ukrainian negotiators, who rushed into talks immediately. Yet, the first round between the two teams ended with some strange side-effects. After a day of talks, three high-ranking members of the Ukrainian delegation experienced symptoms similar to poisoning with an unknown chemical reagent – red eyes, painful blinking, peeling skin on faces and hands. Another member of the Ukrainian delegation was killed in uncertain circumstances a few days later. This is a rather strange way of talking, isn't it? The Russians' message – 'This is what we are going to do with you if you do not accept our terms' – was seemingly aimed at frightening the Ukrainian negotiators and challenging their ability to think rationally and concentrate on the substance of the negotiations. The other explanation was that the Russians were trying to discourage the Ukrainians from participating in negotiations at all. Who would dare to shake Russian hands after this?

One can distinguish two basic strategies in the West's current approach to negotiations with Russia: accommodating Russian demands (the 'peace-making approach' of the French, Germans and Italians), or straightforward rejection with counter-ultimatums (the strategy of the UK and the US). Both have proved ineffective so far, changing neither the behaviour of the Russians, nor establishing an atmosphere of trust conducive to talking about sensitive issues. The Ukrainians have tried to play it differently in the first phases of negotiations, with a strategy that might be termed 'creative improvisation'. Being inexperienced in the handling of professional negotiations, the Ukrainian team simply mirrored Russia's conflicting messages, withdrawing of previous commitments, unclear hierarchy of authority in decision-making, and so forth. Initially, this was effective: the Russians became confused and were unable to predict and offset the Ukrainian tactics. But this may not work in the long-run. The Ukrainians need to create a strategic advantage *a priori,* by knowing and counteracting Russian moves.

In their ability to decode the Russian language of negotiations, Ukrainians are seemingly better placed than their Western partners. Having shared a common Soviet past, Ukrainians are well aware of all the Russian behavioural patterns which might appear in negotiations. Ukrainian knowledge of Russian folklore and culture is another asset, because Russians regularly use folk sayings and proverbs to enrich their statements. For instance, for Ukrainians, it was clear that Putin implied 'silly Europeans' when he supported his argument for high gas prices by saying '*merzni, merzni, volchiy khvost*' ('may the wolf's tail be frozen'). This was a phrase made by a sly fox in a Russian fairy-tale, who got a naïve wolf trapped in a frozen lake. Putin's message was simple: 'I shall fool you, naïve Europeans, and you will get into my gas trap.' It has also been no surprise for Ukrainians to see the flattening of their cities, towns and villages, because they know the old Russian children's game *gorodky* (small towns). In this game, children build small constructions out of special cylinder bricks and then smash them. The winner is the one who destroys the most *gorodky* in one strike. For Russians, destruction equals entertainment, something they learnt in childhood.

One might ask why pay so much attention to studying the Russian cultural component, but it is well known that, in talks, cultural biases have the same impact as a negotiator's individual traits. The latter could contribute about 50% to decision-making and are balanced by upbringing, education and experience. In stressful and highly emotional negotiations, cultural biases tend to prevail over personal characteristics, and a person behaves predominantly by reference to the standards of their culture.

Doubtless, any forthcoming negotiations between Russia and Ukraine over a peace deal are going to be emotional, be they with Western partners or with Ukraine directly. With that in mind, it is crucial to know what elements of Russian culture might surface, and then be prepared to handle them.

Let's consider the main elements of the Kremlin Matrix of Negotiations.

The Western mentality is grounded in a theory of rational choice – promoted by the famous Harvard School of Negotiations – which tends to assume that both sides will consider all the beneficial options and exchange them in interactions with their partners. But one should not expect this from Russians. Their mindset is of irrational behaviour. They tend to ignore seemingly beneficial solutions, which could be measured in direct mathematical calculations. But they are very sensitive to what are called 'intangibles' in negotiations; for example, pride, respect, authority, recognition, inclusion, and so on. These are based mostly on triggers related to the emotional part of our brain. That also means that Russians tend to take decisions after the information has been processed by their emotional brain, without waiting for the rational part (neocortex) to evaluate it. If we take into account that the emotional brain processes the information 20,000 times faster than its rational part, we can

understand that Russians swiftly arrive at decisions which are not properly thought out. This is key to understanding Russians in negotiations.
They would opt for more valuable (for them) intangibles, even if they
incur direct material losses. One should, therefore, expect the Russians to
be rather tolerant towards the direct costs of Western sanctions when they
still achieve some of their valuable intangibles – such as a 'recognition of
authority' and 'respect, based on fear'. Numerous attempts by the West to
communicate with Putin just pour oil on the fire of his ambition and
self-esteem, merely encouraging his sense of greatness. The losses don't
count, they are irrelevant.

Perception of an opponent
As Russians themselves admit, they have a very active 'security mode'
(distrust of their opponent), which induces a desire to fight. This is crucial.
In negotiations, they tend to treat their opponent as a foe, not a partner.
Therefore, the Harvard model of win-win has not taken root in Russian
culture. They immediately switch to an 'offensive defence mode' and
treat negotiations as just another form of fighting. This is also reflected in
their style of approaching the other side, which could be called a 'competitive arrogance'. In their perception, if someone has to win, the other has
to lose (win-lose model). Here, it matters not only how much they win but
also how much their opponent loses. The more an opponent loses, the
greater they feel as it pays well into the intangibles of greatness and success, to which they are extremely sensitive.

Arrogance is subtle and subconscious, but something one can spot in
their manners. It comes from the old imperial thinking of the Great
Russian Empire, which was later replaced by the Soviet Union and the
Russian Federation playing the role of the big brother in a family of 14 sister republics. Independent Russia worked hard to regain this sense of
greatness, and in its modern fight against the entire civilised world, it pre-
tends it has done so. Therefore, in negotiations, the Russians also tend to
treat opponents mostly as minors or subordinates.

These embedded features of the Russian character are reflected in
their choice of strategies in negotiations. There are seven of these, which
scholars have identified based on the Thomas-Kilmann categorisation of
typical behaviour in a conflict: competition (win-lose), cooperation (win-
win), compromise (settlement on fair objective criteria), avoidance

(skipping from negotiations to block them), accommodation (giving up their interests), revenge, and revenge with self-damage. The most popular strategies for Russians are: competition (the one applied currently in talks with the West), avoidance (the one used by Russians in the Normandy format, where they simply abstained from meetings, thus blocking the whole process), self-destructive revenge (the one currently applied in relations with Ukraine in its most extreme form of a war).

A core element of the Kremlin Matrix is the so-called Kremlin School of Harsh Negotiations, a combination of old-Soviet diplomacy tools and KGB emotional pendulum methods, which make an opponent swing between extremes of positive and negative emotions. By applying this, Russians try to switch off an opponent's rational brain and put them in an unbalanced emotional mode, full of insecurity and self-doubt. They also aim to create in an opponent a sense of fear that they will not receive what they so desperately want (Russians also invest a great deal in creating in an opponent an urgent need for something). This emotional instability provides Russian negotiators with an advantage, allowing them to control and lead negotiations in the way they want.

The Kremlin School (basically, KGB methods) suggests five simple steps to swing the emotional pendulum in an opponent:

Step 1: Silence and concentrated listening, and staring at an opponent to make them uneasy. By doing this, the Russians count on common human psychology: if one person is silent during conversation, the other tends to fill in the gaps, saying more than intended. By being deliberately silent, the Russians focus on the opponent and try to find flaws in his logic, as well as conflicting messages.

Step 2: Active questioning. By taking advantage of the information they have collected in the first phase, the Russians begin to fire questions fast, similar to an interrogation. Questions usually point to contradictory statements an opponent made earlier. The purpose of this tactic is to embarrass their opponent and induce self-doubt. This is also one of the means adopted in cross-examinations by lawyers in adversarial situations.

Step 3: Setting a scale of values and depreciating an opponent. The trick here is to play with basic human emotional triggers (appreciation, affiliation, autonomy, status, role) from positive to negative extremes, thus creating in an opponent an identity crisis ('I thought I was a reliable/

responsible/respectable, trustworthy person. But it looks like I am not').

Step 4: Magnanimous gestures. To create a brief sense of relief in an opponent who is already in a fragile psychological condition, Russians might step back by saying that, against all the evidence, (unreliability/irresponsibility/disrespect/mistrust), they believe that an opponent is still reliable/responsible/respectable, trustworthy, and they can prove so by further cooperating with them. The goal here is to make the opponent keen to prove that they are indeed in possession of those qualities.

Step 5: Constructive-destructive ambiguity. In other words, leave the door open and apply the 'wait and see' approach – 'we shall judge you by your actions, you have to prove how good you are'. The Russians create in their opponent a desire to earn their high esteem which renders them more ready to compromise.

Tools and instruments

While assessing their negotiating power, Russians carefully consider three basic elements: positioning power, time pressure (time limit) and urgency (which side is more interested in an outcome). They try to enter negotiations when their positioning power is strong, they are not pressed for time and the other side is more in need of a settlement. If this is the case, they have a dominant position in negotiations, which enables them to apply a power-based model and to play a harsh power game. This is something they are performing now in negotiations with Ukraine. If they have relative positioning power, are pressed for time themselves, or have a higher need for settlement, they tend to apply a manoeuvring defence. The latter is the case in their on/off negotiations with the West.

The most popular tricks from the Russian tactics toolbox are:

1). *Time and energy exhaustion.* The goal is to leave opponents so exhausted, disoriented from tiredness, and unable to concentrate that they are ready to give up and agree to an imperfect decision. Lengthy negotiations (of more than eight hours) in the Normandy format with heads of state/government led to the infamous Minsk-II

Protocol in February 2015. Russians proudly claimed this as their victory and a political defeat for Ukraine, because its provisions (provided they were implemented) effectively destroyed the integrity of the state of Ukraine. In similar cases, Russians are well prepared for such marathon negotiations by fielding two teams; a fresh team replaces the tired one in the middle of talks. They count on the fact that the other side does not have this kind of substitution and has to continue with already exhausted negotiators.

2). *Urgent need or over-motivation.* Russians are infamous for being very instrumental when it comes to creating the other side's urgent need for a negotiated settlement. To create that effect, Russians heat up negative alternatives to show what will happen if their proposals at the negotiation table are not accepted. In such a way, they created the Ilovaisk cauldron (the tragic encirclement and respective shooting of Ukrainian armed forces near Ilovaisk in August 2014) on the eve of negotiating the Minsk-I Protocol in September 2014. Equally, they pressed the Ukrainian side with the Debaltseve cauldron (the most intense fighting of which ran parallel to negotiations in the Normandy format in February 2015). Likewise, each successive round of negotiations after the full-scale Russian invasion in Ukraine in February 2022 has been supported by the heaviest shelling and strikes on Ukrainian cities and civilians.

3). *Bluff.* The trick about power in negotiation is that it is about perception of power, rather than its objective measurement. Therefore, the ability to create an impression of power is very important, and Russians are very good at it. Just recall the recent overwhelming belief that Russian armed forces were among the best trained and equipped in the world, and compare it with their actual humiliation by the Ukrainian Army on the battlefield. There is a very popular Russian folk saying, reflecting this approach: '*glavnoe – ne byt, glavnoe – kazat'sya*'. It means 'it is not important who you are; rather how you are seen to be'. Stemming from this, the element of bluff in the Russian toolbox is another popular instrument. They tend to use it extensively and assume opponents will fall for it and retreat.

4). *Brinkmanship (high risk tolerance).* A historically cultivated sense of supremacy over an opponent is also responsible for an incorrect assessment of Russian appetite for risk, as higher adrenalin and cortisol tend to induce over-confidence and misjudgement of situations.

It is aggravated by a strong cultural bias in favour of relying on luck or good fortune, similar to those the Russians had with their sowing campaigns in the past, when bad and unpredictable weather conditions could ruin all efforts to secure sufficient harvests. Then they learnt that it was not preparedness, but luck and fortune, which governed the result. Hence their over-reliance on something metaphysical, rather than on proper preparation. These superstitions and lack of rational strategies find their reflections also in numerous Russian proverbs and folk-sayings related to destiny. While describing their approach to negotiations, Russians would often say: 'The main thing is to throw ourselves into the fight, and see what happens.'

5). *Personal offence and deliberate depreciation of opponent.* Being explicitly rude in negotiations is common in the Russian negotiating style. The aim is to embarrass an opponent and to distract them emotionally from the substance of talks. Among notorious cases of such behaviour is one exchange between the Russian and Ukrainian delegations during the MH-17 case hearings at the High Court in the Hague. When a senior female member of the Ukrainian delegation raised a question that Ukraine had 'concerns' about Russia, the Russian head of delegation immediately replied, 'Oh, we see that you definitely have some clear concerns' (using a Russian word with dual meaning, hinting that the woman had some sort of sexual obsession), while other members of the Russian delegation began to laugh. The ploy worked and the diplomat was distracted.

6). *Principal-agent duo.* This method is known in the Russian negotiation arsenal as the 'principal-agent trap' when an agent (the delegation) has no authority to decide over any issue without the consent from their principal (in this case, the president of Russia). Russian negotiators in most cases act as simple transmitters of information back and forth, and claim they need some extra time to get consent from their principals. By doing this, the Russian delegation gains more time to work on so-called negative alternatives to pressure opponents into a more agreeable mode. This tactic can link with trick number one, above; they count on the psychological phenomenon of 'energy investment' – when an opponent gets tired from non-productive talks, he eventually agrees to a less beneficial deal.

The assumption of this 'principal-agent game' has been proved on a number of occasions in the current negotiations between the

Russians and the Ukrainians over the Russian invasion of Ukraine. The Russians put forward a delegation composed of an unknown head, Mr V Medinsky (a non-visible advisor to Putin, and ex-minister of culture with zero experience in diplomatic negotiations); a toxic Russian politician renowned for his extreme views on Ukraine Mr L Slutsky (who was put into the delegation as an irritating element to trigger Ukrainian negotiators); and the non-influential Mr B Gryzlov (former head of the Russian delegation in the Minsk Trilateral Contact Group with zero authority even then). When the Ukrainian delegation presented the Russians with draft proposals for a future framework peace agreement at the last supposedly meaningful round of talks on 29 February this year, the Russian delegation pledged to respond officially after consultations in Moscow and stayed silent for months.

7). *Deep anchoring.* Russians are renowned for their habit of speaking the language of ultimatums. They deliberately put forward almost unachievable proposals at the start and press the other party to respond. While reflecting on the Russian wish list, their opponents are forced to become anchored around Russian views, thus moving the zone of possible agreement closer to Russian positions. This is exactly what we observe with respect to the Russian claims to NATO and the US on a new security order in Europe in December 2021. The Western partners, instead of immediately counter-anchoring with alternative proposals, had to reflect and comment solely on the Russian draft. The Russians were not interested in meaningful talks at that point; they wanted simply to use the move to present it as a last gesture of goodwill, which was not met by the West, thus enabling the Russians to resort to unilateral military actions and the invasion of Ukraine. Had these been meaningful talks, the West would have been caught by this trap and would have found themselves revising the Russian draft with respective framing reflecting Russian interests.

8). *Changing commitments.* Russians call this trick 'a low blow'. This implies a sudden change of terms in the middle of a deal, when the other party has already got positive expectations of a beneficial solution. Here, Russians count on the 'positive inertia' of an opponent, which could cause them to pay less attention to the details of a deal. This trick was played by the Russians in negotiations over the prolongation of the stationing of the Russian Black Sea Fleet in Sevastopol (Ukraine) in the 1990s. After initialling the agreed text of the agreement, the Russians swapped one page of the original document with another, which altered the terms in their favour. The spoofing was incidentally noticed by one member of the Ukrainian delegation and the trick failed. Occasionally, Russians might opt for this 'low blow' trick in combination with 'principal-agent duo'. They would justify the sudden withdrawal of previous commitments by appealing to the unquestionable authority of a mysterious 'third party', who has the final word in authorising an agreement.

All the above might leave the reader in a somewhat gloomy mood and with the inevitable question of whether it is worthwhile negotiating with the Russians at all. Would it not be a waste of time to talk to them, if they resort to these kinds of deceitful traps, tactics and unethical moves at the negotiation table? Well, it would be naïve to believe that we can skip this kind of interaction with Russians. Sometimes, negotiations are inevitable, even with an opponent lacking any form of good faith. We cannot avoid negotiating with the Russians over a peace settlement for Ukraine, be it direct negotiations between Ukrainian and Russian teams, or in a wider format. We have to accept that sooner or later it will happen. But we need to be equipped for these kind of talks, with a deceitful opponent. The West needs to learn how to counter Russian tactics and overcome them. It is feasible. There are a whole set of effective measures, which the Ukrainians know. Just ask their professionals in negotiations and you will be well armed.

Reality check. What next for Ukraine?

Moving from a rather academic outlook back to the grave reality of today, we still face a brutal unprovoked war, which Russia waged in Ukraine, and aspire to constructive negotiations to end it. The key question is, when should these negotiations happen? The answer is not now. Here's why.

Negotiation scholars have in their arsenal a concept known as the 'momentum of ripeness', which was originally developed by William Zartman. This approach considers what makes conflicts ripe for resolution. Momentum is generated when both sides are unhappy with the existing status quo and understand that it cannot be improved for them through unilateral actions. They admit then that mutual problem solving is needed, and both become ready to talk substantively, and jointly seek solutions.

At this point, Russia is not ready. It is not yet 'ripened' for meaningful negotiations as it still counts on Ukraine's defeat on the battlefield and shows no signs of stopping its military aggression. For one thing, no single round of negotiations has come with even an interim ceasefire. We should not delude ourselves; Russians are quite stubborn and will continue to pursue their goal of defeating Ukraine. At the very least, they require revenge for their humiliation in the first phase of the war. Even if they do not succeed with their comprehensive plan, they still hope to take some more parts of Ukrainian land in the south and to use it as leverage in negotiations. They are still gambling on that, against all odds. For the sixth consecutive month of war and despite their very limited success (by mid-July 2022 they had not managed to capture one single region in Ukraine within its administrative borders), Russians still claim that a peace deal is possible only on Kremlin terms.

On the Ukrainian side, there is also a firm belief that they should continue fighting. Public opinion polls held in mid-June show strong public confidence (93%) that Ukraine can repel Russia. This belief is grounded on: (1) the amazing military skills of the Ukrainian armed forces; (2) relentless political and diplomatic support for Ukraine from the West, with ever more military equipment coming from them; (3) the effect of sanctions and the international isolation of Russia in weakening the Russian economy; (4) the lost offensive military potential of Russia on the battlefields; (5) the partial retreat of Russian troops from northern areas (Kyiv, Sumy and Chernigiv regions); (6) deteriorating military stocks and morale in the Russian armed forces; and (7) increasing contradictions within the inner circle of Kremlin decision makers about how the military campaign should be further pursued.

These public sentiments are a real advantage for the Ukrainian political leadership, as they do not create moral pressure on President Zelensky to reach a peace settlement at any cost. There is therefore a firm position for the Ukrainian negotiators that, with the accumulation of all the above factors, they are bound to upgrade their negotiating power, and only then should they enter into meaningful negotiations with Russia. Here, the Ukrainians also rely on their unilateral actions, which could create a strong negative alternative for Russia, forcing her to compromise on an initial deep-anchored position.

The momentum for such negotiations is not yet present, for sure. There is no use in numerous calls from some of Ukraine's Western partners to sit down now and talk with the Russians. Neither side is ready for a joint exercise in problem solving; at least, for the immediately foreseeable future. At least until they have both first exhausted their unilateral options.

To ice the cake of complexity, there is another cornerstone point about potential negotiations over a peace settlement between Russia and Ukraine. In the current war, the Ukrainians are not fighting just for their land. They are fighting for the very right to choose their own future, geopolitical friends, partners and alliances. For their freedom to elect the leaders (not necessarily always the perfect ones) they want. This is why the whole nation was infuriated by the claims of the Russian president days before the invasion that he was going to teach Ukrainians how to govern their country and to set up more appropriate 'country managers' than the Ukrainians had. The whole nation has stood up against this. So, it is not just about the land. It is for liberty and freedom that Ukrainians are fighting. Liberty and freedom, which are in the core of the nation's DNA. Liberty and freedom, the most cherished Ukrainian values. Russian demands concerning Ukraine's geopolitical orientation will therefore not be met. And negotiation scholars are very well aware that negotiations over values are particularly challenging to resolve.

Russian destruction of the town of Izium in
Kharkiv region, Ukraine, September 2022.

RISKS OF RUSHING TO RUSSIAN
PEACE DEAL

Alina Polyakova

As many in the West hasten for a quick peace deal between Russia and Ukraine, the search for historical examples that could act as a peace-deal guidebook has become more common. Two specific examples – the 1945 division of Germany and the 1953 Korean armistice – have been portrayed as credible reference models. Yet, a deeper look at both shows that Ukraine's case is very different and any quick settlement with Russia, where it is given permission to occupy parts of Ukraine, will ultimately lead to a much less secure Europe.

A settlement in which Ukraine is pressured to give up large portions of its territory to Russian occupation will not result in a so-called 'frozen conflict', but rather a zone of instability from which Russia will launch future offensives. As such, it will profoundly impact European peace, security, and deterrence as it would create permanent wastelands that ultimately serve the Kremlin's purpose of destabilising Ukraine and Europe from within. This will result in more, not less, regional insecurity. Such a scenario finds little historical reference in the case of a divided Germany or Korea in the wake of the Second World War.

Both historical cases are inapplicable to today's Ukraine as Russia is not only interested in taking over Ukrainian territory, but in destroying the idea of an independent Ukraine altogether. Russia will, therefore, not invest in rebuilding the areas it occupies. Rather, it will turn these territories into zones of criminality and human rights abuses, and use them for staging military activities to undermine Ukraine militarily, economically and politically.

In contrast, the Soviet Union accepted a West Germany that was a sovereign country throughout the Cold War. Russian-occupied territories of Ukraine would also not reflect an East Germany-like model. If the two scenarios were similar, the Soviet Union would have levelled to the ground cities like Dresden and forced German children to study Russian, while sending Germans in East Germany through filtration camps.

Those hoping for a Korean armistice-like deal with Russia will be disappointed as well. A non-occupied democratic Ukraine resembling a South Korea, with a market-based economy that is free to make its own choices about its future, will not satisfy Moscow's imperial ambitions. In Moscow's view, a democratic and economically prosperous Ukraine cannot be allowed to exist and would be seen as a strategic failure.

Moreover, in both Germany and Korea, relative stability was achieved when the US committed to stationing thousands of troops on the border lines. In the case of Germany, West Germany was integrated into NATO in 1955 as 400,000 Western military personnel remained stationed there. In South Korea, the US stationed nuclear weapons beginning in 1958, which served as an effective deterrent. In Ukraine's case, such security guarantees from the US or Europe remain unlikely. To make such analogies, it is worthwhile considering what a future Ukraine would look like if it were to follow the example of East-West Germany or North-South Korea.

A Ukraine similar to East-West Germany
Let's imagine the hypothetical scenario of today's Ukraine as if it were similar to Germany post-WWII.

Certainly, at first glance, there are some similarities. Just as with the German Democratic Republic (GDR), the Russian occupied parts of Ukraine's east are going to be left destroyed by the war. And much of western or non-occupied Ukraine's future depends on decision-making by the West. Lastly, as was the case with East Germany, Ukraine is a priority for the Kremlin's international ambitions. But the similarities stop there.

Most importantly, the Soviet Union had a fundamentally different approach to East Germany than Russia has to occupied Ukraine today. Though the GDR still had to pay substantive reparations to the Soviet Union, East Germany was viewed as a separate satellite communist entity and, therefore, enjoyed a certain amount of autonomy from Moscow. In contrast, whoever was established as leader in occupied Ukraine would be a puppet of the Kremlin. The Soviet Union did not have a goal to fully eliminate the German identity and then fully integrate East Germany as part of the Soviet Union. In contrast, Putin does want to destroy the Ukrainian identity and seeks to absorb Ukrainian land as part of Russia.

Today's Russia also doesn't hold a candle to the economic and military might of the United States, and certainly it is far weaker than the Soviet Union which, despite its eventual failure as an economic power, did effectively compete with the US politically, militarily, and economically for decades. Ideologically, the USSR presented an alternative to the western liberal economic model, embraced by many countries and forced upon many others. With its invasion of Ukraine, Russia has become deeply isolated as a result of global disdain for its actions, as well as significant Western economic sanctions.

In contrast to how post-WWII Germany was viewed by most in the transatlantic community, Ukraine is not despised but rather venerated across the globe for the heroism of its soldiers and civil society. Ukraine is also a vibrant democracy that was brutally attacked by an authoritarian state with fascist tendencies. And though Ukraine is emotionally exhausted, by no means is it demoralised. Indeed, it is more unified and patriotic than ever before since its independence.

Economically, the GDR had a strong export economy, while occupied Ukraine would very likely face the same Western sanctions as Russia. Rather than investing in occupied Ukraine's ability to develop economically (as the USSR did with East Germany), Russia will continue to extract resources without any long-term intention to invest in a sustainable economic model. Whereas the GDR was supposed to be the crowning achievement of state socialism for the Soviet leadership, Russian-occupied Ukraine will be a wasteland.

Those advocating for a hurried Ukraine-Russia settlement must, therefore, clearly acknowledge not just the security implications of such a deal, but the ethical and moral consequences as well. Russian-occupied Ukraine would be a no-man's land of 'filtration' camps, and drug and weapons trafficking. This fate would be imposed on millions of Ukrainians, who would be forced to become Russian nationals.

In terms of non-occupied Ukraine, a negotiated settlement would have to commit to significant Western resources to rebuild and invest in a Ukraine that would quickly integrate into the EU and NATO. As was the case in post-war Germany, where the Soviet Union was trying to win a neutral status for all of Germany, Russia would try to insist on a similar status for Ukraine. But as some historians have argued, the proposition of a neutrality status for Russia is a crafty disguise to further its influence.

For example, in March 1952, Joseph Stalin sent a diplomatic note (now known as the Stalin Note) to the US, Britain and France suggesting a peace treaty with a neutral Germany. As Peter Ruggenthaler, deputy director of the Boltzmann Institute for the Study of War's Consequences, argued in his paper 'The 1952 Stalin Note on German Unification', the Stalin Note was merely a ploy to incorporate the German Democratic Republic into the Eastern Bloc by blaming the Western occupying powers for the division of Germany.

Stalin was not trusted after he decided not to follow through the Yalta Conference agreements and went ahead with establishing communist rule in Poland. And, today, trust towards Vladimir Putin is at a historic low, following the invasion of Crimea and eastern Ukraine, which violated the 1994 Budapest Memorandum in which Russia agreed to guarantee Ukraine's territorial integrity. Furthermore, the Soviet Union was provided with a guaranteed position as a permanent member of the UN Security Council, which provided it with much negotiations leverage in years to come. Russia, too, is using its Security Council membership to slow the West's support for Ukraine.

Nikita Khrushchev followed his predecessor's steps in his first meeting with John F Kennedy in 1961, where the Soviet leader gave an ultimatum – either there be a permanent peace treaty that recognised the sovereignty of both East and West Germany, or the Soviet Union will defend GDR's borders. What followed was more division, human suffering and a less secure Europe as the Soviet Union built the Berlin Wall.

The main lesson to be learned from the post-WWII division of Germany for Ukraine today is that the West will have to do much more than advocate for a so-called peace deal at any cost. Rather, if long-term European security is to be achieved, non-occupied Ukraine should be secured by Western forces, invested in at a significant level, and rapidly integrated into Euro-Atlantic institutions.

A Ukraine similar to 1953 Korea?
A few experts have also evoked the Korean armistice as a potential model for a negotiated settlement in Ukraine.

In 1948, the Korean peninsula was divided between a Soviet-backed government in the north and an American-backed government in the south. War broke out along the 38th parallel in June 1950 as the Soviet-backed side decided to attack as it amassed 200,000 troops. The

UN Security Council responded by adopting a resolution that condemned the invasion. The three-year war claimed the lives of millions of soldiers and civilians.

The US and other United Nations members were willing to position many soldiers in Korea; more than 36,000 US soldiers alone died in the war. President Harry Truman responded to the North Korean threat with what was called a 'police action', where he assembled a group of 22 nations that fought for South Korea via the United Nations Command. Altogether, almost two million US soldiers served on Korean soil back then. Today, neither the US nor any other Western country is willing to station boots on the ground in Ukraine.

The Korean armistice was signed in July 1953 to formally end the war in Korea. South Korea was not a signee; instead, it was signed by US Army Lieutenant General William Harrison Junior, General Mark Clark of the UN Command, North Korean leader Kim Il-sung and General Nam II of the Korean People's Army, and Peng Dehuai of the Chinese People's Volunteer Army. Furthermore, the Korean armistice was not a permanent peace treaty between nations but rather a military document. It was also not a quick negotiation process – more than 158 meetings took place over two years before a final settlement was reached. Lastly, Truman's successor, President Dwight Eisenhower, took on a leading role in achieving the ceasefire, while North Korea had the support of both the Soviets and the Chinese.

But perhaps most important were the security guarantees that the US committed to South Korea via the Mutual Defence Treaty, signed in October 1953. This treaty meant that both nations would provide mutual aid if either faced external armed attack, and it also allowed the US to station military forces on South Korean soil. In order for there to be a similar agreement in today's Ukraine, the US would also have to commit to security guarantees, and Ukraine would have to allow them to station troops there.

As we see in both cases, either a divided Germany or a Korean armistice are both unattainable models for Ukraine without proper commitments in the form of guarantees from Western powers, namely the United States, Germany, Great Britain and France. Furthermore, there are distinct historic differences, both within the developments that led to the conflicts, as well as within the conflicts themselves. For example, GDR had a leader who was independent enough from the Soviet Union and who had enough power to control some of the Soviet leadership's decisions. The Soviets were also interested in extending a communist ideology that would take root in Europe, whereas Russia is interested in fully destroying Ukraine as a nation. The Korean peninsula also had very distinct power dynamics: Stalin was not as interested in Korea as he was in Germany; the Soviet Union received military help from China; and the US was willing to send soldiers to fight for South Korea.

Without specific guarantees, these models have little use. Russia will continue its atrocious quest of destroying Ukraine. This will transform enormous amounts of Ukrainian territory into wastelands under Russian control, and also lead to a less secure Europe.

As an alternative, the ultimate goal of Western policy should be to have a united, prosperous, democratic Ukraine. This entails being committed to rebuilding Ukraine and not allowing Russia to permanently take over Ukraine's territory. In practical terms, this means that the West should not agree to Russia's ceasefire terms that demand Ukraine give up territory. This also means that the West must actively seek for policies and agreements that are aimed at weakening Russia's military and economy while swiftly strengthening Ukraine's.

As the West continues to consume false narratives of a peace deal between Ukraine and Russia, Putin is buying time as he still believes it is on his side: he continues to heavily invest in mobilising more troops, is willing to add pressure on civil society, and is betting on a war of attrition. What's more, we see few signs of oligarchs protesting against Putin's regime, or the rise of anti-war rallies among Russians.

In the end, Putin's strategy might prevail if the West continues to be indecisive in its harshness against the Kremlin – slow weapons deliveries, alarmism over Russia's nuclear threats – and as the window of opportunity to change the trajectory of the war might soon close. Putin has proven to be successful at manipulating the weaknesses of democracies to his advantage: he is betting on the fragility of European unity in light of rising energy and food prices, and upcoming elections where more Kremlin-friendly parties might come to power.

As long as Russia is able to buy time, gain revenue from energy exports and trade with other major economies, such as India and China, Putin will feel comfortable launching missiles into residential districts to terrorise Ukrainians, and threatening to starve millions across the globe by blocking Black Sea freight routes. All of this gives the Kremlin time to plant the seeds of confusion, fear and disunity across the transatlantic community, giving Russia victory at the expense of European security and global stability.

US president Joe Biden ahead of the G20
leaders' summit, in Bali, Indonesia, 2022.

FIGHTING THE GOOD FIGHT

Kori Schake

The international order that the US and its allies constructed from the ashes of the Second World War is under strain. The two main challenges to the order are America's continued ability to uphold it and China's rise. However, the order is much more durable than the frenzy of concern suggests.

Extrapolating from 40 years of Chinese economic dynamism, Western policies are gearing up for the problems of a rising China. Relying on the metrics of gross domestic product, military expenditure, trade volumes, research and development spending, and manufacturing output, China is indeed formidable. But those are all metrics that exaggerate the effect of large populations, and are poor indicators of national power. China has a per capita GDP of $16,842, which is roughly equivalent to the per capita GDP of Iraq, Botswana, or the Dominican Republic. Tracking, instead, geography (number of dissatisfied neighbours), demography (teetering on a cliff due to the catastrophe of its one-child policy and negligible immigration), political institutions (brittle and its bargain of prosperity for autocracy faltering as prosperity stalls), and soft power (caught stealing, committing genocide, revealing its aggressive ambitions), China is precarious. We may be facing the problems of a stalling China rather than a successful China.

China may prove no less disruptive and dangerous stranded in the middle-income trap than it would have been stampeding towards dominance. The Chinese Communist Party (CCP) may perceive a closing window of opportunity to wrest the international order out of Western hands before we realise our relative strength, or are prepared to defend the order we created. Hegemons are often not the wealthiest or even strongest powers in the international order – they are the states willing to set and enforce rules. But we in the West shouldn't doubt that we have the ability to preserve the order. We often lose faith that the truths we hold to be self-evident are universal, but Xi Jinping clearly believes they are, because otherwise he wouldn't need the architecture of repression. And, fortunately, the CCP appears to have given us the time to prepare, having activated the antibodies against its continued rise.

There is concern over whether the United States still believes the international order we have captained since 1945 is in our interests and worth sustaining. American politics are vituperatively partisan, with loud voices – including that of the former president – openly advocating political violence to prevent the democratic transition of power. Both Republicans and Democrats seem convinced that trade has detracted from American prosperity, Wall Street and Silicon Valley acknowledge no difference between the governments of China and the US, and isolationists range on both the right and left.

And yet, American politics, even in the post-war period, have always been solipsistic and often fraught, because of who we are as a political culture. The best description of Americans was provided by historian Bertha Ann Reuter in 1923: 'Americans are a people so extreme in politics or religion or both that they could not live in peace anywhere else.' The characteristic that most makes America diverse from other prosperous and free countries is risk tolerance: we are a country inventive enough to develop Covid-19 vaccines, industrious enough to rush them into mass production, wealthy enough to make them freely available, and also a country in which a third of our population refuses to take them, a country that has suffered a million dead from the pandemic.

Nor are we newly a country full of crazy people run by reckless politicians; that is what we have always been. We have a tendency to mythologise the past into a time when American politicians were statesmen, unhindered by the grubbiness of domestic politics. When they stood like Colossus astride a virtuous country and looked outward to selflessly shape the international order. As a historian, I keep looking for that time and I can't find it.

Take, for example, the year 1954, possibly the zenith of American hegemonic power. Our economy comprised more than a third of global product, amassed preponderant military power that we used sparingly, constructed alliances across the globe to protect allies still recovering from wartime devastation, elected as president a war hero and committed internationalist, and fostered a culture of almost wilful innocence as we recoiled from the experience of the world at war. At the same time, the American military was forcibly integrating schools in the south, President

Eisenhower had sought Senator McCarthy's support during his campaign, and congressional hearings continued to search for communist sympathisers. Furthermore, support for decolonisation didn't extend as far as supporting emergent governments that might choose alignment with the Soviet Union, and that same president would, two years later, side against America's NATO allies during the Suez crisis, threatening to collapse their economies.

It hasn't just become hard to navigate with Americans at the helm, it's always been hard. But that shouldn't cause us to lose sight of the many things the United States has got right: broad and deep capital markets; the rule of law; the revolutionary technological creativity of Silicon Valley; film and music industries that set global style; magnetism drawing hard-working immigrants across the labour market spectrum; the capacity to govern over an ever more inclusive diversity; and a cultural love of failures conjuring up successful second acts. Add to this the truths that we hold to be self-evident: that all people are created equal, that they are endowed by their creator with certain unalienable rights, and that among these are life, liberty, and the pursuit of happiness. The US fails often, but it's legitimately hard for other societies to get right what we have got right.

Possibly the best article written about America and the world was by James Fallows in 2009, titled something boring like 'How Can America Rise Again?'. He wrote about all those enduring strengths listed above, but also about the role of the Jeremiad in American foreign policy. Jeremiah, you'll remember from the Torah, always feared failing God, and that's why he was beloved of God. Fallows's simile is that the US gets motivated for international activism only when it believes it's losing its prominence – so, responding to Germany's *Wirtschaftswunder* in the 1950s, countering Japan Inc in the 1970s, and understanding now that China has rejected the 'responsible stakeholder' vision of mutually beneficial prosperity and power the US offered.

You can almost feel the gears meshing as the American government begins to acknowledge the nature of the challenge: national security and defence strategies identifying China as the main threat; Congress increasing defence spending far beyond what the administration requests; the FBI opening a new counter-espionage case against China every 10 hours; duelling op-ed pieces in business newspapers by Ray Dalio (pro-China) and George Soros (anti-China); Treasury and Commerce departments cooperating on Chinese investment restrictions. This is what the US government slowly getting serious looks like.

Nor is the US just focused on the China challenge. It's broadly understood now – and not just in Washington – that the international order requires defending. Americans are more worried about domestic than international challenges, but they're still worried about, and committed to, an international order. President Biden was elected on returning to traditional post-war American foreign policies; there was almost no opposition to a $40 billion assistance package for Ukraine, and his administration has got its highest marks for orchestrating the allied response to Russia's invasion.

It's fashionable to decry Frank Fukuyama's *The End of History and the Last Man* as claiming history has ended, but that's an unserious response to a serious work of philosophy. Fukuyama advances two important arguments in the book: first, that liberal democracy is the political system that best encourages human flourishing – safety, prosperity, and fulfilment; and, second, that the most serious threat to it is the complacency of people long living under that political system. That's the last man part, and it seems to me devastatingly prescient about the political upheavals we're experiencing in the domestic politics of free societies right now.

What I worry most about is those of us living in free societies conscioning facile, exculpatory nonsense, the most egregious example of which is the gravely intoned 'military force can't solve this problem'. It gets paraded whenever leaders don't want to resort to force, or when commentators object to force superseding other policy tools. But as Russia's brutality in Ukraine is demonstrating, force can and does resolve issues. The sovereignty of Ukraine will be determined by force of arms, and whatever is not achieved by military force will not be accomplished by negotiation, economics, or any other means. Force is historically how questions of power and order are determined; it is only in free countries, living in the arc of safety cast by the liberal order, that the belief is indulged that force isn't the determiner of outcomes. And although we may fecklessly think so, our enemies do not.

Another shibboleth that needs debunking is some beautiful, inspiring rhetoric from Martin Luther King Jr that former President Barack Obama and others interpret literally, which is that the arc of history bends towards justice. It has come to be treated as a natural law, like gravitational pull, and therefore requiring nothing of us to produce felicitous outcomes, which is both an intellectual and a moral failing to believe. The arc of history only bends towards justice when people of goodwill grab hold of it and wrench it in the direction of justice. We should not exonerate ourselves from doing the hard work of building just societies and a just international order; if we do, we become Fukuyama's last man, and the order will collapse around us.

We have been given an important test of the rules-based international order in the form of Russia's invasion of Ukraine. Vladimir Putin could not be clearer that he considers Ukraine Russian and that its subordination is intended to collapse the foundation of Western dominance of the international order. The West has pulled together admirably but is mostly doing what is easy: sanctions that barely touch our own economies, sending weapons instead of soldiers, providing moral support. These fall far short of President George H W Bush repudiating Iraq's 1990 challenge to the ordering principle that state borders change only by mutual agreement.

We're congratulating ourselves on all we're doing, even though it's plainly not enough to produce the outcome our policies are ostensibly directed to achieve. We are not giving Ukraine enough support to cut the jugular vein of Russian aggression, nor even enough to assure victory before winter energy demand in our own countries fractures Western solidarity. The consequences of this are being paid in Ukrainian blood as Russian incapacities slowly engender their failure. The Pentagon is proud of its logistical feat in rapidly shipping arms to Ukraine, as though input measures were the consequential metric, when they plainly are not. Doing enough to ensure Ukrainian victory and restoration of its sovereignty is not only the right objective, it's the stated objective of US policy. By such self-congratulation, we become Fukuyama's last man.

If we are to avoid the fate of allowing the collapse of an international order that has produced our peace and prosperity, we need to close the gaps between our claims and what success requires of us. We need to become serious about the undertaking, and listen to what is required to bend the arc of history towards justice. That will involve strengthening our societies: increasing defence spending; being willing to fight for freedom; not flinching at risks of escalation in conflict; being willing to accept higher prices to impose economic sanctions; and creating incentives for more societies to opt in to the liberal order.

Strengthening our societies will necessarily involve finding ways to use the tools of free societies to protect those societies. We don't want to become what we are seeking to protect ourselves against – authoritarian governments that utilise force and surveillance technologies to repress their own populations, corrupt other governments, and force unequal terms on weaker states. The openness of free societies has allowed our enemies to reach in and steal, influence, and corrupt. But we are not without numerous tools – extant and potential – to use that openness assertively. Civil society, including businesses, is the superpower of free people.

Historian Ernest May, who was on the 9/11 Commission, told me that he thought the biggest mistake the Bush administration made in the aftermath of the terrorist attacks was calling for passivity by the public while the government dealt with the problem. The administration was concerned about vigilantism (they enabled Saudi Arabia to spirit its prominent citizens out of the US, and repeatedly called for tolerance of Muslims) and skittishness giving terrorists a second victory by producing economic collapse. But the threat also persuaded them to adopt policies of 'big government conservatism' that leached initiative from the body politic. May believed American national security would have been better served by the government sharing information and utilising engagement of the public to protect itself – as the passengers on Flight 93 did on 11 September.

Only now, confronted with insidious intrusions by enemies, do we in the West begin to explore how to use our openness as an advantage. The Biden administration defanged Russian propaganda by preemptive declassification and dissemination of disinformation to prepare the public; Western governments developed innovative central bank actions and other financial sanctions. States such as Australia are showing ways to engage citizens and allies by sharing information, taking brave policy decisions (like excluding Huawei from their communication networks and calling for an investigation of Chinese lab experiments that may have been the source of Covid-19), and demonstrating the fortitude of free people when threatened. This is the way. Because Thomas Jefferson's fundamental insight remains true, that there is no safe repository of power other than the people themselves.

AN AUTHORITARIAN
WORLD ORDER?

Russian President Vladimir Putin, 2022.

WHAT DRIVES VLADIMIR PUTIN?

Sergey Radchenko

Towards the end of Fyodor Dostoevsky's timeless masterpiece, *Crime and Punishment*, the novel's protagonist, Rodion Raskolnikov, delves into his reasons for murdering an old pawnbroker lady and her timid sister Lizaveta. He had thought initially he would use the money he stole from the pawnbroker to launch a career (the crime of killing a mean old lady appeared to him insignificant in view of his truly Napoleonic ambitions). But as he goes deeper, it becomes clear that this was not, in fact, a particularly important part of Raskolnikov's actions, and that he committed the crime for a different reason: above all, to prove to himself that he was not bound by the social canon; that he could overcome the artificial constraints of morality; that he had, to use the famous concept of Dostoevsky's near-contemporary Friedrich Nietzsche, the *will to power*.

'Am I a trembling creature,' rambled Raskolnikov, 'or do I have the right?' The right to do what? The right to bend down and pick up that which was his, that was there for the taking, if he only found the inner strength to discard moral objections.

Raskolnikov's struggle with himself – his attempt to rationalise the abominable – uncannily reminds me of Vladimir Putin's reasoning for invading Ukraine. He has put forward various explanations for his aggression, some that might be called 'ideological' in that they highlight Russia's alleged historical rights to Ukrainian territory. Others are based on a skewed interpretation of Russia's core 'security interests'. But behind all this rhetoric lies Putin's preoccupation – an obsession even – with proving to others and, above all, to himself that he has the *right* to Ukraine, the right not in a moral-ethical sense, nor in any legal sense, but in Raskolnikov's sense: to bend down and pick up what was his because he *dared* to do what no one else did – openly challenge the US-led rules-based world order.

America has always occupied a larger-than-life place in Putin's imagination. In his many recent statements on foreign affairs, Putin has spoken of the United States with spite and hatred. A perusal of these voluminous pronouncements reveals that what Putin finds most objectionable is the idea of American 'exceptionalism'. It appears he first used this term to talk about the US in May 2007, in his Victory Day speech, and it soon became a regular fixture of his discussion of foreign affairs.

It is unclear what was the precise moment when Putin embraced this view of US foreign policy: perhaps it was the American intention to set up missile interceptors in Poland and the Czech Republic (publicly announced in January 2007). Putin touched on this issue in his infamous speech in Munich. He also highlighted other perceived affronts, including the US agreements with Romania (December 2005) and Bulgaria (April 2006), allowing for the stationing of up to 5,000 US troops in the two countries. Putin's criticism of American 'exceptionalism' overlapped in time with Washington's greater assertiveness, which challenged Russia's conventional position in Europe and potentially eroded Moscow's ability to threaten the US and its allies with nuclear obliteration.

The build-up of Russia-Western tensions began visibly in early 2007, and led, in short order, to Russia's suspension of its participation in the Treaty on Conventional Forces Europe (announced in July 2007), resumption of strategic bomber flights (August 2007), and, soon enough, to Russia's war in Georgia (August 2008). However, the downward slide in Russian-American relations was briefly arrested with the change of guard in the Kremlin. Dmitry Medvedev's presidency was characterised by the renewal of the Russian-American dialogue, even in spite of the regime's growing obsession with the challenge posed by domestic opposition.

But alongside Putin's 'return' (given he had never left) came also his preoccupation with countering American 'exceptionalism'. He mentioned the issue in his well-remembered op-ed in *The New York Times* in September 2013, where he called for 'caution' in Syria. The op-ed followed President Barack Obama's speech to the US Congress, in the wake of Assad's use of chemical weapons, in which Obama justified US strikes on Syria by referring to American exceptionalism. 'It is extremely dangerous to encourage people to see themselves as exceptional, whatever the motivation…When we ask for the Lord's blessings, we must not forget that God created us equal,' Putin wrote in response. In fact, he personally added this passage to the op-ed written largely by his aides, a reminder of the extent of his personal obsession.

Obama's occasional dismissive remarks about Putin – such as when he compared him to 'the bored kid at the back of the classroom' – added to the sense of a personal affront. It wasn't just that the Americans felt they were 'exceptional'. They also pretended to be teachers. And they wanted to teach him – *him*!

These emotional underpinnings of Putin's conflict with the West were enormously important, more important perhaps than the perceived harm to Russia's security interests from NATO's eastward enlargement. The issue hinged on Putin's perception of himself as the leader of a 'Great Power,' one that, although not America's equal by most measures, nevertheless had the means at its disposal to destroy the United States, and so end in one stroke its arrogant exceptionalism, even if this meant also destroying the world. If he had the means, then did he also not have the *right*?

Putin's ideas were put to a test in 2014, when Ukrainian President Viktor Yanukovych was overthrown in what Putin described as a 'coup' and Ukrainian protesters called the 'revolution of dignity'. Putin perceived an opportunity to cannibalise Ukraine and so prove he could push back against American exceptionalism. 'Those who keep talking about their exceptionalism,' he proclaimed in the wake of his annexation of Crimea, 'do not like Russia's independent foreign policy. Events in Ukraine confirmed this. As they also confirmed that the double-standard model of relations with Russia does not work.'

In speaking about 'double standards' Putin was alluding to America's wars in the Middle East, beginning with the invasion of Afghanistan in 2001, and then Iraq in 2003. The latter was infamous for having benefited from the made-up pretext of ridding Saddam Hussein's regime of the weapons of mass destruction that he evidently did not have. Back in 2003, Putin was careful in his criticism of the Iraq war, and even compared it positively with the Soviet experience in Afghanistan. The Soviets, he argued, had merely tried to 'improve' their position in Afghanistan but instead got mired in a war that lasted for ten years. By contrast, the US attacked a regime that 'had been opposed to the international community for a long time' and that 'brooked no compromise'. As for the US invasion of Afghanistan, that, too, Putin accepted as a necessary measure in the war on terrorism. What doubts he harboured, he kept to himself.

It was only later that Putin would cite Afghanistan and Iraq (and also Yugoslavia and Libya) as examples of American exceptionalism in action, using them to justify his invasion of Ukraine. 'Our Western partners,' he complained bitterly on March 18, 2014, 'prefer the right of might over international law. They have come to believe in their chosen-ness and exceptionalism.' On the same day Russia formally annexed Crimea.

The world looked on in disbelief but there was very little reaction to the crime. The sanctions that were imposed on Russia were of symbolic, superficial character, not so much as a slap on the wrist. It was as if Raskolnikov murdered the old lady in plain sight, and then walked down the street, brandishing the bloodied axe: see, I did it because I could! With Russia promptly annexing a part of Ukraine, and successfully bolstering a defiant tyrant in Syria, it may well be that Putin came to believe in his own manifest destiny.

Indeed, Putin had in effect proclaimed Russia's exceptionalism, ie its ability to intervene in its neighbours' affairs at will, to threaten, to annex. He presented this exceptionalism of his as a response to American exceptionalism. 'Democratisation' of international relations, which Russian propaganda has trumpeted for years as a remedy against the US-led 'unipolar world' came down, on closer inspection, to the assertion of Russia's *right* to do as it wanted at the expense of those deemed weaker, the 'trembling creatures' of global politics, including Georgia and Ukraine.

Putin was especially unwilling to accept the challenge posed by Presidents Petro Poroshenko and Volodymyr Zelensky. It was not because he was terrified of Ukrainian democracy or feared that Russia might catch the 'democratic virus'. Far from it. Russian strategic thinking dismissed Ukraine as a semi-failed state (an important reason why so many in Russia underestimated the strength of Ukraine's resistance). The real reason was that Putin could not accept that his *exceptional right* could be so insolently rejected by trembling creatures that he so disdained.

As he set his mind on destroying Ukraine, Putin's rhetoric about American 'exceptionalism' became shriller. Unsurprisingly, the term crept into his February 24 announcement of the invasion. 'Why is all of this happening?' he raved. 'Where does this insolent manner of speaking from the position of your own exceptionalism, infallibility, and all-permissiveness come from? Wherefrom comes that condescending, arrogant attitude towards our interests and absolutely legitimate demands?' He could well have added, in grim Raskolnikov's voice: 'Am I a trembling creature, or do I have the right?'

Putin had now committed himself to the hideous act of murder. Within hours the Russians launched a full-blown invasion of a neighbouring country, unleashing a gruesome orgy of violence. Few in the Moscow inner circle saw it coming. They thought rationally. They talked about security interests. They weighed the pros and the cons. And they completely underestimated Putin's emotional state, and his pathological preoccupation with proving an *idea* – that he *could*.

'The paralysis of power, of will – this is the first step to degradation and oblivion,' Putin said in his announcement of Russia's invasion of Ukraine. There is something here that bears resemblance to Nietzsche's *will to power*: the desire to do the unthinkable in pursuit of goals, rejecting the seemingly artificial constraints of custom and morality. 'Behold! I bring you the superman!' Nietzsche proclaimed in *Thus Spoke Zarathustra*. Here he was, the Russian 'superman': his face contorted by fear and hatred, facing his own mortality and futility, raining vitriol, asserting himself *in your face, America*.

But Putin's misadventure ran into a problem: the Ukrainians fought back. The Russian offensive stalled. After months of fighting, Putin managed to prove only one thing: that he *could not* do the things he said he would. Not for lack of trying of course; simply, he was no superman, only a delusional despot with a bloated ego. The ego was punctured. Putin blew hot and cold and promised, in one particularly militant speech, that he had not 'even properly begun yet'.

In a rarely-read chapter of *The End of History*, Francis Fukuyama talks about 'men without chests', that is, those who have no ambition to be recognised as superior to anyone else. The problem could arise in a liberal democracy, where all are afforded equal opportunity, and general justice prevails. Such a situation, Fukuyama argues, could lead to a degree of societal degradation: 'If man reaches a society in which he has succeeded in abolishing injustice, his life will come to resemble that of the dog.' He sees redemption in the pursuit of greatness in foreign affairs, citing encouragingly Churchill's statesmanship in the Second World War and President George H W Bush's decision to expel Iraq from Kuwait.

In one particularly controversial passage, Fukuyama even hails the benefits of a 'short and decisive war every generation or so', so that a liberal democracy could 'defend its own liberty and independence'. Putin's Russia is not a liberal democracy by any stretch of the imagination, but he envisioned this war against Ukraine as the short decisive war of his generation – a war that would bring him the recognition he so badly craved. Putin's barrel-chested misadventure thus owes something to a Fukuyamian conception of recognition, perhaps not exactly in the way the political scientist envisioned when the two of them eyed the end of history from their respective perches in the State Department and the KGB.

'I just killed,' Raskolnikov concluded at the end of his famous monologue. 'I killed for myself; just for myself.' But there was a paradox, which he perceived even as he committed his crime. 'Did I not know,' he muttered, 'that if I began to ask and interrogate myself whether I have the right to power – then it follows that I do not have the right to power.' 'I had no right to go there,' added Raskolnikov, 'because I am just a louse like everyone else.'

Eventually, Raskolnikov fully confessed to his crime. He could not live with the guilt, which, for Dostoevsky at least, proved the existence of divine providence. Having risen insolently to assert his *right* against his fellow man, Raskolnikov was stricken down by the hand of God. He fell on the ground and kissed it to the amusement of the passers-by. This, for Dostoevsky, was a sign of Raskolnikov's repentance, the beginning of his return to normality.

Raskolnikov and Putin are very different people. At the very least, they represent men at very different stages of their careers. Raskolnikov was a desperately poor student eyeing the unfair world and rationalising his own place in it. Whether he killed an old lady and her sister to become Putin, or just to prove to himself that he *could* take what was rightly his, he dared not take the next step. He could not overcome. Putin, by contrast, is a highly accomplished murderer. Many an old lady has been dispatched in cold blood on his orders – and innocent children too. Will *he* ever repent, fall on the ground and kiss it? Will he feel the need to, if God – thanks to the criminally pliant leadership of the Russian Orthodox Church – is already on his side?

'Do I then strive after *happiness*? I strive after my *work*!' Thus spoke Putin on emerging from his bunker like Zarathustra from his cave. And, behold, there was death and destruction everywhere.

And he grinned.

'I haven't even properly begun yet.'

Red Army fighters during the Long March,
Shaanxi 1936.

GAZING BACK TO SEE CHINA'S FUTURE

Roel Sterckx

S tudents who embarked on the study of China and Chinese in the 1980s will recall the question most frequently put to them: 'What will China look like two decades from now?' In the higher education sector, training students to be able to divine China's future path was one of the motivating factors behind the establishment of university programmes in Chinese Studies. The 'what will China become' question was the preserve of anyone who had mastered a few Chinese characters, whether one studied Chinese history, art, philosophy, philology, religions, or political science. Nearly four decades on, that very same question still sits on top of the list in almost any conversation China scholars are invited to contribute to. Its answer, however, remains as elusive today as it was back then, albeit that China watchers today have access to more data than ever before. As Simon Leys (1935–2014) once quipped (in an essay bundled in *The Hall of Uselessness*): 'What a successful China expert needs first and foremost is not so much China expertise as expertise at being an expert.'

In a day and age when politicians demand quick answers or predictions about the internal and geopolitical fate of China, there is an advantage to being a historian of ancient China: one can take a *longue durée* view. As much as looking forward is important, taking a reverse gaze at some of the foundational ideas that have shaped Chinese views on society, leadership and power is important for at least two reasons: first, it helps us understand China on its own terms and, second, it tempers assumptions that contemporary developments in China are either entirely new, unexpected, unpredictable or even undesirable.

It is important to remember that the core concepts of Chinese political thought were formed during an age of division, internecine violence, and discord. This was the so-called Warring States period (sixth to third century BC), the classical age that saw China's foundational thinkers, such as Confucius, offering moral, practical and strategic advice to feudal lords vying for power. The map of China was a patchwork of contending states, perpetually vying among each other for military and economic supremacy. De facto, the entire project of empire, initiated by the famous and infamous First Emperor (in 221 BC) and – one could argue – still ongoing today in one form or other, was an attempt to transcend internal social and regional fragmentation. Its aim: to put in place a bureaucratic and military structure that would keep a vast and regionally diverse empire together. This ideal was referred to with phrases such as 'the grand peace under Heaven' or 'great unity', a condition that was to apply to 'all under Heaven'. The notion of harmony and the so-called harmonious society, often hailed in public discourse by Chinese politicians today, represents an aspiration whose canonical roots date back more than two and a half millennia. The underlying tenet in early Chinese political thought was that unity and concord must be the default order of society. Any fissures or cracks that would taint this political ideal were interpreted as ominous and requiring intervention.

Except perhaps for some Daoists, very few Chinese thinkers in the classical age saw social harmony as the spontaneous or natural outcome of human behaviour, or the result of free choice. Norms that generate harmony were to be imposed from the top. Ideally, this was the task of exemplary rulers whose moral force of persuasion would inspire others to be conscious of their place in society. Alternatively, it fell to autocrats, who used a system of rewards and punishments and an all-reaching network of bureaucrats to impose their will. The first tradition represents that of Confucius (551–479 BC) and his followers; the second that of Shang Yang, Lord Shang (fourth century BC), who, for lack of a better term, is often referred to as the founding figure of Chinese legalism. Much of China's political history and its historical portrayals of leadership are footnoted by Confucian and legalist thinking. This continues to be the case today, although people may use a different vocabulary, or fail to place contemporary ideas in their historical context. Therefore, a search for a notion resembling liberty or freedom in the Chinese tradition, however tenuous such a quest may be, requires us to filter such a concept through a tradition of political thinking that appeared Confucian on the outside and legalist on the inside, with various shades and combinations in between.

One might argue that any notion that approximates individual liberty is hard to find in these foundational texts of Chinese political thought. Confucius understood the role of the individual in society as one that is characterised by bounded liberty at best. The individual is not conceived of as an ego but as an embodiment of various social roles: ruler-subject, father-son, teacher-disciple, master-servant, and so on. Humans need to be acclimatised to ethical norms through education and ritual. The underlying premise here is that we live in the plural – not only do we dwell and act in groups with others, but within this social setting we also wear multiple hats. A person is an aggregate of multiple roles, rather than an individual with a one-dimensional personality. Navigating this role consciousness with the help of customary norms, rules and regulations ensures the smooth running of the collective. It is within the unit of the family, household and extended clan that people are sensitised to the fundamental hierarchies that make community functional. This concept, also known as filial piety, is also a political virtue: it implies loyalty to the state and subservient respect for authority. Throughout Chinese history, the state has upheld this familial model that casts the ruler in the role of father to the people, thereby extracting and demanding loyalty. Ideologically, the Chinese state, and the person at its helm, therefore, always knows what is best for its people. The individual, then, is judged and validated on the basis of how he or she fits in. China's social credit system is essentially Confucian. In the Confucian *Analects*, the morally accomplished person is not so much described positively as someone who aspires to liberate himself from social norms and impositions; instead he is (negatively) defined as someone able to free himself from the tribulations and impediments that prevent him from fulfilling his role expectations: free of resentment (5.26), free of great flaws (7.17), free and easy and not worn down by care (7.37), free of craving and desire (9.28, 14.12), free of self-doubt (12.20).

The stated goal is social harmony, if needed, at the cost of the individual. To stand out in the collective one needs to know how to fit in. There have been several visions of the harmonious society throughout Chinese history. They range from egalitarian utopias (as envisaged, for instance, by the Mohists in ancient times, the Taiping rebels in the nineteenth century, or the communist revolutionaries in the twentieth century), to views of the world as strictly hierarchical with everyone conscious of their social station and duties in the service of others. The late-nineteenth century reformer Kang Youwei (1858–1927) (dubbed the 'Martin Luther of the Confucian religion' by his disciple Liang Qichao) branded his own utopian vision of an egalitarian society as a 'Great Union' or 'Great

Community' (*Da tong*). Such archetypes of a harmonious world tend to be projected back to a golden past from which humanity has deviated. 'Reforming' or 'changing' the present can, therefore, be construed as restoring an originally harmonious order; revolution or change can be construed as revolving or returning to what came before.

China's rulers, past and present, have been in the habit of selectively drawing on terms or concepts championed by its ancient philosophers for force of persuasion. During the early 2000s, when China's leadership took stock of how society had changed since Deng Xiaoping's economic reforms of the 1970s (the so-called 'reform and opening up' policy), the ideal of the '(socialist) harmonious society' (*hexie shehui*) became the mainstay in the political rhetoric of the People's Republic. The choice of the classical term 'harmony' in the party's script covered a range of ambitions: tackling corruption and unbridled self-interest, addressing inequality, sustainable development, and care for the environment. 'Harmony' supplied the ideological glue to address or pave over the imbalances and (moral) failings of modern society. Such was the message behind the theatrical display of the Chinese graph for harmony (*he*) during the opening ceremony of the Beijing Olympics in 2008.

Ancient China's philosophers had different views on many of the great questions of life but there was one premise they all shared, namely, the ideal of autocratic monarchy. The ruler ought to inspire obedience and a willingness to serve among his subjects: 'The virtue of the gentleman is like wind; the virtue of the small man is like grass. Let the wind blow over the grass and it is sure to bend.' (*Analects*, 12.19.) The notion that society is best run top-down and that there can only be one person at the top was never fundamentally questioned. Economic, social and military efficiencies were deemed inadequate unless one accepts that, ultimately, only one person can make the final decision. According to Confucius, this person should be a moral exemplar. His mandate to rule is a moral one, but it is one based on competence, not popularity. Chinese political philosophy originated on the battlefield. Every ancient Chinese philosopher or theorist reflects on warfare or draws analogies from warfare. Portrayals of the ruler were often a mirror image of that of a general. Like an army that warrants an enlightened general at its helm, society merits the rule of a vanguard of morally accomplished people, not those elected by the majority, but a meritocratic elite. And since competence leads to the holding of office, authority comes with office, and office alone: 'Do not concern yourself with matters of policy unless they are the responsibility of your office.' (*Analects* 8.14, 14.26.)

Ultimately, the aim is to have the people model themselves, or emulate, those in power: 'The ruler is the sundial; the people are the shadow. If the form is upright, then the shadow will be upright. The ruler is the bowl; the people the water. If the bowl is round, then the water will be round; if it is square, then the water will be square.' (*Xunzi* 12.4.) Realistically, however – and here comes the legalist view of leadership – the person who rules is not always someone who carries moral credit, but someone who is skillful at leveraging power through manipulating those around him: 'The True Monarch prohibits through rewards and encourages through punishments; he pursues transgressions and not goodness; he relies on punishments to eradicate punishments.' (*Shangjun shu* 7.6.) Even when the person in the top seat is unpopular, incompetent, or – as was often the case in imperial China – a child, the institution of monarchy must be preserved. There can only be one Son of Heaven. This premise has never been questioned.

What, then, about the rule of law? In the legal custom of traditional China, the law served to project the authority of the state into the household. It was designed to control those who acted as executors of the state, namely, the bureaucracy, the emperor's automats. Its priority was to assist the ruler in controlling his officials and, through them, the people. Maintaining oversight over officials who act as intermediaries between local and central government has been the constant priority of the Chinese state, from its first emperors to its leaders today. In traditional China, the law was not so much concerned with theories of justice, or the protection of rights, freedoms and privileges of the individual or identifiable social groups (so-called civil law). Instead, the law served the interests of those who rule, not those who are ruled. The law addressed wrongs rather than rights. Collective responsibility within households was a red thread in traditional legal thinking, so was collective punishment. The law also enshrined mutual surveillance and the obligation to denounce others (as well as oneself). On balance, few Chinese thinkers believed that laws could compensate for customary conventions and habits. Behaving legally only touches the surface of what the good society should be. Not violating a neighbour is not the same as treating them nicely. Truly socialised communities warrant customised behaviour in accordance with inculcated moral standards. The law can sanction those who are unfilial and dishonest, but it is unable to turn people into moral citizens.

The balance of historical evidence suggests that it is unlikely that China will witness a major tectonic shift in its political make-up within this generation, and likely beyond. The canon of Chinese political thought, and its long-term imprint on Chinese history, conspires against the desire, expressed by many in the 1980s, that China would somehow embark on some sort of Long March towards liberal democracy in the wake of its economic modernisation, let alone that such liberalisation be one modelled on the West. All signs are that economic liberalisation and political liberalism are not necessarily mutually complementary. As a historian, it is not my task to put a value judgement on this, but we should take this as a cue to become better at learning how to think Chinese. That long overdue exercise should start in our schools, and we will only make progress when the great proponents of Chinese social and political thinking are put on the curriculum alongside the Romans, the Greeks, and the European Enlightenment thinkers. There is a centuries-long history that has forged the DNA of Chinese political thinking, one that should make us aware that the founding of the People's Republic in 1949, Deng Xiaoping's reform era, or Xi Jinping's 'New Era' could turn out to be mere eddies on the surface of a deep stream of historical consciousness. We must study that deep history and make it part of our conversations about today's China.

Russian soldiers in Crimea, 2014.

THE WEST NEEDS NEW GRAND STRATEGY

Adrian Bradshaw

The re-emergence of war in Ukraine this year was the continuation of unfinished business for Vladimir Putin. Like many leaders before him, he has allowed himself to become intoxicated with political popularity gained through the use of armed force, and he has now overreached himself. It is worth remembering that his presidential career was launched on the back of a successful re-engagement of Russian forces in Chechnya, prompted by the bombings of apartment blocks in Moscow and other Russian cities, apparently by Chechen terrorists but which, it is claimed, were organised by him. Putin also gained kudos at home for Russian military action in Syria. As a result of this, he was able to base forces in the Mediterranean; his military acquired valuable experience in the operational use of new weapons systems, such as submarine-launched missiles; and he was seen on the world stage alongside President Obama and others as a mover and shaker in global affairs.

In 2014, the seizure of Crimea was a triumph for him, gaining control over territory originally added to the Russian empire by Catherine the Great and the home of the former Soviet and now Russian Black Sea Fleet. Early this year, he saw a further opportunity (from his point of view, no doubt, a necessity) and, on the back of achieving a degree of freedom of action in Belarus following his support of President Lukashenko, he went for a significant prize – the whole of Ukraine. This would have pushed Russia's effective military security boundary with the West back to the borders of Poland, Slovakia, Hungary and Romania, creating once again a 'near abroad' under effective Russian control. As we know, he failed to achieve his immediate objectives in Ukraine. His attempt at *coup-de-main* did not deliver Kyiv and the country, and several of his original axes of attack have subsequently been withdrawn.

We, and he, will have been surprised by the poor performance of the Russian armed forces and the success and initiative shown by the Ukrainian military. The resolve of the Ukrainian people and their government under President Zelensky's inspiring leadership, and the strong response and unity of the West, has also been better than expected. Putin now seems focused on the more limited objectives of securing the whole of the Donbas, the so-called land corridor to Crimea and, of course, holding on to Crimea itself. At least these seem to be his interim objectives, as he continues to wish to bring the whole of Ukraine under his control, fearing the emergence of a successful liberal democracy in the country, which would demonstrate so clearly to his own people, with their strong cultural ties and multiple familial links to the Ukrainians, an attractive alternative to his form of rule. Nevertheless, it is possible that after achieving some interim objectives we might see a pause in the hot war, depending on the fragility of public opinion in Russia, and the appetites and abilities of both Ukrainian and Russian forces for continued fighting.

Many in the West talk of the expulsion of Russia from the whole of Ukraine, but this is unlikely to be achievable in the short term. While this might remain our ultimate desire, we will most probably have to show patience and resolve of the kind shown by the West during the decades of the Cold War, in order to see this aim delivered. Meanwhile, as the fighting continues, we must quickly deliver to the Ukrainians the means to defend themselves while ensuring that the conflict does not turn into a shooting war between Russia and NATO. Macho bravado of the sort Putin voices is unwise in the face of a nuclear-armed bully, who may at any time face a threat to his very existence from his own people. It would be as well that he does not see us as directly and immediately responsible for orchestrating his personal demise. As far as NATO is concerned, as Sun Tzu suggested in *The Art of War*, the acme of success will be to prevail without fighting.

Our actions when the current fighting comes to an end will be key, and will involve tricky decisions regarding risk. Firstly, we must rapidly make it extremely difficult for Putin to derive any advantage from restarting the war in Ukraine. We must provide the Ukrainians with powerful, defensive means to inflict serious pain on the Russians if they restart their offensive. The key Russian demand before the war of the demilitarisation of Ukraine is out of the question as it almost guarantees future Russian interference. Meanwhile, the resolve of the West regarding sanctions and weaning ourselves off Russian energy supplies must be maintained. Russia must understand that we are not going to forget about their horrific and unjustified invasion of Ukraine, and that their economic isolation will be maintained until their illegal actions are reversed, and war criminals are brought to justice. This will require huge diplomatic effort, although reducing reliance on fossil fuels, whether from Russia or elsewhere, is also necessary to achieve our carbon-dioxide reduction targets, so we have more than one incentive to keep up the pressure on Russia.

Clearly, an enormous effort will be required to support the reconstruction of Ukraine in the aftermath of this war, and international funding should be set aside for that task. The EU might conclude that the rapid accession of Ukraine should be allowed, even if a part of their territory remains occupied. Certainly, favourable trading status will be desirable. Western nations might even consider entering into security agreements with Ukraine, thus significantly increasing the risk to Russia should it restart the war. Of course, there will be enormous scope for mischief on the boundary between Russian and Ukrainian forces, but relative stability has been achieved in places such as Korea with the involvement of the UN.

At whatever stage the current fighting in Ukraine comes to an end, whether by the victory of one side or the other or, more likely perhaps, through a potentially unstable ceasefire, Putin will continue to have motives for further aggression against what remains of free Ukraine and against NATO. His narrative to the Russian people is of an aggressive West that seeks to reduce Russian power and status, and even to break up the country. He has presented himself as the strongman who can protect the Russian people against this threat. He has also reportedly acquired huge wealth through corrupt and criminal means, upsetting many people along the way, and is unlikely to accept being forced from power without a fight; losing his position without a supportive successor would probably pose an existential threat to him. It is highly likely, therefore, that every time he sees his political position threatened and his public support reduced, he will once again feel the need to convince Russians that they need him. Thus, a case for action will once again have to be manufactured, using his experience in dirty tricks and 'false flag' activity, gained in the KGB and in the years since, and some kind of 'defensive' action will follow, probably involving coercion, subversion or the open use of armed force. After Georgia, Ukraine and other neighbours, the next most likely target for such action is NATO; naturally, damage to NATO's credibility and unity would be highly desirable for Putin. Our defences must, therefore, be strong and our deterrence must be smart.

For all of us, the vital requirement will be to prevent future hot conflict between NATO and Russia, that would be highly likely to spiral out of control with catastrophic consequences. In the face of a dictator, who fears only strength, we must prevent conflict by building strong military deterrence which convinces Putin that we are able, quickly and decisively, to defeat any Russian military incursion into any part of NATO territory. If the NATO doctrine of 'flexible response', which was brought in after the near disaster of the Cuban missile crisis, is to be meaningful, our nuclear options must be truly last resort, which means rebuilding credible conventional capability. Our collective military deterrence must be particularly strong in the former Soviet republics and the ex-Warsaw Pact countries. We must never let Putin think he can undermine the credibility of NATO by seizing ground there and then securing any territorial gains through 'escalation dominance', a classic technique in the former Soviet and now Russian playbook.

Furthermore, as war has always been a hybrid business, we must invoke the trinity of deterrence in all areas of national and collective endeavour. Firstly, we must build solid, reliable protection around the assets that sustain our societies: our political systems; our health and social care structures; our banking and business sectors; our key infrastructure; our access to the global commons; and our ability to communicate our values domestically and abroad. In all areas, not just military and security, we must provide strong physical and virtual protection.

Secondly, we must build resilience in all these areas. We must ensure our systems have what military practitioners would call 'reversionary modes', enabling them to continue operating even when compromised. Over-reliance on digital systems and satellite technology are key current vulnerabilities. We must be confident that we have the means rapidly to recover full working capacity in all areas that might be subject to an attack, whether by physical, virtual, economic, informational or other means.

Finally, we must ensure that any attacker knows that they will face an unacceptable cost for their aggression. This requires not only like-for-like but also asymmetric capability. We need to be able, as we have been during the Ukraine crisis, to respond to military adventurism in our sphere of interest through political, economic and diplomatic action, as direct military confrontation might, in some cases, lead to disaster. Such asymmetric, hybrid responses, however, rely on speedy and effective international coordination in the face of the fast-moving situations that are characteristic of this cyber and global information era. Inter-departmental mechanisms within national governments and our international structures need to be very responsive.

Recent events should have convinced even the most vocal advocates of European strategic autonomy in the field of defence that this should not come at the expense of a reduced focus on NATO. The integration of our military deterrence with that of the US is vital for the continued security of Europe, as this recent crisis has reminded us. Furthermore, while we have in NATO an organisation that can formulate and execute excellent military strategy, we should not wastefully duplicate structures within the EU and, in so-doing, not only significantly stretch our manpower capacity for military staff work and command and control, but also reduce our focus on strong transatlantic defence cooperation. Instead, we should look again at the Berlin Plus arrangements agreed in 2003, that enabled the EU's Operation Althea in Bosnia-Herzegovina and Concordia in Macedonia, using NATO command, control and communications support. This mechanism is currently effectively vetoed by a couple of nations with their own regional difficulties. This prevention of in-depth EU-NATO cooperation prevents the achievement of an even more important goal than the efficient use of military forces for EU-specific actions. It prevents the development of a holistic strategy between NATO and the EU, despite 21 nations being members of both. This is highly inefficient and damaging in an era when political, military, security, economic, informational and other actions need to be synchronised in the face of competitors who threaten to become opponents, and who themselves can often manage more effectively to coordinate across such domains because of the strong, unified control they hold over every aspect of their national governments.

In the area of information, we must work hard to ensure that our values of truth and transparency are shared, as far as possible, with the Russian people. We must create the means to enable them to gain access to information about the truth of what Putin does in their name. Given his control of the media and most other sources of information in Russia, this will take imagination and resources. To the extent that it is possible, it will be highly desirable to keep open, or reopen, channels of communication with groups in Russia who may have sympathy with Western alternatives to their form of government. Young intellectuals and entrepreneurs are likely to be attracted to Western freedoms and ideas, and may influence those around them. We must also, for different reasons, try to re-establish links between senior military commanders from NATO and Russia. Regrettably, in something of a political knee-jerk in the aftermath of the seizure of Crimea in 2014, routine military-to-military contact was broken, resulting in an almost total lack of the sort of communication that can prevent conflict breaking out by mistake. Instead, clear direction should have been given down military chains of command regarding approved levels at which communications are permitted, and limitations should have been set on the sort of information that could be exchanged. Now, in the face of Russian atrocities in Ukraine, it is incredibly hard to justify rebuilding communication links. However, if there is a significant lull in the fighting, an attempt should be made to re-establish communications, certainly at the most senior levels.

Similar efforts must be made with China if we are to avoid mistakes and misunderstandings. We must work harder to engender a level of understanding within our own societies about China, and to encourage the Chinese people to see the benefit of our forms of government and to understand that we seek cooperation, rather than confrontation. Indeed, a cooperative relationship will make it more likely that we derive the mutual benefits of trade and collaboration to resolve pressing problems such as global warming and disease.

Of course, protecting ourselves from the aggressive tendencies of autocratic and expansionist regimes is not the only task of our armed forces. While in the area of deterrence the mark of success is to sustain military capability in order to obviate the need to use it; as we know well from the constant action since the end of the Cold War, there are many problems which demand the active use of the military. Peace support, including peace enforcement in a hostile environment, counter insurgency and stabilisation operations all demand a high level of competence from our armed forces, over and above their constant readiness for large-scale, peer-on-peer warfighting, all of which requires specialised equipment and mission specific training. We are likely to see the continued requirement, from time to time, to use military force in areas affected by Islamist extremism, which is growing ever more active and destabilising in Africa since the reverses suffered by the so-called Islamic State in Syria and Iraq. Furthermore, if we are to reduce some of the pressure behind uncontrolled emigration from the Sahel and other parts of Africa and Asia, in particular, we must be more ready to intervene in advance of problems becoming acute. Just as our approach to deterrence must be hybrid, so must we seek to prevent instability through an integrated mix of economic development, assistance with good governance, education, and help with law and order, as well as with military and security assistance.

In summary, we need to bring the current hot war in Europe to an end as advantageously for Ukraine as practicable, but without precipitating a wider conflict. We need then to put a stop to future Russian adventurism in Ukraine. Meanwhile, we must not wait, but must urgently build convincing and effective military deterrence, and we must enable integrated hybrid responses to Russian aggression, both nationally and collectively, right across the North Atlantic, European and Scandinavian region.

Looking further afield, with respect to China and other potential future opponents, we must work on similar cooperation with like-minded nations across the world. I would suggest that we need a new grand strategy for the West, unified by an overarching philosophy which seeks to achieve the support and commitment of our own populations, many of whom have become critical of, and disillusioned with, the very systems we seek to defend. We must put effort into making the case to our own people for liberal democracy, the rule of law and free access to the truth, to stand against the threat from self-serving autocratic and expansionist regimes that seek to keep their peoples in a state of ignorant suppression. At the same time, we must become more willing to act early, with integrated programmes of up-front assistance, to prevent instability developing in Africa and other parts of the globe. This makes them ripe for exploitation by autocratic regimes, creating an engine for uncontrolled emigration, which puts pressures on our resources, societies and political systems.

The continued defence of our values and way of life will continue to be, in part, dependent on maintaining strong military and security forces within united and well-resourced regional and global alliances, guided by strategies that integrate our military and security activity into a multidisciplinary framework with clear strategic objectives.

THE ENDURANCE OF
WESTERN VALUES

Cambridge, United Kingdom.

IS ACADEMIC FREEDOM UNDER THREAT?

Matthew Goodwin

One of the most important forms of liberty in Western civilisation is academic freedom, the freedom of intellectuals to research, teach and express ideas without the risk of facing negative professional consequences for doing so. This type of liberty has long been central to the cultivation, continuation and promotion of Western values. It has helped drive the prosperity of nations. It has helped drive innovation and dynamism. It has encouraged us to challenge alternative ideas, assumptions and belief systems that are at best misguided and, at worst, dangerous. And it has ensured that our students and young people – the next generation – are exposed to a wide range of ideas, beliefs and perspectives, which is not only central to the development of critical thinkers but key to countering the growing polarisation of our politics and societies. Academic freedom, in short, is fundamental to Western societies and has long been central to the advance of knowledge and prosperity.

It also helps to explain why Western democracies are still home to the world's leading institutions of higher education. Between them, the United Kingdom, European Union and United States account for all the top 20 universities in the world and all but five of the top 50. By attracting and educating international students, they are also a source of immense soft power. The UK might have voted to leave the European Union, but it is still home to nearly 600,000 international students, which helps the country entrench Western values and project considerable soft power around the globe.

But today this liberty is under attack. Across the West, rising numbers of academics, as well as their students, no longer feel free to explore a range of different research questions or express their views on certain topics when they are on campus. Increasingly, many of our universities are evolving into highly politicised ideological monocultures that are no longer preserving and promoting academic freedom, where those who do not share the dominant ideological orthodoxy are discriminated against, and where the search for truth and objective enquiry is being pushed aside in favour of political objectives. This is not only weakening our institutions of higher education; it is weakening Western societies more generally.

There have always been intense debates and moral panics about what is happening in universities. The 1960s and 1970s saw these rage across America, Britain and France, over some of the ideas emerging from universities and the extent to which they welcomed a wide range of perspectives, debates which continued into the 1980s. But today, amid the rising polarisation of our politics, something is different. Across the West, particularly since 2015, there has been a rapidly growing pile of research in the social sciences which suggests that something has gone fundamentally wrong in higher education. Specifically, this evidence, derived from large-scale surveys of academics, students and the growing number of university administrators, suggests academic freedom is now challenged in four areas.

Firstly, while universities have always leaned to the left in politics, this imbalance has become much greater in recent years, so much so that some universities have morphed into ideological monocultures which are failing to preserve and promote genuine viewpoint diversity. In the summer of 2022, this was best symbolised by a survey of faculty at Harvard University in the US, which found that 80% of respondents characterised their political leanings as 'liberal' or 'very liberal' while just 1% said they were 'conservative' and not a single one said they were 'very conservative'. Such findings reflect global trends. In 2021, I surveyed academics who are currently working in the most elite universities across the UK, the US, Canada and Australia as part of a project with the Legatum Institute. I found that 76% of academics in these institutions now identify as 'left-wing', with 21% of that group identifying as 'far left'. Only 11% of respondents placed themselves on the right-wing.

In the US, similarly, Sam Abrams has found that the share of professors who identify as left-wing increased from 40% in the mid-1990s to 60% by the early 2010s, while the political leanings of the public remained static. More recent work by Mitchell Langbert, based on a representative sample of tenure track professors, found that the ratio of Democrats to Republicans is 12 to one in the social sciences in major research universities, and 13 to one in 66 liberal arts colleges. Across economics, journalism, history, law, and psychology, just 4% of faculty were registered

Republicans. In liberal arts colleges in areas such as anthropology, communications, and race, gender and sexuality studies, Langbert discovered a perfect monoculture – there were no Republicans at all. This has also been underlined by surveys of my own field, political science, which find that nearly 72% identify on the left.

This is supported by other reliable research, such as the Understanding Society survey in the UK, which suggests eight in 10 academic staff now vote for liberal left political parties, whether the Labour Party, the Liberal Democrats, the Greens or Scottish National Party. If we compare these findings to surveys that were conducted in the UK during the 1960s, then the ratio of left-wing to right-wing academics in countries such as the UK has increased from around three to one in the 1960s to about eight to one today. At the same time, we know that public opinion has remained constant, underlining how university faculty have, overall, become more ideologically disconnected from the societies that surround them.

Clearly, the authors of these studies are not making normative judgements about individual academics. But their findings do raise important and urgent questions about the extent to which academic freedom and viewpoint diversity do exist within many universities today, and whether university faculty and students are being exposed to a wide range of ideas, beliefs, speakers and research questions. When this does not take place, it can have serious implications, not least by encouraging the premature foreclosure of research questions that might challenge the dominant ideological orthodoxy on campus.

Second, it can lead to the negative discrimination of those who do not share these beliefs. As scholars such as Cass Sunstein point out, when ideological monocultures take root, they often embolden more radical members of that community to discriminate against actual or perceived nonconformists, not least because they doubt there will be any repercussions for doing so. This can often lead to a dogmatic and highly moralistic culture on campus which encourages those who do not share their views to 'self-censor' or hide their real views. In the UK, recent studies by the University and College Union, the main trade union for academics, and Kings College London suggest one-third of all academics and one in four students respectively are self-censoring on campus; in other words, they do not feel comfortable voicing their views in seminars and lectures.

Globally, my own research suggests 41% of academics who are currently working in the world's most elite universities – from Harvard to

Oxford – are self-censoring their beliefs on campus, rising from 35% in the UK to 50% in America. To put this in raw numbers, somewhere in the region of 50,000 academic staff in the UK currently feel uncomfortable sharing their views when they are on university campus. Clearly, this might be because they feel the workplace is not a suitable environment to project their beliefs, but it is worth noting that there is a considerable difference in the extent to which people on different sides of the political spectrum feel the need to self-censor. My research finds that while only 35% of academics who lean to the left feel the need to self-censor on campus, 75% of academics who lean to the right feel the same way, revealing how the spread of this ideological monoculture is leading nonconformists to self-censor. This is also supported by research by the Policy Exchange institute in the UK, which finds much the same: people who hold gender critical or conservative views are far more likely to self-censor than others.

Unfortunately, and worryingly, this also now appears to be true of university students. Studies find that while nine in 10 university students in the UK who voted to remain in the European Union feel comfortable voicing their beliefs on campus, fewer than four in 10 students who voted for Brexit feel the same way. In America, similarly, the latest Heterodox Academy Campus Expression Survey, released this summer, found that 63% of college students feel 'the climate on their campus prevents some people from saying things they believe, up from 55% in 2019'. Democrat students were consistently the least likely to say they felt reluctant to share their views on gender, politics, race and sexual orientation, while Republicans and libertarians were consistently the most likely to say they feel reluctant to share their views when they are on university campus. In short, large numbers of faculty and students are now self-censoring their views, though especially the ideological minority.

Thirdly, ideological monocultures also encourage the marginalisation or harassment of nonconformists who do not subscribe to, or merely challenge, the established ideological orthodoxy on campus. On one level, this political discrimination is symbolised by prominent cases, such as Kathleen Stock, who was forced to leave her position at the University of Sussex after being harassed by trans rights activists; Jordan Peterson, who initially had his invitation of a fellowship at the University of Cambridge rescinded; Noah Carl, who was dismissed from Cambridge after student-led protests; or Peter Boghossian, who resigned from his position at Portland State University citing harassment and a lack of academic freedom on campus.

It might be tempting to think these cases are few and far between, but this is not the case. If anything, they represent the tip of the iceberg. According to the Academics for Academic Freedom group, in the UK, there have been more than 100 cases of speakers being banned from speaking at universities or experiencing harassment because of their views. The Foundation for Individual Rights in Education (FIRE) in the States has similarly tracked a sharp increase in the number of academics who have experienced harassment, intimidation or student protests in recent years, finding that most of these attacks come from academics or students who self-identify on the left-wing of the political spectrum. Since 2015, FIRE has tracked 537 incidents of a scholar experiencing some form of professional sanction over constitutionally protected speech, with almost two thirds of those resulting in a sanction and more than one fifth resulting in the scholar losing their job. They were most often targeted for expressing a personal view on a controversial issue (59% of incidents), mainly because of race and racial issues. Almost two thirds of the attacks came from individuals and groups to the political left of the scholar and mainly from undergraduate students

On another level, this (often political) discrimination is also reflected in a rapidly expanding body of research. My own research finds a striking asymmetry in how academics in the world's elite universities feel about different groups in society; while 64% feel positively about people who support left-wing parties, and more than 80% feel positively about people who support Black Lives Matter, only 10% feel the same way about people who support right-wing parties. Recent research by the Centre for Partisanship and Ideology has likewise found that more than four in 10 academics in North America would not hire a known supporter of Donald Trump, one in three academics in the UK would not hire somebody who was known to have voted to leave the European Union at the Brexit referendum in 2016, while only one in four academics said they would feel comfortable having lunch with somebody who opposes the idea of transwomen accessing women's shelters. Most right-leaning academics said they worked in a hostile departmental climate while a significant number of their left-leaning colleagues said they would openly discriminate against their right-wing colleagues when reviewing grant or job applications, thereby essentially making it harder for those who do not share the dominant ideological orthodoxy to rise to senior positions.

Fourth, this research also points to a sizeable and active minority of activist scholars who now routinely prioritise ideological goals over the principle of academic freedom, the search for universal truth, and the traditional emphasis on objective enquiry. My own research suggests that one quarter of academics across the West do not think that limits on freedom of speech undermine the principles on which universities were founded; one quarter think the ideological goal of social justice should always be prioritised in universities, even if it violates the principle of academic freedom; and close to one quarter do not support exposing their students to speakers who might offend them. There is also considerable support across the West's higher education institutions for the ongoing politicisation of these institutions. Increasingly, universities in the United States and, to a lesser extent, the United Kingdom require staff to sign up to the ideological principles of social justice – for example, requiring that job applicants or academics who are applying for major research grants provide statements in which they must signal their commitment to the ideological goals of equity and diversity. My research finds nearly six in ten academics in the world's most elite universities, 57%, now think this is a justifiable requirement. Yet many others, especially those who do not share these views or simply feel that universities should not be organised around political goals, do not support the use of this ideological litmus test. Increasingly, they worry that our universities are being led away from their founding goals and reshaped around the pursuit of social justice and what are openly political objectives.

So, what should be done? One potential answer is in the UK, where the Conservative government, in consultation with a network of academics, has developed and brought before parliament the Higher Education (Free Speech) Bill. Though Conservatives have historically opposed using the state to intervene in such issues, they have come to the conclusion that universities are unwilling or unable to reform themselves. The bill will formally require universities to actively promote free speech, establish a new director of academic freedom who will oversee cases where this is claimed to have been violated, and give regulators the power to fine universities if they do not uphold academic freedom. It will allow staff who feel they are being discriminated against to appeal beyond their own institutions and, by extending that duty to secure free speech to student unions, it will caution student leaders against yielding to pressure to stifle dissent. By authorising the new director of academic freedom to recommend redress, it will also encourage university vice-chancellors to push the issue further up their agendas and help bring about culture change across the sector, which the evidence suggests is clearly in need of reform.

The alternative would be to do nothing at all and hope that universities will reform themselves, but there is little, if any, evidence to suggest that this will take place. On the contrary, if the status quo is not more robustly challenged then it appears likely that rising numbers of students will fail to experience viewpoint diversity, and many academics will leave higher education to pursue alternative careers, while nonconformists – whether on issues relating to sex, gender or race – will face an increasingly hostile environment. All of these problems will not only weaken our universities but also weaken the liberty that lies at the very heart of Western societies and values.

Protests against High Speed 2 rail, the world's
most expensive infrastructure project,
in Aylesbury, UK, 2021.

LIBERTY UNDER ATTACK
FROM ENEMIES WITHIN

Juliet Samuel

L iberty is the theme of this book and, with the war in Ukraine on-going, many essays in these pages understandably focus on the external and immediate threat to freedom posed by military expansionism and NATO weakness. It is easy to look around the world at the building tensions and think that the greatest enemy of freedom comes from a nefarious, despotic regime in Russia, Iran or China.

We should, however, resist the temptation to blame the outside world for the crisis in liberalism. The greatest threat to our liberty isn't truly to be found in some far-off, foreign capital. It is right here, in our own societies. Past generations in the free world created societies that cherished liberty, and developed states compatible with it. But the argument for liberty, whether in the market or in discourse, has to be won anew in every generation, and our institutions renewed or replaced as they decay. The trade-offs between liberty and safety, fairness or cultural cohesion must be constantly adjusted to take account of new technologies, power dynamics and economic imperatives.

In other words, the most serious threats to our liberty come from within. Broadly, they fall into three categories: economic, demographic and technological. I will lay out each in turn.

Economic

At the end of the Cold War, the argument for freedom was easy to make. Freedom not only brought abstract, political privileges, such as the right to vote. It also made us rich. Pop music, cheap goods, home ownership and well-funded public services: these were the rewards of a market-driven economy.

But with the arrival of the Chinese economic miracle and the stagnation of growth in free societies, it started to become clear that freedom and wealth weren't necessarily two sides of an unbreakable bargain.

In the early days, it was common to hear the argument that the Chinese political system couldn't stay autocratic for long. Once the middle classes grew rich, said the received wisdom, they would demand political rights. And for a long time, Beijing played along with this fantasy. Indeed, some voices among its collective leadership prior to 2008 even believed it.

Then the 2008 crisis arrived in the West, with its vast state bailouts, and the argument for a free-wheeling, self-correcting Western model became much harder to make. On the back of this ideological turnaround, a tech-nologically enhanced but fundamentally old-fashioned autocrat called Xi Jinping came to power and set about restoring the primacy of one-party, one-man rule. He could do it because getting rich had not, in fact, triggered a liberal awakening among China's new office classes, but a sense of pride in a uniquely Chinese system.

Shaken by the crash, free societies have now started to entertain the terrifying possibility that dictatorship might actually be more efficient. Financial regulations have been redrawn in Europe with a nod to the 'Asian macro-prudential model'. We now look, with awe, at the transfor-mation of dodgy backwaters like Shenzhen into one of the world's most innovative cities. We see China building eight new airports a year. We see that if Beijing wants to build a new high-speed rail line, it doesn't waste years surveying the newt population or measuring decibels. It just smashes down whatever is in the way and builds.

And we look at our own countries and wonder why productivity and investment have barely grown for a decade. But what is there to wonder about? Just watch the UK government as it enters yet another round of consultations and legal challenges on building a third runway at Heathrow, the country's most crowded and valuable airport. Look and despair at the sight of France's once world-leading nuclear programme bogged down by huge costs and design flaws, and at the wasteful run-down of Germany's entire nuclear industry. Cross your fingers whenever you cross an Italian bridge in case it is the next one to crumble. And mar-vel at the unfathomable cost per mile of the UK's High Speed 2 rail pro-ject, the world's most expensive infrastructure project, or our inability to build enough homes for our population. There is nothing so damning for the future of Western civilisation as our sheer inability to build the things we need.

Yet those who suggest sweeping away many of the regulations and legal norms ensnaring our economies are told that it simply isn't democratic. It's said that everyone must get their say, the regulator needs to double-check this, workers must have their rights, everyone must file their objections, have their cases heard in court, and so on. Or else, the state can't get involved, we must trust the market; we can't afford it, it's all too expensive (no wonder it is). And all of it raises the uncomfortable question: is democracy and respect for everyone's rights, from the local bird-watchers to the local construction guild, just too inefficient to sustain the growth and development we need?

Central banks and governments have generally shielded their populations from the effect of this rising tide of regulation and inefficiency in two ways: by a sustained period of low interest rates and a long period of globalisation. The first has made everyone feel richer by allowing us to borrow to our heart's content. The second has made everyone feel richer by moving large chunks of production offshore, to jurisdictions like China, that aren't bound by our regulations, our limits on carbon emissions, our labour or privacy laws.

This is not a side issue. It is fundamental. Take UK carbon emissions, for example. In theory, the UK has reduced its emissions by 41% since 1990. But by far the majority of that reduction is a result of offshoring production. In other words, we have shut down our own industries by raising costs at home, through measures such as climate and employment regulations, and we now get the goods made elsewhere – largely in countries like China with poor records on the environment and workers' rights – and then import them. Taking this effect into account, number crunching by the World Wildlife Fund shows that emissions related to British consumption of goods and services has, in fact, only fallen by 15% since 1990. This is not a story of emissions reduction, but of emissions displacement.

With the economic and political backlashes now here, the twin strategies of easy money and outsourcing seem pretty clearly to have reached their limit. The potent brew of quantitative easing and stimulus spending unleashed in response to Covid flooded our economies with new money and, combined with the war and sanctions, has fed through into the mother of all inflation shocks. Central banks are now belatedly putting up interest rates to try to avoid a damaging wage-price spiral. Whether they succeed or not, it is clear that the days of printing money without consequences are over.

Meanwhile, we are realising that relying on Chinese production for everything from our telecoms equipment to our nuclear power plants and surgical gloves, far from being cheap and reliable, is risky and fragile. Markets may not yet realise it, but the decoupling of the West from China is already underway. In the name of zero Covid, Beijing is accelerating the process, but that alone won't release us from our own bog of over-regulation, zombie companies and under-investment.

Add into all of this the requirement for net zero carbon emissions in our energy systems (these targets still don't count offshoring) and the increasing care needs of our ageing populations and you have a recipe for pretty stark economic decline. Can liberty and the political norms that sustain it survive if they are seen to deliver a system of falling living standards?

Demographic

Economic decline is being compounded by another factor: demographics. By and large, free countries rely on a Ponzi-scheme system of funding for old-age and health care. Current workers pay in to fund services for the needy. This system works if your population of workers is growing and the population of dependents is shrinking. Unfortunately, in much of the free world (and outside it too – notably, in China), the trends are going the other way. The predictable result is gradually rising taxes and failing services as our models buckle under the burden of ageing.

So, what's the logical, hard-nosed economist's response to this? Well, they say it's obvious. If a labour force is shrinking, one should simply replenish it using the millions of aspiring young immigrants queueing up at the border. But in the typical way of economists, these thinkers are replacing human beings with numbers and ratios and assuming that they are fully fungible, like lumps of coal.

If the migration crisis of 2016 taught us nothing else, it's that our populations do not see it that way. What they see in mass migration is a reckless social experiment performed on their societies without their consent. And when you zoom out to look at the longer history of this issue, they are, in fact, correct. Genetic records from ancient DNA studies suggest that it is rare for a significant 'population replacement event' to occur within the space of a few centuries. Aside from the violent events we know about from imperial expansions, the fastest such event of this kind that's known about from prehistory is the 80% replacement of the British population that built Stonehenge over a 200-year period. Was this a peaceful event? I have my doubts.

In Europe, within a couple of generations we've gone from non-European immigrants accounting for an almost negligible share of the population to comprising 10–20%, and this is rising due to divergent birth rates. Of course, this is not a straightforward 'great replacement', as the far-right sometimes terms it. It involves, rather, the accelerated creation of a new population born of mixing between existing Europeans and immigrants or new Europeans. The speed of this event makes it highly unusual in human history.

Why does this matter for liberty? Well, if you listen to thinkers such as Douglas Murray, you'll hear that a large proportion of the people coming to Europe are steeped in cultures that are at least unconcerned with, if not outright opposed to, freedom. He argues that we cannot expect our organically evolved political and cultural institutions to maintain this wonderful, delicate thing called liberty in the face of such rapid change.

And it's not hard to see examples of this. We've seen a return of religious prohibitions, with the UK cinema chain Cineworld recently cancelling the screening of a film about Mohammed's daughter, due to protests claiming it was blasphemous. We have the case of the teacher at Batley Grammar school in the UK who has been in hiding since the day in March 2021 he dared to show his class cartoons of Mohammed. And then there are the scandals involving the grooming and systematic abuse of young, working class girls by gangs of predominantly Asian men in numerous towns across the country. In Sweden, a country where violent crime was until recently almost non-existent, politics is now being driven by the explosive issue of gang violence by migrant groups in previously safe neighbourhoods. Across Europe, we have seen trucks wielded as weapons, bombs, knife attacks, the harassment of women, and the routine stationing of armed guards outside synagogues and Jewish supermarkets.

Still, others would argue – and they may be right – that the real enemy of liberty is not the immigrants, the vast majority of whom simply move to Europe for a better life, but rather the paranoid, race-based prejudice that immigrants are somehow unsusceptible to the appeal of decent and universal Western liberties. The rise in far-right violence, which has seen politicians murdered, gun massacres unleashed and decent citizens abused, is at least as worrying as its Islamist counterpart. What we should fear, these liberals argue, is not the way migrants change our society, but the way we change in response to migration. Whichever way you cut it, however, we need to view immigration not simply as a mechanical fix for low birth rates, but as a process that should be managed according to social and political needs, as well as economic calculations.

Technological

Few phenomena have disappointed modern liberals as much as the arrival of the internet age. The spread of digital communication is a change as profound as the invention of the printing press, which we tend to associate with the arrival of the Reformation and a great liberation of thought. But the printing press also brought with it other spectacles, such as the frenzy of witch hunts that gripped Europe in the fifteenth century after a deranged text denouncing a scourge of witches went viral for its age. And the Reformation, in turn, brought the counter-Reformation and wars of religion.

It was the same in 1920s Germany, when many intellectuals thought that the spread of mass literacy would bring about a great, democratising liberation. Walter Benjamin talked about the written word being 'pitilessly dragged out onto the street' and pasted up on billboards, stripped of authority and made into a tool for the common man. He thought this would lead to a great revolution for liberty. Instead, it facilitated the rise of the Nazis.

The arrival of social media hasn't yet unleashed a war in Europe, but it is fundamentally changing our societies in ways that traditional institutions, like political parties, universities and workplace bureaucracies, are struggling to manage. The dissemination of ideas between peers has, for good or bad, forever undermined the authority of the office edict or the medical diagnosis. At first, this was supposed to be a technology that made us hopeful. Social media could link up parents of children with rare diseases. It could allow a new clothes designer to sell her wares to the public without a middleman in the way. It was credited with helping to get the US's first black president elected and facilitating the mass uprisings of the Arab spring.

But it didn't take long for us to see the dark side. Nowadays, it's easy to go online and join or initiate a digital witch hunt to drive someone out of their job or push them towards self-harm and suicide. We have seen sophisticated propaganda campaigns persuade people to leave normal lives and travel across the world to join Isis. Algorithms designed to harvest human time and attention have divided the virtual town square into echo chambers that lose the ability to debate one another.

Authoritarian regimes have found in the internet a perfect tool to make efficient their dreams of totalitarian surveillance and control. Even in democratic societies, governments and corporations have responded to the tide of digital horror and lawsuits by putting forward new, centralised ways of policing free speech, including 'fact checking' tools and the UK's mooted Online Safety Bill.

Even if you discount the most sinister effects of this technological revolution, few can deny the corrosive effect of technology addiction and the epidemic of a sense of meaninglessness that comes with it. Philosophical exhaustion, nihilism and ignorance are draining the sustenance from the soil that liberty needs to thrive, and into this void, a new jungle of ideologies, tribal identities and mental health problems is expanding. This is truly the death of God that Nietzsche talked about and, just as he predicted, it is bringing with it the 'revaluation of all values'. The notion of liberty is being rewritten, reclaimed and rejected a thousand times every day.

Just as generations did before us, we are learning that a belief in liberty is not self-evident and its expansion is not inevitable. We cannot rely on the persuasive power of democracy, economic efficiency or cultural riches to make the case for liberty by proxy. We cannot succeed by protecting our decaying institutions from all change, or by going without them. The external threats to the free world from dictatorial regimes are a growing danger. And yet, it's also possible that by reminding us of what the grim alternative to liberty is, these threats will, in the end, be the trigger needed to renew and reunite free societies so they can overcome the greater enemies – the enemies within.

CONTRIBUTORS

KEMI BADENOCH is the British Secretary of State for International Trade, President of the Board of Trade and Minister for Women and Equalities. She was elected the Member of Parliament for Saffron Walden in 2017, before which she was a Conservative member of the London Assembly and a director at *The Spectator* magazine. Badenoch holds two degrees in engineering and law from Sussex University and Birkbeck College, respectively.

JOHN BEW is Professor of History and Foreign Policy at the War Studies Department at King's College London. From 2019, he served as foreign policy adviser to UK Prime Minister Boris Johnson. In 2015, he was awarded a Philip Leverhulme Prize for Politics and International Relations. His books include *Realpolitik: a History* and *Citizen Clem: a Biography of Attlee.*

ADRIAN BRADSHAW KCB OBE DL has degrees in Agriculture, Defence Studies and International Relations. He has been a Visiting Defence Fellow at Balliol College, Oxford and is Senior Associate Fellow at RUSI and Visiting Professor at King's College London. He joined the 14th/20th King's Hussars in 1980 and has served in armour, aviation and special forces. He completed his Regular service as Britain's most senior officer in NATO as Deputy Supreme Allied Commander Europe in 2014–17.

RICHARD CHARTRES is a crossbench member of the House of Lords. He was appointed a life peer after more than 20 years as Bishop of London and serves on the House of Lords Appointments Commission. He studied history at University of Cambridge and was subsequently Professor of Divinity at Gresham College. Currently he is an Honorary Fellow of Trinity College. He has a longstanding commitment to caring for the environment and has served as an ambassador to the World Wildlife Fund.

CHRISTOPHER COKER is director of LSE IDEAS, a foreign policy think tank at the London School of Economics and Political Science. He is a former member of the Council of the Royal United Services Institute, for whom he wrote the monograph *Empires in Conflict: the Growing Rift Between Europe and the United States.* He is also a former editor of the *Atlantic Quarterly* and the *European Security Analyst.*

MARIE DAOUDA teaches French language and literature at Oriel College, Oxford. Dr Daouda works on the reception of antiquity in nineteenth- and twentieth-century French and English literature, and on the representations of good and evil in literature, music and painting. Dr Daouda writes for British newspapers and magazines about education, diversity and social politics in the UK and in France.

PETER FRANKOPAN is Professor of Global History at the University of Oxford, and Professor of Silk Roads Studies at King's College, Cambridge. He works with the United Nations Industrial Development Organization on the future of sustainable cities and on the Belt and Road Initiative. Frankopan's books include *The Silk Roads: a New History of the World*, *The New Silk Roads: the Present and Future of the World* and *The Earth Transformed: an Untold History.*

FRANCIS J. GAVIN is the Giovanni Agnelli Distinguished Professor and the inaugural director of the Henry A Kissinger Center for Global Affairs at Johns Hopkins SAIS. In 2021, Professor Gavin was named a 2021–2022 Ernest May Senior Visiting Fellow of the Applied History Project at Harvard's Belfer Center for Science and International Affairs. Gavin is the author of *Gold, Dollars, and Power: the Politics of International Monetary Relations, 1958–1971* and *Nuclear Weapons and American Grand Strategy.*

MATTHEW GOODWIN is Professor of Politics at Rutherford College, University of Kent, a Senior Fellow at Policy Exchange and has served as Senior Visiting Fellow at the Royal Institute of International Affairs at Chatham House. He is the author of six books including the bestseller *National Populism: the Revolt Against Liberal Democracy* which was listed among the *Financial Times* and *Times Literary Supplement* books of the year.

KATJA HOYER is a German-British historian and journalist. She is a Visiting Research Fellow at King's College London and a Fellow of the Royal Historical Society. Katja is a columnist for *The Washington Post* and writes for *The Spectator, The Telegraph, Die Welt* and other newspapers on current political affairs in Germany and Europe. She is the author of the bestselling *Blood and Iron*. Her latest book is *Beyond the Wall: East Germany, 1949–1990*.

JEREMY JENNINGS is Professor of Political Theory at King's College London. He holds a visiting professorship with the Fondation Nationale des Sciences Politiques and was founding editor of the *European Journal of Political Theory*. His publications include *Revolution and the Republic: a History of Political Thought in France since the Eighteenth Century*, which won the Franco-British Society's Enid McLeod Literary Award. His most recent book is *Travels with Tocqueville beyond America*.

ROB JOHNSON is the Director of the Changing Character of War Centre at the University of Oxford, and a Senior Research Fellow of Pembroke College. A former army officer familiar with the development of irregular warfare, his specialisms include military thought, strategy, operational history, and new technologies. He has acted as an advisor to NATO, to UK parliamentary committees, and to military commands. He has recently taken up the appointment as the first Director of the Office of Net Assessment in the Ministry of Defence. He has published on war, strategy, operational histories and local forces, including the award winning *Lawrence of Arabia on War, The First World War and the Middle East*, and the co-edited *Military Strategy in the 21st Century* and *The Conduct of War*. He is currently writing on Anglo-American strategic decision making in the two world wars.

ALEXANDER LEE is a Fellow in the Centre for the Study of the Renaissance at the University of Warwick. Educated at the universities of Cambridge and Edinburgh, he has previously held positions at the University of Oxford, the Université du Luxembourg and the Università degli studi di Bergamo. He is the author of five acclaimed books, including *Humanism and Empire: the Imperial Ideal in Fourteenth-Century Italy* and *Machiavelli: His Life and Times*. He is currently writing a new history of the Venetian Ghetto.

JANNE HAALAND MATLÁRY is Professor of Political Science at the University of Oslo and the Norwegian Command and Staff College. Her more than 20 books include *Military Strategy in the Twenty-First Century: the Challenge for NATO* (co-edited with Robert Johnson) and she is a columnist for *Dagens Næringsliv*. She represented the Norwegian Christian Democratic Party as Deputy Foreign Minister from 1997 to 2000. In 2001, she was appointed Dame of the Sovereign Military Order of Malta and, in 2020, Dame of the Order of Merit of the Republic of Hungary.

RICHARD MILES is Professor of Roman History and Archaeology and Vice Provost at the University of Sydney. He was previously a Fellow in Ancient History at Trinity Hall, University of Cambridge, and a Newton Trust lecturer in the Faculty of Classics. He has written and presented documentaries for the BBC, including *Ancient Worlds* and *Archaeology: a Secret History*. His books include *The Donatist Schism: Controversy and Contexts* and *The Bir Messaouda Basilica: Pilgrimage and the Transformation of an Urban Landscape in Sixth Century AD Carthage*, the latter of which he co-authored with Simon Greenslade.

FRASER NELSON is a leading British journalist and commentator. He is the editor of *The Spectator*, a weekly columnist for the *Daily Telegraph* in London and a regular broadcaster. He is also a director of the think tank Centre for Policy Studies and for the charity Social Mobility Foundation. In 2013, he won the British Press Award for political journalist of the year.

IULIIA OSMOLOVSKA is director of Globsec Kyiv office, chair of the Transatlantic Dialogue Center and an executive director of the Eastern Europe Security Institute Ukraine. She is a member of an ad-hoc emergency informal network of Ukrainian analytical centres adjacent to the Ukrainian Ministry of Foreign Affairs and Ministry of Defence. She is a career diplomat with 15 years of diplomatic service at the Ministry of Foreign Affairs, with a particular focus on European security and EU integration.

AGNÈS C. POIRIER is an award-winning journalist, writer and broadcaster based in Paris and London. She is the UK editor for the French weekly magazine *L'Express* and the author of, among others, *Left Bank: Arts, Passion and the Rebirth of Paris (1940–1950)* and *Notre-Dame: the Soul of France*.

She holds degrees from Sciences-Po, Sorbonne and studied at the London School of Economics and Political Science.

ALINA POLYAKOVA is President and CEO of the Center for European Policy Analysis as well as an adjunct professor of European studies at the Johns Hopkins University's School of Advanced International Studies. Polyakova is a recognised expert on transatlantic relations, European security, Russian foreign policy, digital authoritarianism, and populism in democracies. She is the author of the book *The Dark Side of European Integration*, as well as dozens of major reports and articles.

SERGEY RADCHENKO is the Wilson E Schmidt Distinguished Professor at the Johns Hopkins School of Advanced International Studies. He has written extensively on the Cold War, nuclear history, and on Russian and Chinese foreign and security policies. He has served as a Global Fellow and a Public Policy Fellow at the Woodrow Wilson Centre and as the Zi Jiang Distinguished Professor at East China Normal University. Radchenko's books include *Two Suns in the Heavens: the Sino-Soviet Struggle for Supremacy* and *Unwanted Visionaries: the Soviet Failure in Asia*.

CHARLY SALONIUS-PASTERNAK is a Senior Research Fellow at the Finnish Institute of International Affairs, Helsinki, where his primary areas of research are foreign, security and defence policy. He has been a commentator for TV and radio in several countries, and was previously an international affairs adviser to the Plans and Policy Unit of Defence Command, Finnish Defence Forces, and a visiting lecturer at Tufts University, Boston.

JULIET SAMUEL is a columnist for *The Telegraph* newspaper in the UK and has spent her career covering finance and business. As a reporter for various newspapers, she has covered the Euro crisis, Brexit and the boom and crash of the last commodities supercycle. As a columnist and essay-writer, her subjects range from Covid to climate, monetary policy, the growing influence of China around the world, supply chain mayhem and Putin's relationship with the Russian Orthodox Church.

MARY E. SAROTTE is the Kravis Professor in the Kissinger Center of the Johns Hopkins School of Advanced International Studies. Her six books include the trilogy *1989: the Struggle to Create Post-Cold War Europe, The*

Collapse: the Accidental Opening of the Berlin Wall and *Not One Inch: America, Russia, and the Making of Post-Cold War Stalemate*, which were named *Financial Times* Books of the Year in 2009 and 2014. Sarotte earned her BA at Harvard University and her PhD at Yale University.

KORI SCHAKE is the director of foreign and defence policy at the American Enterprise Institute. She was previously a foreign-policy adviser to the McCain–Palin 2008 presidential campaign. Schake obtained her PhD in government from the University of Maryland and did her undergraduate studies at Stanford University. She is the author of *Safe Passage: the Transition from British to American Hegemony* and is a contributing writer at *The Atlantic*.

MARK J. SCHIEFSKY is the C Lois P Grove Professor of the Classics at Harvard University and the director of Harvard's Center for Hellenic Studies. His research centres on the history of philosophy and science in the ancient Greco-Roman world and its transmission and reception in later periods. He is the author of a commentary on the Hippocratic treatise *On Ancient Medicine*, as well as numerous articles on ancient philosophy and science.

BRENDAN SIMMS obtained his PhD from the University of Cambridge, where he is a Fellow of Peterhouse and director of the Centre for Geopolitics. He is founder and president of the Henry Jackson Society, a London-based think tank devoted to the spread of democracy and human rights, and president of the Project for Democratic Union, a Munich-based student-organised think tank. His books include *Britain's Europe: a Thousand Years of Conflict and Cooperation* and (co-authored with Steve McGregor) *The Silver Waterfall: How America Won the Pacific War at Midway*.

ALEXANDER MCCALL SMITH is the author of over 100 books. He was formerly Professor of Medical Law at the University of Edinburgh before becoming a full-time writer. He has recently completed volume 24 in his series of novels set in Botswana, *The No 1 Ladies' Detective Agency*. Last year saw the publication of a collection of poetry, *In a Time of Distance*. He is a librettist for composers of operas and song cycles.

ROEL STERCKX is Joseph Needham Professor of Chinese History, Science and Civilisation at the University of Cambridge and a Fellow of Clare College. He was trained at the Katholieke Universiteit Leuven, National Taiwan University, University of Cambridge and University of Oxford. His books include *The Animal and the Daemon in Early China* and *Chinese Thought: from Confucius to Cook Ding.* He is a Fellow of the British Academy.

MERRYN SOMERSET WEBB is editor in chief of *MoneyWeek* magazine and a contributing editor to the *Financial Times* where she writes a weekly column. She is also a non-executive director of two listed investment trusts in the UK. She is the author of *Share Power* and *Love Is Not Enough: a Smart Woman's Guide to Money.* She was named the Headline Money Awards Financial Commentator of the Year in 2019 and the Harold Wincott Personal Finance Journalist of the Year in 2018.

Image rights ©

LIBERTY
The Evolution of an Idea

Published by Bokförlaget Stolpe, Stockholm, Sweden, 2023

© The authors and Bokförlaget Stolpe 2023

The essays are based on the Liberty seminar held at
Engelsberg Ironworks in Västmanland, Sweden in 2022.

Edited by
Kurt Almqvist, president, Axel and Margaret Ax:son Johnson Foundation
Alastair Benn, deputy editor, Engelsberg Ideas
Mattias Hessérus, director of the Ax:son Johnson Institute for Statecraft and Diplomacy

Translation of the song in the introduction: Ruth Urbom
Text editor: Andrew Mackenzie
Picture editor: Tove Falk Olsson
Design: Patric Leo
Layout: Petra Ahston Inkapööl
Cover image: *Déclaration des droits de l'homme et du citoyen* (Declaration of the Rights of Man and
the Citizen), Jean-Jacques François Le Barbier, 1789. © Musée Carnavalet/Roger-Viollet
Prepress and print coordinator: Italgraf Media AB, Sweden
Print: Printon, Estonia, via Italgraf Media, 2023
First edition, first printing

ISBN: 978-91-89425-93-4

Bokförlaget Stolpe is a part of Axel and Margaret Ax:son Johnson Foundation for Public Benefit.

BOKFÖRLAGET STOLPE

AXEL AND MARGARET AX:SON JOHNSON
FOUNDATION FOR PUBLIC BENEFIT